Susann Ludwig
La chance

Culture and Social Practice

Susann Ludwig, born in 1987, is affiliated with the University of Leipzig, Germany. She did her doctorate at the Centre for African Studies at Universität Basel (ZASB). As a social anthropologist in African studies, she is fascinated by the every-day play of people doing things, and by questions related to chance, space, relationality, and possibility. Overall, she has spent two years doing ethnographic fieldwork in West Africa, particularly in Bamako, Mali.

Susann Ludwig

La chance

Uncertainty, Knowledge Production and Gameplay among University
Graduates in Bamako, Mali

[transcript]

The Swiss National Science Foundation SNSF generously funded the research activities as well as the publication of this book possible. The Basler Freiwillige Akademische Gesellschaft (FAG) funded the late writing-up period of the thesis.

This book is a revised version of the Ph.D. thesis submitted in conformity with the requirements for the degree of Doctor of Philosophy in African Studies Faculty of Humanities and Social Sciences, University of Basel

Title: "La chance: An Ethnography". University Graduates Making Sense of Uncertainty in Bamako, Mali.

Submitted November 2017, defended April 2018

Doctoral commitee: Prof. Elísio Macamo (first supervisor) Centre for African Studies Basel, University of Basel
Prof. Richard Rottenburg (second supervisor) Social Anthropology, University of Halle-Wittenberg

Bibliographic information published by the Deutsche Nationalbibliothek
The Deutsche Nationalbibliothek lists this publication in the Deutsche Nationalbibliografie; detailed bibliographic data are available in the Internet at https://dnb.dnb.de

This work is licensed under the Creative Commons Attribution 4.0 (BY) license, which means that the text may be remixed, transformed and built upon and be copied and redistributed in any medium or format even commercially, provided credit is given to the author. For details go to https://creativecommons.org/licenses/by/4.0/
Creative Commons license terms for re-use do not apply to any content (such as graphs, figures, photos, excerpts, etc.) not original to the Open Access publication and further permission may be required from the rights holder. The obligation to research and clear permission lies solely with the party re-using the material.

First published in 2024 by transcript Verlag, Bielefeld
© Susann Ludwig

Cover layout: Maria Arndt, Bielefeld
Cover illustration: Susann Ludwig
Copy-editing: Matthias Müller, Rotterdam
Typeset: Jan Gerbach, Bielefeld, Francisco Bragança, Bielefeld
Printed by Majuskel Medienproduktion GmbH, Wetzlar
Print-ISBN 978-3-8376-6989-3
PDF-ISBN 978-3-8394-6989-7
https://doi.org/10.14361/9783839469897
ISSN of series: 2703-0024
eISSN of series: 2703-0032

Table of Contents

INTRO 9
VIGNETTE: *La chance* makes a difference 9
Jeunesse diplomée - "sans emploi?
This book is about *"la chance"* 16

THIS BOOK: chapter description. 27
Part One: Ethnography of *La chance*. Or, What Graduates Know
and What They Know They Don't Know. 29
Part Two: Assemblage of *La chance*. Or, The Emergence
of *La chance* in the Encounter. 31

Part 1: Ethnography of La chance 35

1 Knowledge | Situating *La Chance* in Graduates' Knowledge. 37
[We are here] 37
KNOWLEDGE: On the presence of *la chance* 38
   Le bras long | A case of privilege? 39
   Le concours | A case of random selection? 47
   THE KNOWN | What they DO know 50
KNOWLEDGE: On the absence of *la chance* 51
   L'homme propose, Dieu dispose | Nothing is certain 51
   THE UNKNOWN | What they know they DON'T know 56

2 Graduates | Situating *La Chance* in Graduates' Everyday Lives. 59
[We are here] 59
PEOPLE 60
UNKNOWNS 71

Part 2: Assemblage of *la chance* 91

3 A Manual 93
VIGNETTE: Dieu donne *la chance*, mais toi aussi tu peux
t'ouvrir *la chance*. 93
INVITATION: Dear Reader,... 94
　　[MAP] 96
What is *la chance*? 97
What is *la chance* – yet, again? 102
Now, I put these two layers together. 103
In an assemblage. 103

4 *La chance* | Emergence. 109
Assemblage: *la chance*. 113
　La chance is a prerequisite. 114
　　KNOWLEDGE: PREREQUISITES. 129
　La chance is a sprout. 131
　　KNOWLEDGE: SPROUTS. 149
　La chance is an outcome. 151
　　KNOWLEDGE: OUTCOMES. 164
[Tracings] 166
　Tracing L1: KNOWLEDGE: prerequisites, sprouts, outcomes. 166
　Tracing L2: Clues on *la chance*. 170

5 *La chance* | Encounter. 173
Assemblage: Opening up *la chance*. 176
　Looking for *la chance*. 176
　　KNOWLEDGE: PREPARATION. 192
　Finding la chance. 195
　　KNOWLEDGE: IDENTIFICATION. 206
　Working with *la chance*. 208
　　KNOWLEDGE: TRANSFORMATION. 218
[Tracings] 220
　Tracing L1: KNOWLEDGE: preparation, identification, transformation 220
　Tracing L2: The game of opening up *la chance*. 221

GAMEPLAY: The game of opening up *la chance*. 231
[Argument] 231
   I Graduates are playing the game of *la chance* 232
   II Implications of Gameplay 236
   III What we see now 239

Bibliography 245

Acknowledgements 253

INTRO

VIGNETTE: *La chance* makes a difference

The university graduates I met in Bamako are working on the realization of their future – some of them have achieved their goals already, and some have not, or not yet. So, if personal effort is what they all invest, what is it then, to them, that makes the difference? *La chance* makes a difference, it is distinctive and it distinguishes. [...] To provoke *la chance* is to look for *la chance* in the sense that individuals provide themselves with the skillset required in order to make sure they are able to identify la chance by the time it appears (extract from a round table presentation in Bamako, 9 January 2017).

I begin with the moment that marked the final stage of my research. In January 2017, our research group "Construire son Avenir",[1] met for a final workshop at the University of Bamako in Mali to discuss our findings and present results of our individual research within the project. We had also organized a round table with the thought-provoking title "La jeunesse d'aujourd'hui – et de demain?" (Youth today – and tomorrow?), during which local stakeholders would discuss the issues raised. The audience consisted of students, professors, and administrators – some of whom were my informants – and some external participants who happened to come across our minimal advertising. I was nervous and I was meant to talk for no more than five minutes to

---

1 The project "Construire son Avenir: Self-Conception and Career Practices of Young Graduates in Burkina Faso and Mali" was based at the Centre for African Studies at the University of Basel and funded from 2013-2016 by the Swiss National Science Foundation. The project was led by Prof. Dr. Elisio Macamo. The other team-members were: Dr. Michelle Engeler, Prof. Dr. Manfred Perlik, and Dr. Noemi Steuer. My PhD colleague Maike Birzle (MA) covered research in Burkina Faso.

present the core of my findings from ten months of fieldwork with university graduates in Bamako. I decided to present *la chance*.

During the round table discussion, a well-known politician responded in his first comment: "Moi, je n'accorde pas d'importance à la chance." ("I don't attach any importance to chance.") Later, he explained that in his own life, he "had *la chance* to study in France." His success though, he said, came once he started working fifteen hours a day. Another participant depicted university graduates as victims of a system that fails to properly educate them. If today's youth wanted to succeed, they only had to work hard. They could start businesses, move to the countryside in order to become farmers; they should stop demanding, stop complaining and stop doing nothing. The message was clear: a university degree is no guarantee; only hard work will pay off. However, those who "sit around waiting for *la chance*" will undoubtedly fail.

I felt misunderstood; it was neither my intention nor the point of my presentation to create an image of "university graduates sitting around waiting for *la chance*." I considered explaining my point again, but I decided not to. The audience predominantly affirmed the participants' remarks; some were thankful and presented themselves, their stories, their ambitions, and their efforts. Others asked how they might pursue a career in politics. However, a female student's comment "There are no jobs in Mali!" was completely ignored. The discussion did not reveal their thoughts on my preliminary findings on *la chance*; only later did I realize that this round table revealed a discourse based on the categorization of *la chance* as luck – and not as merit or something else.

On an earlier field trip to Bamako, I made a similar categorization myself:

> Coming from downtown Bamako, Moudou[2] and I are headed to the second bridge. On the driveway next to the administrative part of the city, dozens of young men are selling sunglasses. Everybody sells sunglasses, the exact same sunglasses. "Why are they all standing right there? All at one spot?" I ask. Moudou answers: "La chance will bring them clients. Every day, it's going to be someone else... and, you know, there are also some vendors walking around town all day" (field notes, September 2011).

---

2 All research participants' names are changed in order to protect their privacy and to ensure anonymity.

As a concluding remark, I jotted down: "Everybody's going to have *la chance* at some point in time. Apparently, selling is not about skill, but about luck. Making money is luck, not merit." Soon afterward, I recognized that I was wrong: the very fact that dozens of people sell sunglasses at this exact spot turns this driveway into a customer hot spot – which benefits every seller. I was also wrong in assuming that *la chance* is just the French word for luck. In fact, to my informants in Bamako, *la chance* is a type of common sense and it "lies so artlessly before our eyes it is almost impossible to see" (Geertz 1975, 25).

Jeunesse diplomée – "sans emploi?"

Universities change, graduates change.

The changing role of higher education from being "valued as a public and intellectual good" to being made essential to the foundation of the nation state in its development (Zeleza and Olukoshi 2004, 3) is a global trend. All over the world, young people are more likely to go to university than ever before (France 2007, 60). In the West, higher education has become "part of the normal, taken-for-granted, experiences" and due to its expansion, higher education is no longer exclusively accessible to middle- and upper-class students (Furlong and Cartmel 2009, 121). In the US, the role of the university has changed with globalization from promoting reason, to advocating culture, to today's emphasis "on the techno-bureaucratic notion of excellence" (Readings 1996, 54), which, according to the author, "lacks a referent".[3] With a particular focus on Africa, Zeleza and Olukoshi observe a shift from the "'development' university" of the 1960's and 1970's to the "'market' university" of the 1980's and 1990's, and with this development, "threats to academic freedom became less political and more economic" (Zeleza and Olukoshi 2004, 43). Higher educa-

---

3 Bill Readings, The University within the Limits of Reason, 1996: "The characteristic of the modern University is to have an idea that functions as its referent, as the end and meaning of its activities. [...] in general the modern University has had three ideas. The story begins [...] with Kant, who envisioned the University as guided by the concept of reason. Kant's vision is followed by Humboldt's idea of culture, and more recently the emphasis has been on the techno-bureaucratic notion of excellence. The distinguishing feature of the last on this list is that it actually lacks a referent."

tion became more dedicated to meeting the demands of the labor market, and private universities grew (Thaver 2004) and ultimately led to the "massification of higher education" (Zeleza and Olukoshi 2004, 3). In accordance with that global trend,[4] in Mali, too, the number of students in tertiary education has increased significantly during the last fifty years. In 2018, for instance, according to official government numbers, there are about 85,000 students enrolled at the public universities of Mali, which is almost one fourth more than a year before (Ministère de l'Education Nationale 2018, 20).

After independence, several key institutions took the lead in educating the nation's emerging elite, the so-called "grandes écoles". These included a university for public administration (l'École Nationale d'Administration [l'ENA]), university for engineering (l'École Nationale d'Ingenieurs [l'ENI]) and the university for higher education (l'École Normale Superieure [l'ENSUP]). Despite different training foci, these institutions participated in a common project: they produced "professionals who were being trained to operate the burgeoning machinery of the state" (Engeler 2017, 10)". These particular higher education institutions still exist today, and there are others that have also arrived on the scene more recently. For example, the University of Bamako was established in 2006, making its debut with five faculties,[5] two institutes, and 11,250 enrolled students in its first year (Imperato and Imperato 2008, 104). By 2010, there were more than 80,000 students (Diakite 2011), which exceeded the accommodations available in the university's infrastructure (Daou 2010). As a result, a government decree transformed the University of Bamako's former faculties into four separate universities. For instance, la FLASH, i.e. the faculty of languages and social sciences, became l'Université des Lettres et des Sciences Humaines de Bamako (U.L.S.H.B). During the 2015-16 term, a total of about 62,000 students were enrolled at the Universities of Bamako. Though most graduates I talked to found the quality of education provided by the professors satisfying, they all expressed dissatisfaction with the conditions at the

---

4 All over the world, young people are more likely to go to university than ever before (France 2007). "[I]n many western countries" higher education has become "part of the normal, taken-for-granted, experiences" and due to its expansion, higher education is no longer exclusively accessible to middle- and upper-class students (Furlong 2009) .

5 i.e. Faculté des Lettres, Langues, Arts et Sciences Humaines (FLASH), Faculté des Sciences Juridiques et Politiques (FSJP), Faculté des Sciences Économiques et de Gestion (FSEG), Faculté des Sciences et Techniques (FAST), Faculté de Médecine, de Pharmacie et d'Odonto-Stomatologie (FMPOS).

Universities of Bamako[6]: too many students, no library, insufficient resources, packed courses, power outages, slow administration, and unfairness regarding the distribution of grades and scholarships. Numerous strikes, held by personnel or students, became an everyday routine of university life, as staff and students voiced their discontent over their salaries, their scholarships, and the examinations. In 2011, classes were canceled for more than three months due to strikes. In response, the whole term was declared an "année blanche," an empty year in which no student advanced or graduated (Ludwig 2011, 9).

Experiencing university today is significantly different compared to the times of the protesters against the Moussa Traore military regime in the 1970s (see Steuer 2017) and the student movement of the 1990s (Smith 1997). In other words, for their parents' generation, a university degree secured public sector employment and elite status (Behrends and Lentz 2012, 139), but those days are long gone (Engeler 2017, 14). So, rather than age, gender, class or subculture, my informants share the experience of university education and of uncertainty with regard to the current labor market situation. The idea of a shared and, therefore, connecting experience relates back to Karl Mannheim's concept of generations, which consists of multiple and even opposing units of people, united by a common overarching experience that significantly differs from experiences of the former generation (Mannheim 1928). Academics in Mali constitute a small, yet, due to their elite qualification, highly relevant generational unit of people.

La jeunesse diplomée. Sans emploi.

Whenever I introduced myself and what I was doing to neighbors, relatives, secretaries, taxi drivers or government officials, I said that I was conducting research on university graduates in Mali – "une étude sur les jeunes diplomés ici au Mali". The reaction was usually this: "Sans emploi? Sur les jeunes sans emploi." – "Unemployed? The unemployed youth?" In the beginning, I always passionately corrected people, saying "No, no. Young univer-

---

6 Students enrolled at the Universities of Bamako as of term 2015-16: l'Université des Sciences Sociales et de Gestion de Bamako (U.S.G.B) 16,350; l'Université des Lettres et des Sciences Humaines de Bamako (U.L.S.H.B) 20,980; l'Université des Sciences, des Techniques et des Technologies de Bamako (U.S.T.T.B) 9,300; l'Université des Sciences Juridiques et Politiques de Bamako (U.S.J.P.B) 15,989. (Source: Scolarité de l'ULSHB in private communication 2017-10-18).

sity graduates!" but they would almost always respond sweepingly, "Yeah, sure, the unemployed young people". At some point, I accepted this response, maybe because I experienced similar responses when I spoke to university graduates. I was interested in what they were doing after graduation, and they answered, "Rien" – "Nothing". However, as the conversation progressed, they talked about all kinds of activities in which they engaged (see also Langevang 2009, 748; Hansen 2005, 6).[7] While most of them were not working on a fixed or secure contract, they were working for a living or in an internship that was directed towards some future opportunity. Some helped their parents, and some worked on their vocational training. No matter what they did, most of them were busy doing something: they were busy opening up *la chance*.

This relates to what Billy Ehn and Orvar Löfgren analyzed as "doing nothing" (Ehn 2012). By questioning everyday phenomena such as waiting, routines, and daydreaming, they challenge the notion of "doing nothing". People always do something, they say. However, we refer to "doing nothing" whenever nothing appears to be happening, or when something just happens too fast for us to recognize, when something happens in disguise, or when something that is happening is not considered to be worth mentioning for some reason.

"Employment may not be normal worldwide, but it is normative" (Kwon and Lane 2016, 5). Unemployment being the negatively connoted counterpart of employment arguably puts everything we value at stake, i.e. health, life in our societies, the future (ibid. 17); it leads to long-lasting disenfranchisement (ibid. 3) and compromises to social recognition and blocks young people's path to gaining adult status in their societies (ibid. 6).

With university graduates in Bamako, however, the situation seems to be quite different. They are busy, healthy and happy. They start building their own houses, marry and have children, they are respected by their families and peers regardless of their employment situation, but with regard to what they do on an everyday basis.

---

7 Both describe "doing nothing" as a discursive metaphor, which symbolizes a young people's feeling of "being stuck" (Sommers 2012), i.e. in "social and physical immobility" (Langevang 2009)

Doing nothing?

Unemployment is a global phenomenon, but it is experienced locally and, therefore, made sense of in different ways (Kwon and Lane 2016, 5). Looking closely at these experiences and practices, unemployment emerges as "a site for forging new ways of working, being, and thinking in these precarious neoliberal times" (Kwon and Lane 2016, 7) and we are able to see what people do when they do not find work: they work (see Lane 2016, Mains 2016, Fisher 2016).

This resonates with a great body of research on African youth focusing on practices in response to the challenging and uncertain labor market situations in their countries and, as a result, the "prolonged decline and drastic reduction of social possibilities" (Vigh 2006, 96). Liberian youth hustle (Munive 2010, 323; Kaufmann 2017), youth in Accra manage (Langevang 2008, 2046), youth in Cameroon muddle through everyday life (Waage 2006), and youth in Mali engage in small businesses (débrouillage) (Ludwig 2013). A few publications on university graduates in Africa relate their present practices to imagination and anticipation, carving out a future-oriented way of dealing with uncertainty. In Goma, Congo, a university diploma affords young academics the ability to imagine "a better future and provides the belief that [...] opportunities to find work are better than without it (the diploma)" (Oldenburg 2016, 17). Imagination also informs graduates in Burkina Faso presenting responses to uncertainty, who actively "hope and thus create accessible gateways" (Birzle 2017, 54). University graduates in Tanzania respond to career uncertainty deploying various practices, such as attracting potential employers, running businesses, changing careers, and accepting temporary jobs (Sambaiga 2017). Female Guinean graduates' take agency as they stay flexible in their progress towards heterogeneous future goals (Ammann 2017, 116). Similarly, male Guinean graduates strive for economic and political participation as "political entrepreneurs" (Engeler 2016).

In this book, I do not argue for the value of what graduates in Bamako are doing, neither do I contrast their practices to something I think they should be doing, instead I focus on graduates' knowledge of their situation and describe what they are doing based on that knowledge.

This book is about *"la chance"*

This book is about *"la chance"* (French for luck, chance). *La chance* is a concept which accounts for everyday knowledge production in uncertain contexts in Bamako, Mali as well as in the social sciences.

In Bamako, university graduates constitute an educational elite strongest affected by unemployment. With reference to *la chance*, university graduates make sense of their situation and they play what I call "the game of *la chance*".

Examining graduates' knowledge about their situation, we see that *la chance* is much more than its translation of "luck" or "chance" reveals. Throughout the book, we see how *la chance* emerges as a product of graduates mending the intersection between what graduates know and what they know they do not know. *La chance* is known to make a difference between those who get employed and those who do not. *La chance* makes sense. However, *la chance* is elusive in the sense that it appears to be self-explanatory in concrete contexts, but it escapes our grasp as soon as we try to approach its essence.

In 2015, about seventy percent of all university graduates in Mali were registered at the country's agency for the promotion of youth employment (APEJ 2015). Undoubtedly, the employment situation in Mali is challenging. For years, the public employment sector has been saturated, while the bulk of the country's economy continues to be based predominantly on agriculture. Young academics encounter severe difficulties entering the labor market, let alone finding a job that corresponds to their qualifications.

Against this background, three consecutive questions arise:

1. How do university graduates deal with uncertainties?
2. What is *la chance*? The phenomenon: *la chance*.
3. Why do graduates keep opening up *la chance* despite their knowledge of the circumstances?

Let me explain:

(1) Uncertainty

Uncertainty is a fundamental paradox that "humans live in history, in a situation where the future cannot be known and the past cannot be changed and, therefore, where the unpredictable is constantly turning into the irreversible" (Graeber 2012, 25; see also Luhmann 1991, 4; Macamo 2017, 184; Whyte 2009, 215). Since the outcomes of our actions are never fully predictable (e.g. Calkins 2016, 3; Luhmann 1991), uncertainty is a universal human phenomenon, however, in the 21st century, uncertainty has come to be considered a resource of creativity, innovation, growth, but also a source of precarity and insecurity (Leccardi 2005, 131}. Especially in African contexts, uncertainty is used to either "imply unpredictable outcomes, often of a negative kind that make life precarious" (Haram 2009, 13) or as a simple umbrella term for contexts characterized by poor conditions shaped by societal hardship, such as economic crisis (Langevang 2008), political change (Vigh 2009), conflict or post-conflict or war (Kaufmann 2011; Vigh 2015), unemployment (Langevang 2008), disease (Whyte 2015), migration (Nunzio 2015), existential needs, shortage of food supplies (Calkins 2016; Gilbertson 2015) or material – insufficient monthly salaries (Archambault 2015). Nevertheless, "we all navigate"[8] (Vigh 2009) and, yet, the extent to which we do so and the way we do so varies (Calkins 2016, 2) depending on the environment around us.

On an everyday basis, uncertainty is a matter of knowledge.

Uncertainty can be described "as a structure of feeling – the lived experience of a pervasive sense of vulnerability, anxiety, hope, and possibility" (Cooper and Pratten 2015, 1), but uncertainty is also a matter of fact rooted in the unpredictability of the future as well as in the lack of knowledge in present situations (see Cooper and Pratten 2015; Beck 1986). The core of uncertainty is the unknown: the unknown future and the unknown present.

We cannot know the outcomes of our actions for certain. With everything we do, we take risks inherent to action itself and, therefore, impossible to avoid (Luhmann 1991, 37). To calculate risk means to calculate the unpredictable "and it is by these calculations that societies create frameworks of pre-

---

8 According to Vigh, "[T]he concept [...] highlights motion within motion; it is the act of moving in an environment that is wavering and unsettled, and when used to illuminate social life, it directs our attention to the fact that we move in social environments of actors and actants, individuals and institutions, that engage and move us as we move along" (Vigh 2009). Vigh uses the concept of social navigation in order to grasp empirical action such as *dubriagem (debrouillage*, muddling through) analytically.

dictable social action"[9] (Krüger 2003, 51). The foundation of these calculations is knowledge. So, the more that is known in the present, the easier it is – or seems to be – to predict the future outcome of an action. Conversely, the less that is known in the present, the poorer the ability to predict the future.

University graduates in Bamako face three kinds of uncertainty: everyday uncertainty, immediate uncertainty, and no uncertainty.[10] These uncertainties vary in their relationship with knowledge: everyday uncertainties describe situations in which current knowledge is evaluated, part of that knowledge is the awareness of conditions which are impossible to know. Immediate uncertainties are triggered by ruptures or new situations which require new knowledge. Situations with no uncertainty are defined by a present which is sufficiently known.

(2) Knowledge production

Accounting for *la chance*.

Against uncertain backgrounds in Bamako, *la chance* answers the question of what creates the difference between graduates whose imagined futures become reality and those whose imagined futures do not, or have not yet. Individual effort, qualifications, creativity, persistence, flexibility, hope, networks, structural conditions, and God also provide answers; *la chance* embodies all of these factors.

Through the documentation and problematization of the relationship between *la chance* (layer one: empirical phenomenon) and *la chance* (layer two: concept), this book explores uncertainty as a social phenomenon in Bamako as well as a conceptual conundrum for me as a social scientist.

The phenomenon: *la chance*.

Chances are present from the very start. We have a very clear idea of what *la chance* is. Some think of chance, luck, opportunity and others more familiar

---

9 My translation. Original quote: „Risikokalkulationen sind Formen des Umgangs mit Unsicherheit, anhand derer Gesellschaften Rahmen für berechenbares soziales Handeln schaffen" (Krüger 2003).

10 Please note that "no uncertainty" does not equal "certainty".

with the Malian context might associate *la chance* with Muslim religion and humbleness. The aim of this book is to make *la chance* visible by opening it up for complication and, thereby, allowing for *la chance* to reveal its own meaning throughout the process of analysis. *La chance* is not simply out there, on the contrary, *la chance* is accomplished by graduates. So, rather than rely on our own assumptions, we get to listen and explore graduates' descriptions of *la chance*.

> *Le bonheur* exists, but you have to work for it. Work is preconditioned by *la chance*. And if you're working, you're going to have thousands of chances to be happy. [...] 'Inchallah', the reason for saying 'inchallah' means 'If God likes it, it will happen'. And it's true, whatever God does not decide is impossible. [...] In Islam, God says 'Help yourself and heaven will help you, too.' So, those who do not help themselves, those who do not work, those who tell themselves 'I have my diploma, so I will stay home and *la chance* will come.' ... But seriously, do you think that *la chance* will come? *La chance* won't come! [...] You've got go out and look for *la chance* first, and if you're looking for it and with the help of God, you're going to have a job. (My translation, 2014, interview with Moussa, Physics graduate.)

La chance is contrasted to the concepts of '*bonheur*' (luck') and '*être heureux*' (being happy, happiness). *La chance* is further connected with the ideas of accessibility, i.e. 'work' and 'God', as well as the ideas of success and failure. The relationship between work and luck is causal. "Happiness" is associated with what happens after or because of "work". In other words, there will be luck only if you work. Thus, "work is also a result of *la chance*". There is an order: first, *la chance*, then work, followed by *bonheur*. In other words, luck and happiness are preconditioned by "work", which is again preconditioned by "la chance". It all starts with *la chance*. "Inchallah", as explained, "means that if God likes it, it is going to come true". Put differently, God's word is the ultimate word; God's decisions precede *la chance*, work, and *bonheur*, as well as happiness. "*Dieu* said: 'Help yourself and heaven will help you, too.'" Individual effort represents a way to indicate your preference for the future. People who rely only on the power of the acquired diploma do not seem to gain God's recognition. "*La chance* is never going to come!" Not making an effort leads to failure, while making an effort leads to success.

Conceptualizing *la chance*.
***La chance* is many things and *la chance* does not equal *la chance*.**
Analyzing graduates' common sense understanding of *la chance*, I identified three different kinds (see Chapter 4, Layer 1), which I call prerequisites, sprouts, and outcomes. Prerequisites of *la chance* constitute the context into which individuals are born and socialized, e.g. family, environment, education. They are often referred to as *ma chance* (my chance) – *la chance* in possession and are considered to be a privilege that potentially enables further *la chance*, i.e. sprouts. Sprouts of *la chance*, like a sprouting plant, are what university graduates refer to as an opportunity or coincidence. A sprout of *la chance* needs to be identified by an individual who is prepared. Sprouts can be transformed into outcomes of *la chance*, such as a work contract that follows an internship or a position in the civil service following a passed *concours* (the government system distributing public sector employment). Outcomes constitute the product of individual effort, a result of personal effort. Unlike prerequisites, outcomes of *la chance* are connected with the idea of merit.

Moreover, graduates know how to attend to *la chance* (Chapter 5, Layer 1): "looking for *la chance* (*chercher la chance*)"; preparation, "finding *la chance* (*trouver la chance*)"; identification, "working with *la chance* (*bénéficier de la chance*)"; or "transformation." To look for *la chance* means to be prepared, in order to create or identify *la chance* when it appears, and to transform *la chance* into something one could possess.

We see that *la chance* is not another word for a concept we already know. *La chance* is not the same as, for instance, 'luck', which is philosophically conceptualized as hazard that is either perceived as positive or negative; it is not a product of individual action (Rescher 1990), nor does *la chance* capture the idea of 'hazard' or 'fate' towards the result of strategic action (Pankoke 1997, 75). *La chance* is not the same as the feeling of being lucky or happy (Bargatzky 2010; Gilbert 2006), nor is it exclusive to events or circumstances shaping individual biographies (Becker 1994; Chimanikire 2009; Bandura 1998). And even though there are similarities to 'serendipity', a 'happy accident happening by chance', an unanticipated but appreciated by-product of an action (Merton 2004; Chimanikire 2009) or the idea of 'luck' being based on a timely, or perhaps life-long preparation for opportunities (Hettlage 2010, 11)[11], neither of these concepts fully capture *la chance*.

Knowing *la chance*.

University graduates know that:
La chance makes the difference.
La chance makes sense.
La chance accounts for uncertainty and certainty.
La chance is common sense and extraordinary.
La chance accounts for the past and the future.

What sounds contradictory or confusing actually makes a point of *la chance* being both stable and unstable. As soon as we think we got it, it escapes our grasp. Only for us to find it in a new and different shape. Again. And again.

Consequently, the follow-up question is:

What is *la chance*?

This simple question is relevant, because of the very relations and questions it provokes, for instance: what does *la chance* do and what do graduates do with *la chance*?

La chance is how things work in Mali.

In Bamako,[12] I met university graduates at different points in the process of realizing their futures – some of them had already achieved their goals while others had not or not yet. Degrees, internships, and efforts are important, but they are not enough to make a difference. Graduates know that *la chance* makes the difference: it determines the future outcome of their present actions.

---

11 Original quote: „Je nachdem, wie man sein Leben in die Hand nimmt, wachsen die Chancen, etwas Vernünftiges oder wenigstens Tragfähiges daraus zu machen. So gesehen wäre Glück eine Art rechtzeitige, oder vielleicht lebenslange Vorbereitung auf Gelegenheitsstrukturen oder – wie Novalis es zuspitzte – ‚Talent für das Schicksal'" (Hettlage 2010). Note that in his description of luck, he uses three different concepts, i.e. chance, fate and opportunity (Chancen, Schicksal, Gelegenheit) in order to describe 'luck' ('Glück').

12 The setting of my research is Bamako, a West African capital city. However, I do not consider my work as research on the city (see Förster 2013), nor do I conduct research in the city of Bamako as the center of higher education in Mali.

Everyone looks for *la chance*, but it does not appear for everyone – it is distinctive and it distinguishes. Using *la chance*, graduates make sense of what does not make sense. *La chance* reveals how graduates make sense of their experiences and observations in Bamako. For instance, if 100 graduates apply for one job, 99 of them will not get the job. Graduates understand that; they know they have to work hard in order to get the job, but they are also aware of the fact that not every hard-working person is going to succeed. For the one applicant who gets the job: "It is *la chance!*" That is common sense. *La chance* explains the difference between 99 and one, it explains randomness and why things happen the way they happen. *La chance* explains "how things work in Mali."

La chance works.

> "The reality of everyday life is taken for granted as reality. It does not require additional verification over and beyond its simple presence. It is simply there, as self-evident and compelling facticity. I know that it is real" (Berger 1991, 37).

La chance is common sense knowledge.

La chance is many different things, but what exactly are these? And how do graduates know that "getting a job" and "meeting someone", for instance, is *la chance*? What exactly do graduates categorize as *la chance*? To graduates in Mali, *la chance* is common sense. Common sense is "just life in a nutshell" (Geertz 1975, 7) and it "lies so artlessly before our eyes it is almost impossible to see" (ibid 25).

Common sense constitutes a starting point for investigation (Francis 2004, 26). Common sense is considered a "practical accomplishment" (ibid. 25) produced by its members, i.e. graduates. Therefore, graduates are experts on *la chance*. Drawing from that idea, this chapter will illuminate the ways in which *la chance* is "'produced' to be recognizable" (ibid. 33) as common sense. This will allow me to turn the "normally taken for granted" categorization of an employment opportunity "into an object of reflection" and analyze the categorization of *la chance* as a "practical accomplishment" (ibid 25). Following that approach, *la chance* appears as a practical accomplishment of graduates' making sense of uncertainty. *La chance* reveals how graduates make sense of their experiences in Bamako as they "produce and gain knowledge, and thereby make a situation more predictable and meaningful" (Hänsch 2017, 8). As a systematic explanatory framework, *la chance* creates certainty in uncertain situations with regards to opportunity for income and arbitrariness with regards to selection processes. Graduates understand the randomness of the situation they live in.

(3) Gameplay

Ultimately, my work on the previous two questions allows me to approach an overarching and probably even more puzzling one:

Why do graduates keep opening up *la chance* despite their knowledge of the circumstances?

As much as this question seems specific to the study of youth in Africa, in this case university graduates in Bamako, it also is a general question concerning the absurdity of life (Camus 2014). Graduates are like Sisyphus trying to push a rock up a mountain, however, I argue that this is neither a punishment nor fun. They are opening up *la chance* voluntarily and they are happy. This is similar to the work of social scientists who keep working on the description of phenomena despite acknowledging the elusiveness of that endeavor.

As opposed to game theory, playing games is not about the strategic decision-making in anticipation of a desirable outcome prior to action, but rather about the continuation of action itself. Playing games is the "voluntary attempt to overcome unnecessary obstacles" (Suits 1925). In a utopian world in which everything were accessible to us, one could argue, all we would do is play games. Considering the Malian situation of university graduates, the situation appears much more like a dystopia in which graduates are forced to draw on the elusive promises of *la chance*, rather than engage in it voluntarily. And yet, every graduate I met seems to be living a fulfilling life. That is a paradox. But only if we assume that the key to a life like that is a successful career. Claiming that graduates are playing the game of *la chance* seems like a provocation, however the graduates are not the ones targeted, but rather our own scholarly assumptions. I argue that graduates' practices are not a response to the precariousness of their situation, but a voluntary action. In other words, graduates are not playing because they have no other option, but they play because they want to.

I argue that the practice of opening up *la chance* is a game, a "voluntarily attempt to overcome unnecessary obstacles" (Suits 2014 (1925), 43). To say that graduates are playing the game of *la chance* has three implications: (1) *La chance* matters within the game only (prelusory goal). (2) The game of *la chance* has constitutive rules. (3) The game of *la chance* is played voluntarily (lusory attitude).

Anticipating Criticism.

To say they are playing a game of *la chance* invites criticism:

It might come across as if I were diminishing their actions and their agency and not taking them seriously. And given the difficulty of their situation, it seems graduates have no choice but to play. To say they are playing a game, sounds almost like their actions did not matter anyway. Yet this is only true if we assume that the fixed goal is an employment that corresponds to their qualifications, for instance.

It might also seem as if I were romanticizing their difficult situation and at the same time being too lenient with those responsible for causing it. However, due to their particular circumstances, university graduates actually know and do something from which we can learn.

Graduates find themselves in a situation in which they can really say for sure that they are not going to get the job they had been promised when starting their university studies. They do not believe in the promises the labor market or the society once made to them. They know these promises are not true. Rather than being in denial about that, they deal with the situation and do not focus on a fixed goal. They do not try to run for that carrot. They just refuse to have that version of success and failure imposed on them. Precisely because it seems almost impossible to ignore that reality.

Gameplay is not game theory.

Whereas game theory is about acting as a result of strategic decision-making in anticipation of a desirable outcome, the idea of gameplay (see Suits 2014 [1925]) is about the action itself, in which the goal of playing games is the action. So, there is no strategy other than – one could argue – the decision to take a particular route of action.

Game theory is about competition and about strategy. It is about the logic justification of players' actions with reference to expected outcomes. It is about maximizing utility, about intention.

The setting of game theory is the unknown. Precisely because the players assume they are dependent on other people's actions, they cannot fully know the outcome of their own actions. Therefore, they are forced to strategize about their moves. So, one might argue that the fact that graduates play games is a strategic decision in response to the unknowns they face. However, the decision itself is not directed towards employment as the outcome, but towards playing games. In other words, their strategic decision is to play games. In doing so, they deploy an option game theory does not consider in its models.

In the infamous "prisoners' dilemma", for instance, the goal is to be able to leave the prison as a free person, and the two ways to reach that goal are defined by either confessing the crime or remaining silent. The players strategize or gamble based on probability, but they do not play. Game playing is not even an option in that particular situation. The reason is because the player is committed to being able to win the game. In game theory, the player wants to win. Therefore, the actions are directed towards winning.

But what if the prisoner played the situation by storytelling (see the 2015 movie *True Story* by Rupert Goold)? What if the prisoner fell in love with the detective? In both cases, the goal of the game shifts from getting out of prison towards continuous play and, therefore, maintaining the situation, which allows the prisoner to keep telling stories or keep flirting, for instance. The goal is no longer getting out of the situation and consequently out of the game. Rather, the goal is the situation itself. It might be hard to imagine that a person would voluntarily want to remain in interrogation. But it might be easier to imagine if we acknowledge that the prisoner understands that the interrogation is a set-up and, therefore, will most likely not get him out of prison. Thus, this understanding renders the goal of being set free simply not worth strategizing for. Game playing is not primarily about pleasure and fun, but more importantly, it offers an alternative option which both responds to the setting and corresponds with an individual's understanding of it.

THIS BOOK: chapter description.

Approaching *la chance* and *la chance.*

Three blind people examine an elephant by the means of touch. They do not know they are dealing with an elephant. They investigate by the means of touch. They compare the surface and the structure of what they touch to what they know and conclude accordingly: "It's a snake". "It's a rope". "It's a tree". "It's a fan". The elephant consists of a snake and a rope and a tree (even four trees) and a fan (but only at times: sneezes, breathes or does other elephant things). Though the results of the men's analysis seem incommensurable (compare Kuhn 1962), all these elements make an elephant. The parts, and the whole. But also, how the parts speak to the whole and vice versa. The elephant is only complete in its relations and connections.

"Methods, after all, are not neutral devices" (Hine 2005, 7). In other words, the methods we apply in order to see our research object define the way we see our research object in the end. In that sense, we do not see *la chance* as it is, but *la chance* how it appears through a particular method or lens. Examining *la chance* with this approach, all we are going to end up with is particularities. We won't find *la chance* (the elephant). We only find single *la chances* (a snake, a tree...).

The empirical phenomenon of *la chance* is an experience (phenomenology), a practical accomplishment (ethnomethodology), a narrative (narrative analysis) ... *La chance* is all of these things and not just one in contrast to the others. *La chance* is defined by the way a person sees it. And yet, though different to each and every individual, *la chance* is out there – not as a pattern, not as one phenomenon, not as an experience... – *la chance* is out there in relation. Therefore, this book is an attempt to describe *la chance* in relation. I am blind and I approach *la chance* by listening to those who conclude "it's *la chance*" and examine how they came to these conclusions.

What are university graduates dealing with when they are dealing with *la chance*? And what are we dealing with when we are dealing with *la chance*? What can I learn about the world if I take *la chance* into account? Through the exploration of these relations in which *la chance* emerges, i.e. between graduates and researchers, individuals and all of us, between Bamako and the world, this book offers a unique view into what we take for granted.

This book is an ethnography (part one) and an assemblage (part two).

Part One of the book ethnographically situates the empirical phenomenon of *la chance* in graduates' lives in Bamako. Part Two is an assemblage (see Deleuze and Guattari 1987) which sets out to analyze the phenomenon of *la chance* and develops a conceptual framework of *la chance*. It is based on graduates' knowledge accessed through narrative interviews.

As a method, the combination of both approaches helps me describe and grasp the (in)stability of *la chance*. Whereas the ethnography empirically situates *la chance* in graduates' lives, the assemblage is a tool which epistemologically accounts for emergence and, therefore, captures the general logic of *la chance*, while keeping it open.

The second part of the book is in the form of an assemblage which allows it to be entered at any point, encouraging an explorative reading experience. Offering the schemes extracted from coding with MaxQDA, and a map for orientation, you will be able to move around in the book, not reading it in a linear fashion, but moving through its parts at your own pace and according to what you would like to read about.

Let me explain:

To me, *la chance* is a fascinating and continuous puzzle, an omnipresent token in my thinking and, ultimately, a provider of a career in the social sciences up to this point.

My first answer to the question of "What is *la chance*?" is inspired by ethnomethodological thinking (see Chapter 4 and 5. Layer One). This first layer offers a systematic account of what *la chance* is to university graduates in Bamako, i.e. prerequisites, sprouts and outcomes. Overall, *la chance* emerges as a product of graduates making sense of circumstances that do not make sense. I continue with a second investigation of that very same question "What is *la chance*?" two years later. Of course, I did not start from scratch here, but used the data I had organized during my initial research process.

And whereas the first time I concluded "It's a fan!", the second time, my conclusion sounds more like "It's a tree!".

Thus, the picture I will be able to paint is a bit more complete, yet far from being comprehensive and far from being clearer. Both conclusions are far from "It is an elephant!" However, put together and in relation (see Assemblage), they show that *la chance* is not only part of graduates' lives in Bamako and of my life, but also inherent in the research process.

To you, *la chance* might be the same, but chances are you draw your own conclusions about *la chance*. My mission here is twofold: It is to make visible how both graduates account for *la chance* and how I see *la chance*, but also to encourage you to develop you own understanding of *la chance*. This is what "The assemblage of *la chance*" in the second part of the book attempts to accomplish. It provides both the conclusions and constraints resulting from my own thinking and opportunities for you to explore by yourself and draw conclusions of your own.

Part One: Ethnography of *La Chance*. Or, What Graduates Know and What They Know They Don't Know.

The first part of the book ethnographically situates the empirical phenomenon of *la chance* in graduates' lives in Bamako.

Chapter 1: Situating *La Chance* in Knowledge.

What do university graduates know about their society in relation to the national labor market? And how do they account for that knowledge?

Uncertainty is inherent to action, since the outcomes of action are never fully predictable. "We all navigate" (Vigh 2009). However, when navigating uncertainty, people know and understand their environment as they go along; they have to be able to analyze and evaluate it. Navigation requires knowledge, which is essential to certainty. In accordance with the main concern of the sociology of knowledge, I understand knowledge as "everything that passes for 'knowledge' in society" (Berger and Luckmann 1991, 26), and that includes "common-sense 'knowledge' rather than 'ideas'" (ibid. 27). Examining graduates' common-sense knowledge about their everyday lives and the Malian society, I show how they make sense of an environment that appears static for the most part and and then suddenly moves sometimes. I argue that uncertainty is about knowledge, which includes both what is known and what is known to be unknown.

There are official systems of job distribution, but nevertheless graduates know that getting an employment is actually *la chance*. I examine "le bras long" ("the long arm", with reference to social networks) and "le concours" (the national system for the distribution of employment in the civil service). We will encounter both as cases of ordinary and extraordinary situations, i.e. situations in which graduates find themselves knowing about the circumstances that led to the situation at hand (knowledge about the presence of knowledge) and knowing they do not know about these very circumstances (knowledge about the absence of knowledge). The commonly used expression "l'homme propose, Dieu dispose" (man proposes, God provides) accounts for graduates' knowledge of what they do not know. This intersection between what graduates know they know and know they do not know is right where *la chance* kicks in.

Chapter 2: Situating *La Chance* in Graduates' Everyday Lives.

Graduates — who are these people? What are their questions? What do they know (they don't know)?

In this chapter, I investigate the relationship between graduates and situations that raise questions for them in order to find out what they know and what they know they don't know. The focus on everyday situations in individuals' lives allows me to relate the known and the unknown and in doing so carve out challenges of everyday life. We will see that the unknown is not the counterpart of the known, but a part of it. Ultimately, I use these situated empirical accounts and questions as an entry point in approaching conceptual unknowns.

The first part of this ethnographic chapter starts off with vignettes (a soccer game and a wedding) connecting the two respective protagonists with each other (Madou and Amadou, Simone and Safiatou), followed by an introduction of each university graduate individually with a short biography and a vignette accounting for an everyday situation I extracted from participant observation. The fragmented character of this part of the chapter allows the reader to get to know the four graduates exploratively just like they get to know *la chance* in the next part of the book.

The second part of this chapter presents situations that raise questions for the graduates introduced above. The sections are arranged according to questions highlighting aspects of their professional and family lives, as well as their temporal dimension, i.e. present and future.

Part Two: Assemblage of *La Chance*. Or, The Emergence of *La Chance* in the Encounter.

The second part of the book is an assemblage, which sets out to analyze the phenomenon of *la chance* and continues to develop a conceptual framework of *la chance*. This part is based on graduates' knowledge accessed through narrative interviews.

Chapter 3: A Manual.

What is an assemblage? How is it used in this book and in relation to *la chance*?

The purpose of this chapter is twofold: The reader is directly addressed and provided with a map and manual for orientation in the assemblage and an invitation to explore. For orientation, I describe the following two chapters (chapters 4 and 5), their layers and tracings, which are based on different methodologies. I further invite readers to explore the assemblage either in a linear way, which then tells the story of a journey of discovery documenting my research process, or in a fragmented way, which will allow readers to explore *la chance* on their own.

Overall, the content and the shape of an assemblage allows us to get from a perceived idea of *la chance* and its elusive character towards a systematics of the unknown. The assemblage of *la chance* has two layers which guide us through chapters four and five.

In the first layer, I approach the questions: "What is *la chance*? And what does *la chance* do?", applying Membership Categorization Analysis (MCA), which helps me to systematically account for graduates' knowledge. Scanning the devices that members, i.e. graduates, employ describing *la chance*, I focus on predicates (in order to find out what *la chance* is in chapter one) and activities (in order to find out what *la chance* does in chapter two). All in all, MCA shapes the first layer of analysis, which I call systematization of *la chance*.

In the **second layer**, I revisit this systematization of my data. This time playfully exploring the accounts' contents, I go through them looking for conceptual clues independent of the Bamako context. Later on, I arrange these clues which account for the emergence of *la chance* (in chapter 4) and *la chance* in the encounter (in chapter 5).

At the end of each section, I offer **tracings**, which summarize my findings and abstract from them. I use the word tracing because I understand that the map allows for more connections in addition to the ones I see and it is up to the reader to add to the assemblage.

Chapter 4: Emergence Of La Chance: Types and Relations.

What is *la chance*?
Layer 1 (L1). Systematization of *la chance*.

To graduates in Mali, *la chance* is common sense. Common sense is "just life in a nutshell" (Geertz 1975, 7) and it "lies so artlessly before our eyes it is almost impossible to see" (ibid. 25). This layer makes *la chance* visible as it analyses *la chance* as a members' category.

Conducting Membership Categorization Analysis, which originates in ethnomethodology, I present a systematization of graduates' knowledge of *la chance*, which consists of three types: prerequisites, sprouts, and outcomes. Prerequisites are constituted by graduates' social context, their families, the environment they grew up in, and their education. Graduates possess prerequisites which have either been assigned to or accomplished by them. Prerequisites have the potential to further enable *la chance*, namely, sprouts of *la chance*. Sprouts of *la chance* are opportunities; they appear and they need to be identified by graduates. Sprouts potentially advance new paths which can be established by graduates as they turn sprouts of *la chance* into outcomes. Outcomes of *la chance* are opportunities grasped and transformed by graduates. Employment contracts based on an internship or the successful participation in a *concours* are instances graduates refer to as *la chance*.

Layer 2 (L2). *La chance* in relation.

In this second layer, by means of an explorative content analysis, I show how *la chance* emerges in relation to others and to oneself, to what is taken for granted and the everyday as well as to what is not *la chance* and la *malchance*.

We will see that:

La chance is the exception, not the norm.
La chance is to accomplish something highly unlikely.
La chance is the preferred option, not just any option.

Drawing from the relational character of *la chance*, I examine the unequal distribution of *la chance*. We see that *la chance* plays by its own rules and therefore cannot be enforced or predicted by graduates. Rather, *la chance* emerges between structural and agentive factors. Furthermore, we learn that there is an important difference between the agency of a graduate and the agency of *la chance*. Whereas graduates' agency is constituted by practices of preparation for *la chance* and its identification as well as its transformation, *la chance*'s agency is characterized by its presence and its absence. In other words, the agency of *la chance* reveals itself in its emergence.

Chapter 5: Encounter: The Practice of Opening Up *La Chance* and The Game of *La Chance*.

What does *la chance* do? How is la chance accessed?
Layer 1 (L1). Opening up *la chance*.

Led by the question of how graduates open up *la chance* and again by applying MCA, I reveal that most of the activities surrounding *la chance* are bound to sprouts of *la chance* (see chapter four). Sprouts of *la chance* are a bit like serendipitous events, which cannot be planned, so "[a]ll we can do is [...] put ourselves into a favorable position to profit by unexpected occurrences" (Merton 2004, 191). In other words, sprouts are special; they are a rupture of the everyday, which is why they require an explanation.

I present graduates' practices, "looking for *la chance* (sprouts)" or preparation, "finding *la chance* (sprouts)" or identification and "working with *la chance* (sprouts)" or transformation. Graduates "looking for *la chance*" anticipate *la chance* in a concrete or abstract manner and prepare for it accordingly. These practices of preparation are conducted in the present based on their prerequisites, but they are geared towards the future – towards a sprout of *la chance*. Graduates identify and evaluate them, and again, graduates' ability to do so depends on their preparation. Once identified, graduates work on the sprout's transformation into a concrete and anticipated outcome. In contrast to preparation, transformation is not an activity directed toward a sprout of *la chance*, but a response to a sprout. The intersection of these two kinds of activities is marked by the identification of a sprout of *la chance*.

Layer 2 (L2). The game of *la chance*.

Drawing from the clues extracted in layer two through an explorative content analysis, I develop the idea of the game of *la chance*, which is not about winning, but about playing.

La chance is found in the encounter, i.e. in the relationships and in the collaboration between the players. I describe the players and their relation to *la chance*. I focus in particular on the relationship between player one and *la chance*, which is characterized by knowledge and practices of deciding, preparing, seeing and influencing.

Furthermore, I introduce various plays (workplace, friendship, business, success, by-product and parenthood) in which *la chance* emerges in the encounter between the players. This is also where we find out about the difference between having *la chance* and having the ability to have *la chance*, the co-constitutive relationship between the players characterized by the difference between players seeing and being seen as well as the interchangeability of players one and two. Ultimately, I use these considerations to illuminate what is unknown to the players.

I argue that the practice of opening up *la chance* is a game, a "voluntary attempt to overcome unnecessary obstacles" (Suits 2014 (1925), 43). To say that graduates are playing the game of *la chance* has three implications: (1) *La chance* matters within the game only (prelusory goal). (2) The game of *la chance* has constitutive rules. (3) The game of *la chance* is played voluntarily (lusory attitude). As a result of the discussion of these points in dialogue with the empirical material, we will see that graduates play the game of *la chance* because they want to, not because they have to. We further see that graduates do not obey the rules of the labor market which is ultimately targeted to procuring employment, but the rules of the game of *la chance* targeted to the continuation of play. In doing so, they play with the rules of the labor market. Playing the game of *la chance*, graduates know they cannot win against the background of the labor market. However, within the game of *la chance*, they do succeed and thereby appropriate the labor market.

Part 1: Ethnography of *La Chance*

1 Knowledge | Situating *La Chance* in Graduates' Knowledge.

[We are here]

In Bamako, there are institutionalized systems of job distribution which are supposed to make sure the most qualified applicant gets the job. However, graduates know that employment is *la chance*. How come?

This puzzle invites the examination of the relationship between knowledge and employment focusing on common-sense knowledge. The overall purpose of this chapter is to situate *la chance* in graduates' common-sense knowledge. The leading questions are:

What do university graduates know about their society in relation to the national labor market? How do they account for that knowledge?

To university graduates, it is common sense that getting a job is *la chance*. But what constitutes the conclusion of that being common sense? There are three kinds: observational common sense, which is a result of external senses' perception of the environment; judgmental common sense, which is also referred to as "good judgment" as it is based on understandings of everyday experiences; and consensual common sense, which relates to facts everyone knows and agrees on (Rescher 2005,12). Common sense facts "appear to be transparently true through the circumstance that they are obvious and (in a certain way) self-evident" (ibid. 29). Common sense is "shamelessly and unapologetically ad hoc" (Geertz 1975, 23), and even though or maybe because every "solid citizen" is an expert on common sense (ibid 24), it "remains more an assumed phenomenon than an analyzed one" (ibid 9). It is in that sense that I proceed to examine what is "obvious" and "self-evident" about how to get a job in Mali according to university graduates.

Departing from the common-sense statement "employment is *la chance*", I will describe three systems located at the intersection between employment and *la chance*, i.e. "le bras long", "le concours", and "l'homme propose, Dieu dispose". I will elaborate graduates' knowledge about each system's routinized way of distributing jobs. My informants know that *la chance* makes the difference between those who gain employment and those who do not, or not yet.

One of the aspects that are crucial here is the question of employment and more specifically: who gets employed? Approaching this question, we are going to examine the relationship between knowledge and employment. In other words, what do graduates know about who gets employment?

On this journey, we look at the case of *le bras long* and *le concours*. We will encounter both as cases of routine and non-routine situations, which means as situations in which graduates find themselves knowing about the circumstances (knowledge about the presence of knowledge) that made up for the situation at hand and knowing they do not know (knowledge about the absence of knowledge) about these very circumstances.

Knowledge includes the known and the unknown. Knowledge is what is known and what is known to be unknown. Both are ways of knowing. *Le bras long* and *le concours* account for what graduates know, "l'homme propose, Dieu dispose" is a case of knowing what they don't know – which is right where a *la chance* kicks in.

KNOWLEDGE: On the presence of *la chance*

If uncertainty is about knowledge, the question is: what do graduates know? And again, what do they know about what?

Throughout the next section, I focus on graduates' common-sense knowledge about how to get a job in Mali. Examining this relationship between knowledge and employment, I focus on the case of *le bras long* (the long arm) and *le concours* (competition for government employment), both of which make a difference when it comes to getting employed or staying unemployed. *Le bras long* refers to social networks and plays a significant role when it comes to accessing employment, internships, information; passing *le concours* based on qualification and performance allows for direct access to steady life-time government employment.

Le bras long | A case of privilege?

> It's difficult to have a job here in Mali, because there is this kind of relation...
> Like, you are my sister and I have a company, so I take you. Even if you aren't
> qualified. It's like that in Mali. But if by chance we do find somebody who is
> qualified, of course we're going to employ that person. (My translation, inter-
> view, 2014, with Mohamed, graduated in Administration.)

That "certain kind of relation", also referred to as *le bras long* (the long arm)
is given as the reason why it is difficult to find a job in Mali, but at the same
time, it does enable people to get employed. Family members are prioritized
over qualification and graduates know that: "It's like that in Mali".

> *Le bras long* is best explained as advantage. If nature favors your parents, they
> might come up with an adequate and concrete solution for your situation.
> This means that you are going to be employed at a company because of their
> relations and not because of your merit or because of the studies you did. [...]
> I don't have this *la chance*. I don't have *la chance* of having parents with a long
> arm. (My translation, interview, 2014, with Amadou, graduated in Interna-
> tional Law.)

Amadou explains that *le bras long* offers concrete solutions, such as employment, which is *la chance*. Some parents have *le bras long* to the benefit of their
children; it is a primordial advantage. The power of *le bras long* lies in its
ability to provide access to employment without the consideration of either
merit or qualification. In fact, Amadou's account is about the expectation
that jobs are distributed to those who deserve it based on their qualification,
while the reality is that *le bras long* employs those who have influential family
members. Amadou calls that *la chance*. To sum up, family and qualification
lead to employment: if there is a business, and you are family and looking
for a job, you get the job. At the same time, if there is a business and you are
qualified when no family member is, you get the job. "Everybody has their *la
chance* in life... maybe it's just like that, that there are people whose parents
have *le bras long* and others' parents have short arms". Everybody possesses
individual *la chance* and the length of one's arm is part of it.

Imagine *le bras long* as a branch of a tree which comes in different shapes
and sizes, different qualities and quantities, with dense and sparse bifurca-

tions, some flourishing others dry, maybe just temporarily due to the season of the year; every single one of them pointing into a different direction.

The tree image is productive here, because it helps us to see and remember that every graduate has successfully climbed up the stem of a tree by graduating from university.

Up there, graduates engage with the trees' traits in terms of (1) movement and in terms of (2) fostering. (1) Moving around, they climb and descend branches, they jump and swing between them, a branch might fall off taking the graduate down with it. In the following accounts we see graduates accepting to stay on and reach for a branch, switch between branches, making their way from one branch to the next. (2) They also invest in growing branches, leaves and fruit, which might or might not pay off. Sometimes they find help, fertilizer, or too much sun for a sprout to take off.

Yet, it is not only about the graduates' actions, but also about the nature of the trees around them. Some trees are further apart, others grow closer together, some branches might fall off and some branches might even connect different trees, which then allows for the movement of graduates between trees.

Le bras long is always both about origin and destination, it has heterogeneous origins, i.e. family, friends, colleagues, and it might (or might not) take various paths: directly and via intermediaries, towards an initial or a new goal emerging on the way. Graduates know that "here in Mali", employment is *la chance* and it is provided by *le bras long*, which is *la chance*, too. The following empirical examples show how the length of one's arm mobilizes and constrains graduates' access to employment.

So, the following section is a description of *le bras long*, its constitution and its capabilities. With the help of graduates' knowledge, I am going to describe what *le bras long* looks like, what it does with graduates and what graduates do with it. We will see how graduates take and grow branches.

TAKING branches.

Accepting a branch (Amadou).

Le bras long has been crucial throughout Amadou's life: his family's arm brought him to Bamako for his university studies. Thanks to his aunt and uncle, who looked after him and provided him with a room in their house, he was able to go to university. He lived on his scholarship, bought a moto and did little jobs from time to time in order to be "a bit independent". Amadou also worked at the telephone stall attached to his uncle's house and later took over the business. This job was provided by his uncle. Later on, Amadou tried to set up a cleaning business and reached out to influential people like the mayor of one of the six communities in Bamako, though none of them could pay him on time. The network he created for that purpose came into existence, but its arms remained too short. After some time managing his own telephone stall with the profits diminishing, he started working at his auntie's cafeteria. Though he did not earn much, he liked the responsibility and the fact that he was finally able to return a favor to her. In 2015, Amadou is back in Segou working at a mediating company affiliated with a well-known brand company. It is his own business, and he is one of the first in charge of a business like this in Segou. Initially, it was not his idea, but his other uncle's, who lives abroad. He provided Amadou with the capital to start off this new business.

His family's arm worked how it was supposed to work according to common sense knowledge: Amadou received a job at his auntie's restaurant and his business was funded by his uncle. That is not a surprise. However, to Amadou, the fact that the *bras long* worked is *la chance*. He did not get any money from the professional contacts he acquired himself, which is no surprise either. "C'est comme ça au Mali": it is common sense that family helps out family members – depending on what is accessible to them. You see, Amadou is a lawyer, but his auntie owns a restaurant and not a law firm. Amadou wants to set up a cleaning business, but his uncle, who is also a businessman, does not credit Amadou's idea and instead wants his nephew to execute his own ideas. In this case, *le bras long* leads into directions determined by others. Grateful, yet, also for the lack of other options, Amadou has to accept the helping hand.

Switching branches (Simone).

Simone always wanted to be a journalist. Two arms lead her to an internship at national TV: the family arm of her uncle and the professional arm of her university professor rewarding her for being one of his best students. She says her uncle had nothing to do with her getting the internship – unlike common sense about *le bras long* would suggest. Today, people at the station know and appreciate her journalistic work. In the end though, neither of her long arms, i.e. her uncle, her professor, colleagues at the TV station were long enough to get her the contract she wanted. Instead, there was another family arm pointing to a different employment opportunity:

> I have an uncle, who works for the UN. [...] He suggested that I should go see an Indian businessman. In fact, I sent him my CV and he then sent it to my current boss. And he was pleased and interested, so he called me. (My translation, interview, 2015, with Simone, graduated in Law.)

Here, Simone talks about her current job at the International Airport Bamako-Senou. She had learned about the job through her uncle, and he was also the one to send her CV over. Ultimately, Simone was employed in airline administration. Though her uncle was involved here, Simone presents it as the long arm putting her in a favorable position by delivering access to the information of a job vacancy, as well as access to the hiring person. Simone switched from one branch to another once her preferred one did not extend any further.

Swinging from one branch to the next (Madou).

Similarly, Cheick swings from one branch to the next. Cheick (see people) wanted to do his PhD in physics after his studies. In order to accomplish that, he needed to go abroad. His parents had the money to pay for the flight, a history of reliability that convinced the embassy to give him a visa, and a place to stay in Germany. Madou's dad used to be a lecturer at that university, but he was a linguist. Because Madou wanted to become a physicist, the long family arm brought him there, but not to the physics department. It was Madou himself who contacted the physics professor, who then offered him a scholarship for his doctoral studies. In the end, he was unable to take advantage of his scholarship and stayed in Mali looking for a job:

> Mom gave me that idea saying, 'Did you talk to your uncle at the company?' [...] Getting that internship took me more than a year, even though I have relatives over there. I didn't even know the person who ultimately decided to take me as an intern. I was introduced to him when I got there. Also, the people with whom I work... I didn't know them. Same with my boss, I didn't

know him... he's a burkinabé. My boss is a burkinabé. (My translation, interview, 2014, with Madou, graduated in Physics.)

Madou's long arm is a prolonged arm that stretches via his mother to his uncle to his boss, and it pointed towards a telecommunications agency. At first, this account seems to present a long arm situation, but not quite, because there are two facts that Madou presents as unusual: one, it took him so long to get a job, and two, he received the job even though he did not know the person who employed him. Had *le bras long* worked in accordance with his expectations, he would have received the job instantly. Instead, Madou had to remain persistent for over a year. In the end, he got the job, not because of his arm, but because of his enduring effort and a decision made by his boss, whom he "did not even know" and could not possibly have known, since his boss "is a *burkinabé*". From his emphasis, I conclude that it is unusual to get a job without having any relatives in the company and that he assumes I think he received his job because of his uncle. Madou did not get the internship because of his long arm, which is itself *la chance* since it usually ensures a job; Madou got employed anyway.

Reaching a branch (Oumar).

When Oumar was still a kid, his father lost his job as a government official. Ever since, his family has faced financial problems and has had difficulties affording their children's education. During university studies, his best friend Adama had his back. He also introduced Oumar to the company they are both working for today:

> My friend Adama works over there and sometimes they organize soccer tournaments, in which their company plays against another company. They called me and I played. And when they were recruiting new employees, they called me as well. That's how it all happened. (My translation, interview, 2014, with Oumar, graduated in Economics.)

Adama invited his friend Oumar over to a soccer tournament organized by his company. Oumar, who used to play for a second league club, accepted the invitation and obviously impressed them. Initially, he did not apply for a job, but after the match he received an offer. Consequently, when asked how he got the job, Oumar refers to a soccer event and his friendship with Adama – not to an application or a job interview, for example. It was his friend's long arm Oumar was able to reach for.

GROWING branches.
A flourishing branch (Safiatou).

Safiatou kept working at the radio station long after her internship was over. She made a name for herself; she even had her own radio show and collaborated on various TV projects with other journalists. Just like for Simone, this professional arm never led to a contracted employment at the station, so, she decided to get into communications via another professional arm originating at the TV station:

> It all happened because of me. In order to get to national TV, I've had a professor who suggested us to go there and get in touch with them. So, I benefited from that and networked for real. After that it was easy for me to get access to other internships. Voilà, that's how I found myself over there. And it was the same contacts that got me into the other communications agency. I played my relations I created at the TV station. It all started with these contacts, and it is because of them that I'm here today. (My translation, interview, 2013, with Safiatou, graduated in English.)

Today, she works for a well-known communication and marketing agency. Starting off as a private student in journalism, Safiatou received the opportunity to conduct her internship via a professional long arm. She points out that she was the one who created a professional network for herself, which has been beneficial to her ever since. Safiatou "played her relations," knowing that the long arm provides access, she put herself in a position to use it once it flourished.

A dry branch (Mohamed).

Just like Safiatou did at the radio station, Mohamed worked on his professional network during his internship at a bank. He studied economics, because he thought that this decision might enable him to work both in the public and the private sector. His parents are on good terms with the university, especially with the faculty of social sciences and languages. His dad was professor and his mother occasionally cooks at university events. Mohamed always helped his mom at the restaurant as a supervisor and accountant. He also received the opportunity for an internship as an accountant at the faculty of social sciences, as suggested by his mother. He is not getting paid with money, but with experience, he says. In this case, the long arm of his family suggested another direction; Mohamed followed and ultimately benefited from that. He would have preferred to work for a bank in the private sector, particularly at a bank in the capital where Mohamed did an internship several years ago. Back then, he did not get a contract, but he is still in touch with his boss, who promised to find him a job.

> People at the bank appreciated me a lot. They wanted me to work there, but they didn't have the means to recruit me... This happens via concours, you know. But the concours, we don't even talk about that anymore. [...] So, they want to help me, but they don't know how. (My translation, interview, 2013, with Mohamed, graduated in Administration.)

Mohamed extended his professional network by conducting his internship at a bank. Afterwards, it seemed as if everything was set for him to get employed: he worked well, people liked him and wanted to recruit him, but then there was no official recruitment scheduled, i.e. there was no vacant position he could apply for. In other words, qualification, effort, and *le bras long* combined cannot overcome the fact that there is no job. Within the framework of his internship, Mohamed grew a professional long arm, which turned out to be dry. At least for the time being, it is worthless in terms of potential employment, due to the overall job situation at the bank. Unlike in Safiatou's case, in which her self-grown professional long arm in journalism created an opportunity for them in copy writing, Mohamed's *bras long* was not able to achieve that.

Let's recall:

To Amadou and Simone, *le bras long* is like a tree with branches attached to the root and reaching only so far. Other more attractive trees are too far away for them to reach via the branches they have access to. To Madou, *le bras long* allows him to move like Tarzan in the jungle from one vine to the next, which again provides him with the necessary momentum to reach even further towards destinations interesting to him. Oumar is the guy looking around on the ground and is suddenly being grabbed by a friend swinging on a vine. Each of them acts in relation to the environment they find themselves in. We see that *le bras long* is about the environment and about the person engaging with it.

We saw that family members, friends or colleagues might play a significant role in graduates' entry to the labor market. However, graduates made sure to emphasize that in their individual case, it was different and the fact that they had procured jobs was explained by something other than *le bras long*. In Madou's, Oumar's, Simone's, and Safiatou's cases, their contacts were mediators between potential employers and the graduates themselves. They provided access to information, which in turn facilitated access to the job, rather than furnishing the job itself. It is striking, though, that neither of these arms points into directions they would have preferred professionally.

Maybe things would have been different if Amadou, for instance, had not been willing to execute his uncle's business idea instead of his own, Madou switched from physics to marketing, and Safiatou from journalism to copy writing. They identified these opportunities and, consequently, decided to work with them.

For some of my informants, *le bras long* unlocked spaces which otherwise would have stayed closed or at least unnoticed. Madou's uncle provided him with information[1], Amadou's uncle with money, and Oumar's friend with an important contact. *Le bras long* represents the idea of favoring family members, especially when it comes to employment distribution. If one member of a social group gains access to certain kinds of resources, any other member of that same social group is more likely to be provided with at least the possibility to access those resources as well – by the means of that very first member. *Le bras long* is *la chance* to those who have it; *le bras long* reproduces *la chance*. Similar to 'social capital', *le bras long* is constituted by both the actual and potential resources available to the individual (Bourdieu 1983, 190). Graduates either have a *bras long* already or they create one of their own themselves.

Up next, we see how Safiatou and Mohamed grow branches of their own, yet again, with different results. University graduates know about *the bras long* and the way it operates ("C'est comme ça au Mali"), and yet, every individual experiences it differently. There is no single *bras long*, but each one is

---

1 For further reading on the nature of exchange networks and its benefits in terms of access to information see Powell 1990.

different in its constitution, and its function is dependent on both external circumstances and ways in which individuals engage with it.

Le concours | A case of random selection?

The *concours* is an official government system of recruitment for public service – a competition for employment positions – and is equally open to everyone who has the educational degree required. People who meet certain qualification criteria compete as they take an exam. Ultimately, people are selected with reference to their performance.[2] Yet, the number of those who pass is determined from the very beginning. This means that the difference between the results of the last ones who pass and the first ones who fail is minimal. However, the actual effect of passing or failing a *concours* produces permanent and brutal discontinuities (Bourdieu, 1983, 190). For instance, also somebody who brings up the rear in the *concours* will receive a life-long contract in public administration, which comes with a secure monthly salary and possibilities for promotion. The last one passing will be as privileged as the first one, the one following the last one though will not have anything – just like the other thousands of participants.

In October 2016, the Ministry of Labor and Civil Service announced a *concours* for civil service in the categories B and C (Walanta 2016). Applicants for category B are required to have at least a baccalauréat diploma and not to be older than 35. Applicants for category C need a DEF (diplôme d'études fondamentales) at least and their age needs to be between 18 and 32. University graduates qualify for category A, but at this point in time, there are no vacant posts for that category. Graduates are, however, free to apply for categories B and C. In that *concours*, 230 civil servants will be recruited in various domains, such as technicians (health, mining, and agriculture), controllers (treasure, finances, customs) and administrators. There is one month between the announcement and the application deadline, at which point applications are processed and lists with participants' names are published. The actual *concours* takes place at the end of December. The test consists of a technical part, a professional part, and a general part, each lasting two hours.

---

2 This is in contrast to the lottery system, e.g. the green card lottery system (Piot, 2010, chapter three), in which winners or losers are determined by batch. The system of selection is based purely on hazard.

According to a grading coefficient, the results of the technical part and the professional part count three times more than the general part. Applicants need to achieve a minimum of 10/20 points in order to qualify. Here are some numbers[3] of participation: there were 873 people applying for 30 category C jobs in administration (Anon 2016). This is thirty people applying for one job. There were 1,644 people applying for 13 category B jobs in treasury controlling (Anon 2016). Again, this is 126 people per job. And there were 8,498 applicants for 10 category B positions in finance controlling (Anon 2016); in other words, 850 people applying for one job. All in all, not a single position corresponds to a university graduate's qualification and the ones for which they can apply count thousands of other applicants.

When I conducted fieldwork in 2011, I visited a *concours* and most of the applicants I talked to that day said they only participate in order to able to say at least they tried – not because they really believe in being chosen. So, the following section is about university graduates' experiences with the *concours* and their knowledge about how *le concours* works. Malian university graduates know how the *concours* is supposed to work, but it is common-sense knowledge that the *concours* is a pro-forma event and decisions are made according to the rules of the *bras long*. It is said that ministers' and employees' kids and friends are preferred by *le concours*. However, there is another factor even more significant to the results of the *concours*: *la chance*.

La chance intervenes (Mohamed).

Mohamed knows that passing a *concours* does actually not depend on knowledge:

> They ask you questions which are fundamental for a financier. So, if you don't manage to respond to those... honestly, you shouldn't even participate in the concours. [...] But there is another criterion for selection. [...] For example, you need 100 people, and more than 350 knew (all the answers to your questions). How are you going to make your selection? That's where *la chance* intervenes. [...] The questions asked are simple. That's how it is with le concours! (My translation, interview, 2014, with Mohamed, graduated in Administration.)

---

3 I have chosen these examples because graduates in economics are more likely to apply for these positions in administration, rather than for positions in nursing or mining.

1 Knowledge | Situating *La Chance* in Graduates' Knowledge. 49

Passing the concours depends on *la chance*, because if you are an economist and people ask you questions about economics, you will be able to answer them for sure – and so will any other economist participating in the *concours*. Now, if everybody knows the answers to all the questions asked, the distinguishing criterion can no longer be the performance in the *concours*; it has to be something else, which Mohamed says is *la chance*. *La chance* picks the one who will be employed. Consequently, the distinguishing feature is not the performance only, but performance plus *la chance*.

Le bras long intervenes (Boubacar).

Boubacar, an economist, is the only graduate I know, who passed the *concours*. Several family members – his father, mother, older sister, and one of his two younger brothers – work in government offices. When Boubacar started working at the ministry of commerce shortly after his graduation, people say it was his family connections that put him in this position. In the following account, I ask for his opinion on that issue:

> Susann: So, your parents didn't help you?
>
> Boubacar: No, no! My parents didn't help me. They helped me, of course, of course they helped!
>
> Susann: No. Since they are also working in...
>
> Boubacar: No, no! Not at all. No! We are not in the same domain. And imagine, how many functionaries are there here in Mali? Now, if everybody helped their children, how could we get out? [...] Your parents can't do anything for you. We were more than 1,000, more than 3,000, 4,000 candidates and they were looking for 5 or 10 people. Imagine the probability of getting le concours. I told myself that maybe, if I have *la chance*, if God is with me, I can have the concours. (My translation, interview, 2013, with Boubacar, graduated in Economics.)

This interview extract is interesting, because there seems to be a difference between helping and helping. So, let's get a bit into detail here: Boubacar's parents "did not help him, but they did help him. I did not explicitly ask if his parents worked on his examination results, or if it is because of them that he received the government job; I did not ask about *le bras long*. However, he instantly understood that this is what I was meaning to ask. His reaction highlights the common sense of the *bras long*, which is about parents ensuring their children's employment. "No, no! Not at all. No!" He insists being fully aware of the usual assumption about parents putting their children into civil service. Then he switches saying "they did help me", which gives credit to their parenting. He acknowledges their contribution to the fact that he was in the position to become a civil servant. His parents were the ones to put him into that position that enabled him to do the rest of it himself. They helped him in general and throughout his life; but they did not make him pass. In the conversation, I then try to justify my question and at the same time I insist: "Since they are also working...". He quickly interrupts me saying, that they are not working in the same domain, so they could not have possibly made him pass. "Tes parents ne peuvent rien pour toi!" – "They cannot do a thing for you". He adds some numbers: 1,000 to 4,000 competing for 5 to 10 jobs. Statistically, it is highly improbable to be amongst the five or ten people that pass. So, even if you do, it is *la chance* and God. Departing from the assumption that it might have been his family arm that gave him access to public administration employment, he introduces me to probability and statistics and ultimately, to *la chance*.

THE KNOWN | What they DO know

In Mali, the *concours* results determine future public service agents; however, graduates account for the selection process of the *concours* with reference to *le bras long*. Malians know how both systems operate: the *bras long* puts family members first; the *concours* puts performance first.[2] Yet, there are cases in which these official rules of *le concours*, or *le bras long* do not apply – and still, they are not perceived as arbitrary. Either way, graduates are not surprised; they know how things work in Mali.

Now we know that:

1. Getting employment is *la chance*.
2. *Le bras long* is a way to get employed. *Le bras long* is *la chance*.
3. *Le concours* is a way to get employed. Passing *le concours* is *la chance*. People pass *le concours* via *le bras long*. *Le bras long* is *la chance*, too.

KNOWLEDGE: On the absence of *la chance*

Now we know what graduates in Mali know about getting an employment. But if employment accounts for the presence of *la chance*, does that consequently mean that unemployment accounts for the absence of *la chance*?

Let us look at this by asking the opposite question: what do graduates know about not getting a job?

L'homme propose, Dieu dispose | Nothing is certain

"L'homme propose, Dieu dispose" (Man proposes, God provides) is a frequently used expression. It highlights the connection between individuals' efforts and God's plan, which is unknown to the individual. The underlying principle of the expression is the recognition of effort; it is about making God see that man wants something. Now, if God provides in response to what man asked for in the first place, it is *la chance*. Most of the situations concerning the long arm and the *concours* which I have described earlier in this chapter are situations in which graduates did receive *la chance* in the form of employment. However, graduates also know that hard work does not always pay off. As we are going to see, sometimes God just does not provide – at least, "differently" or "not yet".

> The difference between God and *la chance*? That's difficult, but it can be explained. I'm going to put myself in the position of all these people now... I'll say that God provides *la chance*. God is the programmer. [...] According to religion, God is the foundation of everything, of *la chance*, and everything that's going to happen to you. Even if I'm going to have a job tomorrow, it's God's plan. God will create the conditions for me to have *la chance* to get that. (My translation, interview, 2014, with Amadou, graduated in International Law.)

The difference between God and *la chance* is not a difficult question to answer for a believer. As "the creator", "the provider" and "the programmer", God is the "foundation of everything". Being the "programmer," God created the past and the present, just as God knows and will create the future accordingly. Everything that happens is designed and provided by God and so is *la chance*. Talking about the origin of *la chance*, university graduates refer to

God's plan in relation to their own.[4] *La chance* is an interplay best summarized by the common expression: "L'homme propose, Dieu dispose." However, God's plan is only revealed as it unfolds.

Mohamed, for instance, passed his exams. He says that he did so because he studied hard, and because "un peu de chance" was granted to him – he was healthy.

> I've been working, so I was given a bit of *la chance*, hein! I can work, I can even spend all night studying... and I do not pass. God making things right... During the exams, I might have malaria or get sick... think I'm going to pass? We can't control sickness. Voilà, this is *la chance*! I've had *la chance* to be healthy and so I made it. (My translation, interview, 2014, with Mohamed, graduated in Administration.)

Being healthy on exam day was a bit of *la chance*. "God making things right" provided him with the conditions enabling him to open up *la chance* on his own as he passed the exam. This was preconditioned by his previous studies, but also by his health. Preparation for the exam is in Mohamed's control, but it is God to determine *la chance*, which is out of his control. He could have been sick that day, and this would have been out of his control. Being healthy, though, put him in a position to prove that he studied hard in the first place. In his account, Mohamed acknowledges that things could have happened differently. *La chance* is that all the negative things that *could* have happened did not happen and everything worked out as he desired. In this case, the two driving forces of his success were himself and God. Both were directed towards the same goal: Mohamed wanted to pass the exam, God approved.

God provides differently: quality.

Sometimes God provides *la chance*, but differently from what people had expected. In the following account, Mohamed talks about "God's plans":

> *La chance* comes from God. I think that everything is written down already. Everything that I have to do, the way I have to take... I think everything is well-traced already. But *la chance*, that is really what you want... so, pray to God

---

4 Except for Simone, who is Christian, all of my informants are Muslim.

1 Knowledge | Situating *La Chance* in Graduates' Knowledge. 53

for he can give it to you. If he doesn't, don't get mad, hein! Because he saves
something even better than that for you. [...] In everything I do right now,
there is improvement. And I think that maybe we can influence *la chance*, but
not every *la chance*. (My translation, interview, 2015, with Mohamed, graduated in Administration.)

Mohamed says that *la chance* comes from God. Everything that happens is
predetermined in God's plan. *La chance* is what you really want; *la chance* is
if God provides you with what you have been praying for all along. This also
means that God's plan and an individual's wishes do not always coincide. In
that case, it is important for the individual to not get mad, but to trust that
what God provides is even better than what has been wished for, and this
can be good, but not necessarily *la chance*. However, it is considered *la chance*
when an individuals' plan coincides with God's.

Mohamed wanted to become a successful soccer player, but God provided
something else for him. Though his career as a soccer star did not work out,
everything else he did, such as his career in administration and his wedding
plans, has been rewarded with improvement by God. Mohamed concludes
this thought with the idea that individuals might be able to influence some
kinds of *la chance* and others not. The difference between these various forms
of *la chance* remains unclear.

Sometimes God's plan is different from the one people imagine for
themselves. Here is an example of how God provides "differently", which
is a different *la chance*. Mohamed's father was a hardworking professor at
the University of Bamako, but he never intended to climb up in administra-
tive hierarchy, all he wanted was to teach and research. Now, the research
proposal his father submitted for funding was denied and, yet, without any
intent and effort, he became head of department at the University of Bamako.
God's plan was different from his own and it did not include research abroad,
but it made him become head of the department. "L'homme propose, Dieu
dispose différentement." – "Man proposes, God provides." Mohamed
describes the situation as follows:

La chance will come! It's on God to agree. Because I'm a believer... It's God who
provides *la chance*. [...] Nobody can do anything when it comes to *la chance*. It's
what my dad has been telling me about him not wanting to become the head
of department or the dean or vice-dean. All he wanted was his passion: he

didn't need anything else. But he told me that if *la chance*, if God really wants him to be the boss... he will have *la chance*. They almost forced him to become head of department then. But this is really what he told us: Don't do anything, it's *la chance* that... but, me, I'm being honest with you: do it and do it right and the rest will follow. Voilà! (My translation, interview, 2015, with Mohamed, graduated in Administration.)

La chance will come, if God agrees. *La chance* is provided by God. Mohamed frames this as his religious belief. He further confirms this with the example of his dad becoming the head of the department as a result of God's plan. *La chance* comes just like that. There are two different frames of reference Mohamed uses: him "being a believer", saying God only provides *la chance* and him "being honest", saying doing things right leads to *la chance*. The frame of "belief" is supported by a story of his father, who did not fight for a higher position, simply because he did not desire it. Because God wanted him to be promoted nevertheless, there was nothing he could have done about it. Mohamed, on the contrary, argues that there is something individuals can do about *la chance*. Following up on this, I argue that his dad was a bright, hard-working man, and if this was not the case, nobody would have wanted him to be in that position and that *la chance* might not have come if it was not for his work. Mohamed responds that "Everyone else in the department is bright and hard-working, too!" Here again, *la chance* intervenes as a difference-maker. There is a mass of people that are perceived to be the same, then one happens to have *la chance*, and all of a sudden, that person is different from the others. That person suddenly has an advantage that cannot be explained by anything but *la chance*. Everyone is the same, but those who have *la chance* are recognized as exceptions.

God does not provide yet: temporality.

What happens if an individual's and God's plan do not coincide? Or, put differently, what happens to *la chance* when it is absent? According to Safiatou, the two will coincide "certainement un jour" – "one day for sure":

The biggest success in life is not that of finishing studies. That's only one part of it. But the most difficult thing is to find yourself a job. Now, finding a job is *la chance*. I believe in God and I say that God gives you *la chance* of finding one.

1 Knowledge | Situating *La Chance* in Graduates' Knowledge.

> If you don't find a job... maybe it's not the right time. So, I suggest to young people to fight, to not give up and to continue looking for a job. It'll come one day, for sure. Even if it's going to be years later. (My translation, interview, 2015, with Safiatou, graduated in English.)

La chance is finding a job, which, along with finishing one's studies, is one of the most difficult and biggest successes in life. God provides *la chance* of finding a job. Safiatou speaks from the perspective of somebody who found internships quite easily in the past and is employed today. Nevertheless, Safiatou knows that finding a job is difficult and that there is the possibility of not finding one. If that is the case, young people should continue to fight, try to find a job and be persistent, because "one day" or "years later" they will find a job "for sure". In other words, Safiatou does not doubt the existence of *la chance* in general, but believes in its temporal absence. She knows *la chance* will appear, provided people keep looking, she just does not know when *la chance* will appear. What is important when it comes to *la chance* is this: effort, God and timing. Individuals are responsible for the effort; God is responsible for the timing of *la chance*. If people did not find a job, they do not find *la chance* – yet. However, this does not mean that they will never find a job.

Just as Safiatou says that *la chance* will come "one day," Boubacar argues along the same lines in referring to *la chance* "next time". He is in charge of the distribution of internships in his ministry and he encourages people to keep applying. "Maybe you did not have *la chance* this time, but next time, you will," he says.

> There are so many people graduating every year. [...] We have to look for people we are going to employ. Now, if we don't take you the first time, don't get discouraged. Maybe you did not have *la chance* this time. Next time, you're going to have *la chance*. You have to go and apply again! But the people are always discouraged saying "it's because of personal relations and if we don't have *la chance*, if we don't have parents there, it's not going to work. (My translation, interview, 2015, with Boubacar, graduated in Economics.)

La chance is to be chosen for an internship at the Ministry. Boubacar talks about the situation in which somebody is not chosen to be an intern given the enormous number of applicants. The reason a person was not chosen is because this time, s/he did not have *la chance*. *La chance* is "maybe not this time" but "next time". He distinguishes between two different times: "this time" and "next time": "This time" with no *la chance*, when the person did not become an intern, and "next time" when the person will be provided with *la chance* and will be taken as an intern. Interestingly, Boubacar speaks from an insider's perspective; he decides which interns the Ministry is going to accept, he knows the criteria according to which he chooses the candidates, and yet, he refers to *la chance* – as if it were not up to him to decide, but *la chance*. If people are not selected, they get discouraged and they blame *le bras long*. This is not going to work, he says. Rather, people should apply again. Boubacar acknowledges the fact that not everybody will be an intern due to missing *la chance*, and not due to missing relations. Note that he does not say there is no such thing as *le bras long*; he says that those who blame *le bras long* and do not apply again will not get the job. Only those who keep applying qualify for *la chance* "next time". The distinction between "now" and "not now" is interesting. "Now" is the time in which *la chance* is absent. Something did not work out. "Not now" is "next time", "later" or "one day" is the time of *la chance*; it is when something has worked out. In other words, God might not provide *la chance* "this time", but "next time". This turns the "now"-absent *la chance* into a *la chance* which is "not yet" provided by God. Consequently, the absence of *la chance* is not absolute, but temporal.

THE UNKNOWN | What they know they DON'T know

In its absence, *la chance* has "not yet" come into being in the present and is, therefore, still to come in the future. *La chance* might also be present, but in a "different" shape. *La chance* continues to exist in its absence. *La chance* is not questioned by its absence; it is "protected against induction" (Silverman 1998, 75). The presence of *la chance* in its absence is a practical accomplishment which contributes to the common-sense knowledge on *la chance*. As a result, the absence of *la chance* is explained by its "different appearance" or "temporality".

1. The focus on content presents *la chance* as subjective, because sometimes *la chance* is different from what people expect it to be. Mohamed's father recognized it was *la chance* for him to become head of the department, and Madou decided it was his *la chance* to start working at the telecommunications com-

pany. Both had imagined another *la chance* for themselves. The recognition of *la chance* here is a matter of perspective. So, while a graduate might not get the job he or she wants, they might be able to get another job. In other words, *la chance* is not absent; *la chance* is there, but unrecognized.

2. The focus on time presents circumstances as temporal instead of as absolute givens. Absent *la chance* is *la chance* still to come. So, if someone does not get a job despite all efforts, it is just "not yet". If *la chance* depends on timing, *la chance* might emerge from its very absence at any point in time – just that the exact time is unknown. To Ernst Bloch, the notion of "not-yet" status is essential to hope: "[...] the power of hope as a method rests on a prospective momentum entailed in anticipation of what has not-yet become: 'a relatively still Unconscious disposed towards its other side, forwards rather than backwards. Towards the side of something new that is dawning up that has never been conscious before [...]'" (Bloch 1986 in Miyazaki 2006, 14). In other words, looking at things retrospectively is limited to "what has become" already. Though by looking at "what has not yet become" opens up spaces for the future in the present.

Summary.

La chance is an empirical phenomenon university graduates experience and know about. *La chance* is knowledge in a sense that it indicates the very intersection of what graduates (1) know they know and (2) know they do not know.

Absence and presence co-constitute each other. Absence is recognized through an idea of something being present, i.e. something used to be there before, or is supposed to be there, but is not. Jean Paul Sartre notes that absence has the power to make disappear what is actually present (Bille et. al. 2010, 5). For instance, when a friend does not show up to a meeting, we sometimes forget what is present around us, in other words, the person's absence overshadows whatever is present. Similarly, the absence of employment potentially disguises other activities, or the absence of knowledge about one thing disguises knowledge about others. However, as much as absence has the power to disguise presence, it also has the power to create it. "The paradox of immateriality", for instance, describes that in the absence of an object, an objectification is created, which addresses that very lack (Baudrillard in Bille et. al. 2010, 10). Research uses this constitutional relationship between absence and presence when accessing absence through the presence of, for instance, materiality, experience, the body, the memory and discourse (Tali 2018, Malmström, Bille et al). Analyzing absence in the context of a museum archive, Tali (2018) says that it "is only through comparison and in reference to what is present that I can come to analyse these different forms of absences" (Tali 2018, 2).

In a similar manner, analyzing the relationship between absent and present knowledge among graduates, I put non-knowledge in relation to knowledge. More specifically, by examining the frequently used expression "L'homme propose, Dieu dispose", which accounts for something graduates do not know, yet knowing they do not know. Through that lens, we were able to see that they know THAT (fact) something will happen, however, they do not know WHAT (content) it is and WHEN (temporality) exactly it is going to happen.

We have seen that there are systems of job distribution, which are supposed to work in accordance with different maxims: *le bras long* favors family members, *le concours* employs with reference to performance and "l'homme propose, Dieu dispose" rewards effort. University graduates know how these systems are supposed to work, but they also know that these systems do not work accordingly. The discrepancy between the jobs available and the graduates applying reached a point at which the criteria set for the distribution of jobs no longer apply. Graduates know that job distribution works differently: *le bras long* does not provide jobs, but it does provide information about jobs. *Le concours* employs according to the rules of *le bras long*. And God provides some version of what man proposed in the first place.

Simply put, we now know that:

Employment is a result of the presence of *la chance*. Graduates know that employment is *la chance*. Unemployment is a result of the absence of *la chance*. In the absence of *la chance*, *la chance* is made present.

2 Graduates | Situating *La Chance* in Graduates' Everyday Lives.

[We are here]

This chapter focuses on the graduates themselves. The first part portrays their everyday lives while the second part offers insight into their experiences and questions. I start off with vignettes (a soccer game and a wedding) connecting the two respective protagonists (Madou and Amadou, Simone and Safiatou), followed by an introduction of each university graduate's short biography and a vignette accounting for an everyday situation. The second part presents situations which raise questions for these graduates. The sections are arranged according to questions highlighting aspects of their professional and family lives, as well as their temporal dimension, i.e. present and future. The key questions here are: What are our graduates' questions? What do they know they do not know?

We will see that present-related questions refer to unknowns concerning dependencies and transitions into new situations, whereas future-related questions refer to unknowns concerning details about present knowledge and the consequences of present decision-making.

Investigating situations which raise questions is an entry point to what graduates know and what they do not know. The focus on everyday situations in individuals' lives allows me to relate the known and the unknown and in doing so elaborate challenges of everyday life. We will see that the unknown is not the counterpart of the known, but much more a part of it.

Throughout the entire chapter, *la chance* is absent and, yet, its purpose is to situate *la chance* in graduates' everyday lives.

PEOPLE

In this first part of the chapter, I will present four graduates. I start off with the vignette "the wedding", which presents and connects Safi and Simone. Safi getting married and Simone facilitating for her. I will then introduce both of them properly by giving some background information on their family and their education. I end this part with a vignette that describes each of them individually in an everyday situation in the now. Safi at home with her kid right after work and before preparing dinner, and Simone in her car on an errand for purchasing a business dress.

I continue with a vignette of a soccer match which connects Madou and Amadou. Madou is playing on the field having fun and Amadou is on the sidelines analyzing the game. They are cousins and live in the same household in Bamako. Here too, I will introduce them properly by providing some details about their family and educational backgrounds, before closing with vignettes of Madou and Amadou in everyday situations at their workplace.

[MAP]

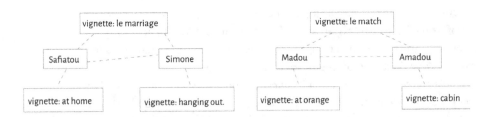

VIGNETTE: the wedding.

It's a Saturday in 2014 when Safi and Abdoul get married. Around 2 pm, I meet the girls in ACI2000 at an American style beauty parlor. Safi is already wearing her white wedding dress, her hair is done and she is waiting to have her make-up applied. Simone, her best friend, is running around the parlor, answering and making phone calls with both her two phones and Safi's two phones. There is another friend of Safi's from Mauritania and an older lady who is observing the scene with a serious air.

I would find out later that this is the woman who is going to introduce Safi to the secrets of love and marriage. "There is TV and internet, so it's not like we have no idea, but, you know, this is our tradition", Safi jokes some days

2 Graduates | Situating *La Chance* in Graduates' Everyday Lives. 61

after the wedding. Right now, Safi does not have time for anything. However, she's not busy, but calm and seems to be in her own world and just lets things happen. All of a sudden, she realizes she forgot to buy a white veil. Her facial expression changes from relaxed to eyes opened wide and eye brows up high. Simone takes care of this: one phone call and thirty minutes later a guy on a moto arrives carrying a white plastic bag with three different veils inside. Safi chooses the most transparent one, because obviously she is not getting her hair styled for no one to see it, she says. Her face is now covered in a mask of whitening make-up. Her eyes are silver; her lip gloss is shiny. Her dress is white and made out of heavy high-quality fabric. European style. The corset covers her pregnancy belly and pushes up her breasts. She's wearing a gigantic silver bracelet with about fifty white pearls attached to it. She's decently accessorized with a white brooch attached to her hair, white pearl studs and a silver bracelet around her wrist.

> She's standing there and everything around her is fast and busy; we pause for a second to look at her. "Ma cherie, il faut pas pleurer dehh!" – "Honey, you're not going to cry, huh!" Simone is joking with a raised index finger and a serious face. Safi's eyes fill with tears. "Tu es maquillée!" – "You've got make up on!", Simone exhales and gives her a long hug. "Ce sont les emotions!" – "It's emotions!", Simone later explains to me.

It's getting even noisier now: Abdoul arrives. He looks like a great marabout in his gigantic white Boubou and his long white cylinder hat. We take some pictures; he's laughing and teasing as usual. Everyone is busy dressing up, so it's just the two of us going outside and looking at the car he parked at the back of the parlor to benefit from the shade. It is a white and shiny 2001 SUV Mercedes-Benz from 2001. There are some colorful, glittery flowers in blue, red and pink attached to it. "It's got air-conditioning, so we won't be sweaty by the time we arrive at the mayor's office", Abdoul tells me. But first, they are off for a photo session in front of a small hotel in ACI2000. The couple poses in front of green trees and bushes. First some couple shots, then one with mom and grandma and the other grandma and auntie and all of them together and friends. Quick quick. We don't even waste ten minutes at that spot. Safi and Abdoul climb back into their car.

Arriving at her family's house "la maison de la grande famille" in Missira, Safi sits next to her mom and grandma; they're preciously embedded in the female wedding society and balloons and artificial flowers. It's about 16h45 when Abdoul arrives to pick up his very-soon to-be wife. The house is about 500 meters away from the mayor's office, so the whole crowd heads off on foot. On the street, of course. No one minds the traffic; the traffic doesn't mind us. No one seems to be in a hurry and no one seems to care. "Le dimanche à Bamako, c'est le jour de marriage" – "Sunday in Bamako is wedding day". There are weddings all over the city. Men sit outside under a plastic tent on blue metal chairs. They all wear bazin boubous of various qualities in discreet colors. The women, in colorful bazin dresses and huge fulas on their heads, sit in the house's courtyard on their blue metal chairs. In front of the mayor's office, there is a huge crowd waiting. Some of them belong to Safi's and Abdoul's company, but half of them is waiting for another couple to appear. Safi and her future husband go in. I stay outside and talk to a close friend of Safi's, a journalist. He's proud of her and that she is doing everything right.

As they emerge from the mayor's office about thirty minutes later, they are holding hands. Everyone wants to take a picture with the newlyweds now. The guys tap Abdoul's back and he doesn't even know from whom he is receiving all those congratulations. Beads of perspiration cover his forehead. Safi's face looks tired, but she's smiling. (Field notes, August 2013.)

SAFIATOU

Safiatou (born 1989) is *bamakoise* – born and raised in Bamako. Her father is a businessman and her mother travels all over the world for an international network-marketing company. She has two older brothers; one is working at the American embassy, the other one is a loafer, she says, and is employed at the ministry of environment in Bamako. Her younger brother is still in school. In her family, Safiatou is the first one with a university degree. In fact, she's got four. She adores writing, exploring new things, traveling, being on the move. "So do journalists", she says. Universities in Mali do not offer journalism as a subject of study, neither public nor private. That is why she decided to study English at the University of Bamako as well as Communication/Marketing at one of the best and most expensive private universities in the capital. Convinced of her talents, one of her teachers provided Safiatou a two-week internship at the state broadcasting station ORTM. After that time, she voluntarily kept working at the station, got in touch with journalists, benefited from their experience and started her own show on the radio about culture and fashion. After receiving two bachelor degrees in Mali, she moved to Casablanca, Morocco another two masters studies in Communication/Multimedia and Journalism at the French Institute of Press. In her free time, she has been working for radio stations in Morocco and Mali. It was tough to meet the high demands of the Moroccan educational system and also to encounter daily racism in Casablanca, but nevertheless worth the effort, she reflects. Safiatou is convinced that she has gained a better education than the majority of her former fellow students; a better qualification for the Malian labor market and a head full of ideas for innovation.

In 2013, she marries Abdoul, a 25-year-old Malian, who just finished his studies in economics at a university in France. One of her former colleagues introduced them. Shortly after, they email and have Skype calls every day, before deciding to get married. "On était pressé!" – "We couldn't wait," she explains with a smile on her face. They marry religiously on the 20th day of Ramadan, which is said to provide special blessing. At the civil registry office, they register their marriage as monogamous, because they are convinced that their love is unique. Since she became responsible for her husband, his family, and herself, her life changed; no more clubbing with the girls.

VIGNETTE: At home.

I knock at the mint metal yard gate and shout the boy's name "Abdrahamane!" He opens the door after quite some time and tells me that Safi is upstairs. She always is. I enter the house, everything is dark in the basement, I take the steps. I take off my flip-flops as I enter the living room. Safi and Abdoul are sitting on a white leather couch facing the TV. TM2 is on, but they do not look as if they have been watching consciously. They hang out snuggling, they look tired and blessed. First thing she does after welcoming me to their home is to lead me to their bedroom where the baby is sleeping. The room is about 25 square meters, no windows, a door that leads to the bathroom. The walls are painted pale blue. Two tubular fluorescent lamps that shed blue light onto the scene. There is a king-size double bed right next to the entrance door, there is a huge wardrobe in front, a bassinet fills the empty corner on the left. The small corridor to the bathroom is filled with shoes and DVDs. Bakary is bedded like a little treasure in the middle of the mattress on a couple of baby blankets; two tablets lie on the very edge of the bed. The aircon is turned off; only the fan provides a soft breeze. Bakary is breathing hastily and softly at the same time. Safi looks at him with a blessed smile, slightly touches his head. The baby wakes up slowly while she looks on, delighted by every move he makes. Ten minutes later, she passes the baby on to her maid Aissetou so that we can talk. (Field notes, May 2014.)

SIMONE

Simone was born in 1989 in Bamako in a "famille mixte" – her mother muslim, her father catholic. Her father is her advisor and role model. "Je le considère comme le meilleur des meilleurs. C'est mon idole [...] Il a réussi", she says. Her dad was a successful entrepreneur and intellectual. When she was a kid, they watched the news on TV and talked about it afterwards. That is how she got to love journalism – her childhood dream and her passion.

She studied law at the University of Bamako. At the same time, she was enrolled at a private university, where she studied communication and journalism. During her studies in Bamako, she worked as an intern at ORTM and a communication agency. For her Masters, she left for Morocco, where she was finally able to study journalism. It is her father who paid for her studies in Mali and in Morocco and she is thankful for that. She and Safiatou basically shared all of their student life in and outside of Mali.

VIGNETTE: Hanging out.

Her room is all tidied up, the walls are blue, the classic Mali blue, like a neon sky blue, and there are some traces of dust. Her tiny TV with a decoder is running. And so is the ventilo. Her wardrobe has a big mirror. There are pictures of her and her friends attached to it, most of them show her though. The interview lasts for a little more than an hour. After that, we go see her parents sitting on the terrace clicking peanuts. We get into her car. It's a grey Toyota Starlett. She is the only girl I know in Mali that owns a car. Still, she is being laughed at because of it. No air condition and the doors only open from outside. So, if you want to get out you either have to ask someone to open the door for you or you have to roll down the window and unlock the door from outside on your own. She makes fun of her car as well, but if others do so she is there to defend her baby. She plays it cool and cruises through the dusty roads of her neighborhood. No music, but we sing; she says hi to people she knows and doesn't know and complains about bad drivers for no reason. After Simone has had her afternoon lunch at her Senegalese friend Awa's beauty parlor, we head to Halles de Bamako. Simone is looking for a dress she could wear at a fancy din-

2 Graduates | Situating *La Chance* in Graduates' Everyday Lives.

ner her boss from the airport company invited her to. He is from Dubai. And the dinner is at some fancy place in ACI2000. She wants a dress that looks like business, but not overly respectable. Awa suggested a nice boutique. We park the car too far away from the store because Awa does not want to be associated with it. The staff shows us dresses. Simone tries everything on. It feels like we're in a luxury boutique because the girls comport themselves that way. They are the queens here. Heads held up high, they look down at the staff, their eyes barely open. One of the guys suggests a white dress and Awa doesn't even bother to look at it closely, waves it aside and says with a voice full of boredom: "Chose djeman-là, nous on est pas tellement dedans quoi!" One dress is nice, but Simone's belly looks too gigantic in it, she says, and she does not want to bother about that for the whole evening: "It's a dinner and I am sure going to eat!" We leave the place without buying anything. Awa has got a nice dress at home. We go look at that. Simone looks pretty in Awa's dress and there is a lot of space around her belly. They add earrings and Awa's glasses to her outfit, because that makes her look professional. "Now, back to the salon, chop chop! We need to get your hair straight!"

VIGNETTE: *Le match.*

It's on a Tuesday that Mohammed tells me that there will be a game on Sunday. "Madou's team against ours. We do that sometimes. Just for fun. I'm organizing this. Come!" On game day, I arrive ten minutes early to find Mohammed and his teammates warming up. His team is AS Faladie, a third division team; they train and play together regularly. They are all dressed in their team shirts with black and pink stripes saying "Coupe Beidi Niang Premiere Edition". No one knows what that means. 13 is Mohammed's squad number. They are all wearing cleats and their socks are pulled up right below their knees.

Madou's team is called DjeLaFa United – like Manchester United and like Faladie, but with the syllables inverted. They used to wear second quality red and white Manchester home jerseys. You get them for 3000 Franc CFA all over Bamako. Back in the days, they were the best team in the area, but ever since they graduated and started working, they play irregularly and just for fun. Madou and his two best friends Djeli and Oumar arrive by the time the match was supposed to start. The three of them plus the funny, but unexperienced goalie Soufi are the only ones of Madou's team present. They have a laugh as they pick up their phones and make some calls to friends who might want to join their team quickly. Within the next 15 minutes, four more people show up.

In the meantime, Mohammed wants me to take a picture of his team. They align like soccer teams do: five in the back, their arms on each other's shoulders and five in the front with slightly bent knees. Professional, strong-willed faces. I take a couple of pictures, before I start teasing them for being so serious. They laugh, I take some more pictures.

Now, Madou and Alpha roll the ball around a little, do some relaxed dribbling. Whenever a guy their age passes the field, they scream: "Ehh, toi-là, vient jouer!" They laugh and high five each other. It's been a while since AS Faladie is done warming up. Their faces are sweaty. Adama, who is said to be the most talented kid in the neighborhood, passes by and and decides to join Madou's team. He's only 17, trains every day; and he's quick and cheeky. Finally, Djelafa United is complete and ready to roll. No debrief. They magically organize themselves as a team even though they have never played in this formation before. They are all wearing soccer jerseys: all of different colors, all of different teams. Madou's wearing Di Maria's white Real Madrid jersey with the squad number 22, white AC Milan pants, black Adidas soccer socks, Umbro cleats in black and white. He's going to score: "Je suis Christiano!!"

Amadou is standing at the sideline watching as the match starts. He used to be a passionate soccer player himself, but then he injured his knee. Now, he takes a lot of pride in coaching a local football team. Adama over there is one of the teams' best players and regularly approaches Amadou for advice concerning the game, but also girls and school. "I'm unemployed right now, I've got the time to do these kinds of things. I really want to help these kids." Playing soccer on Amadou's team is preconditioned by good grades in school. Soccer only is not enough. "Dans le foot, tout ça, c'est *la chance*. Mais il faut au moins avoir un diplôme" – "Everything depends on *la chance* in soccer. You have to have a degree, at the very least." Adama wants to become a successful player; that's his dream. Amadou is aware of the fact that despite all of Adama's talents he is probably not going to be a professional soccer player. However, there's no point in destroying the kid's dream, so Amadou told him to combine soccer and education in order to be on the safe side. Every famous player had *la chance* one day, Amadou says. Playing soccer is not about individual fulfillment and passion, but about gaining huge amounts of money fast – "et c'est ça" – and that's it. Samuel Eto und Didier Drogba never wanted the huge career, they just wanted to get paid, he says.

On the soccer field, there is no referee. Things regulate themselves. Conflicts suddenly appear and disappear. Fifty minutes later, a referee arrives. His inexperience makes everyone laugh. His judgement is respected though. The game is fast and dynamic. Everyone wants to win. Mohammed gets fouled quite often; he falls down three times and gets up quickly without complaining. Whenever the ball gets close to the goal, the few spectators would scream "But! But! But!" – "Goal! Goal! Goal!" In the end, the result is 1:1. Mohammed prepared a goal. Madou made one. Match tied. No celebration, little frustration. They both won, both lost. Adama playing for Madou's team was unfair, Mohammed says. Madou exchanges "bien joué"'s ("well played") with his friends and teammates for one day. (Field notes, March 2014.)

MADOU

Madou finished school with a BAC in Sciences Exactes in 2005 and then enrolled at the University of Bamako. He wanted to study informatics, because he wanted to become a researcher. "Informatics is the future", he says. It was exceptional for a kid in Mali to know what he or she wants to become, so his parents were proud of him and his dream. In fact, he reflects, it was his family that made him appreciate education. Unfortunately for him, there is no such subject as informatics at the University of Bamako, but people told him to start with physics at the Faculty of Natural Sciences (FAST), because this is where some informatics courses will be offered, at least in the later semesters. This, ultimately, was not the case. So, his studies became frustrating and money became his primary motor to keep going: He failed some exams, passed some, received average grades until he finally made a bet with his dad: if he passed his exams with very good grades, Madou would get a gift. And there was also the scholarship: "That was kind of my motivation, you know." In his third year, he studied until late at night to get the grades he wanted – for the money. And ironically, it was during that time that he learned to really like studying physics, which then made him want to become a physics researcher.

After his graduation in 2010, he did not want to continue studies in Mali, because this would have meant to study either at ENI in order to become an engineer or at ENSUP in order to become a professor, neither of which Madou aspired to. Plus, he did not want to restart. He wanted to continue with his studies and since there were no consecutive study programs offered in Mali during that time, he needed to go to another country – which he did. In 2011, Madou went to Bayreuth in Germany, where he approached a professor at the physics department who appreciated him. Plus, it's even less expensive to study in Bayreuth than at a private university in Mali. He received a PhD-scholarship. Madou does not think that his interest in science and research has anything to do with the fact that his father was a scientist, who did his PhD in Germany. The difference between the two of them, however, is significant: "I know he loved doing research; he loved publishing articles. To me, this is different... I always wanted to become a star! Invent something, you know." In the end though, he could not accept the scholarship due to Mali's 2012 coup d'état, which made it impossible for him to leave the country. In the meantime, he found himself a job at Orange, where they made him conduct another studies program in Marketing Management.

He says, he still dreams of becoming a researcher, but it's expensive to continue your studies. Marketing management is the profile Orange wants him to have. "It's a bonus" – A bonus that is going to take him three years. He tells me that he still wants to go to Germany to do his masters studies, but the priority for now is the scholarship that was given to him by Orange. It's important to have as many diplomas as possible, because "this way you can work a little everywhere".

VIGNETTE: At Orange.

On Saturday, Madou and I chill in his room. We talk about his father, business and love. His colleague calls him saying that she's about to pull into Orange. He hadn't planned on working today, but ultimately decides to take advantage of the ride. He's getting ready to leave in an instant. "Have fun!", I say. He seems confused and says that he's going to go and work and not to have fun. I tell him that I always felt like he seems to be enjoying his work and that is why I told him to have fun. He asks me to come along and I'm happy to. 15 minutes later we're on the road and Madou is driving. His colleague is taking the back seat, he calls her big sister. She doesn't enjoy Bamako traffic all the way to

2 Graduates | Situating *La Chance* in Graduates' Everyday Lives.   69

ACI2000. Orange occupies an entire building, it looks all shiny and clean. The elevator on the inside isn't working, so we take the dusty stairs. There's security at the entrance. We're cleared. The office is spacious: 40 work stations, 5 people working. Of course, it's the weekend. They're working on things they didn't get done during the week. The airco is running at full blast, there's a water tank providing ice cold and hot water. Every worker has a desk and a PC with their name tag on it. Lots of boxes, lots of chairs, clean. The internet connection is incredibly fast. Everyone is talking either to each other or on the phone, sometimes both. I sit on a desk next to Madou and type up some notes. He's focused. Every once in a while, he gets up to fix himself a bowl of cereal, to chat, to listen to and sing along with music, to perform a few dance moves. He is constantly listening to music. He does not react to the others calling for him. Tunnel vision. Only interrupted by him singing a couple of deeply emotional lines. Always staying in his tunnel. After an hour, cleaning staff arrives. Everybody is talking, teasing each other, discussing work with each other. "This client right here has four million F CFA in his account", Madou says. His colleagues are astonished: "4 million!". Back to work. I actually do think we are having fun. On a weekday, Madou spends approximately ten hours a day here. He says, his boss keeps on distributing tasks to him.

AMADOU

Amadou (1983) was born as the oldest of eight children in Segou. His father died when he was in his teenage years and his mother lives today in Bamako as a business woman. Amadou is proud of his education because he has not only been educated by school and Islam, but also by the street. He started his school career in Segou at a public school, which he perceives as an advantage because that is where he learned to take his education seriously. At the time of his first years in school, teachers used to love their profession, they did not teach in order to make a living as they do today. In fourth grade, he moved to Sevare where he was at the hands of a strict teacher who employed violence to force his students to study. Amadou hated that, but has realized today that this is the pressure he needed in order to study effectively. He acknowledged that laziness hurts. After another move to Bamako, he put a lot of effort into his studies voluntarily and he even aspired to be better than the most intelligent girl in his new school. He obtained his baccalauréat with a focus on human sciences in Segou, which is the most difficult branch because it requires advanced knowledge in both languages and mathematics.

Amadou then decided to study international law at the University of Bamako because his idea was to work for an international company, or even for the United Nations one day. He therefore returned to Bamako, where he lives with his aunt. His studies at the University of Bamako are paid by the government, but he has been engaged in some kind of business or other ever since. As a child, when there was no electricity in Segou's villages, he sold petrol to Bozo fishermen. Amadou also fabricated tiny toy cars and made his friends do some advertisement by playing with them. "Almost every kid wanted to have my cars!" As a student, he received from his uncle the keys to a telephone cabin right in front of the house. People from the neighborhood made all their phone calls at Amadou's cabin. He gradually transformed the cabin into a business and meeting point for the neighborhood's youth. Every night, Amadou hosts tea sessions.

VIGNETTE: At the Cabin.

Tonight is some final match in the Spanish premier league: it's FC Barcelona against Real Madrid. The telephone cabin is closed. There are only a few reasons that justify the fact that he closed his business: Friday prayer, evening prayer during Ramadan and soccer. Not even the need to sleep is a justification to close it. He postpones his daily closing hours as much as possible: sometimes his eyes fall shut involuntarily. His friends would be talking, teasing, laughing around him, but he just wouldn't mind them. Amadou would then sit in his metal chair, with a straight neck and back, eyes closed. From a distance you wouldn't even be able to say that he's sleeping, only if you take a closer look at his face. His friends have stopped telling him to go to bed a long time ago, but I did it once. He was suddenly more than awake: "If a client wants to buy credit with me and would find the cabin closed, he'll probably never ever come back", he explains. "Tu as bien compris?" – "You get me?", that is how he punctuates extended monologues. I nod. He continues. He would take the risk, though, for important things: God and soccer. And yes, at the time of important prayers and important matches, most people are at a mosque or in front of a TV. (Field notes 2011.)

2 UNKNOWNS

The following section is about questions in graduates' lives concerning the future or the present horizon. Both questions regarding the present and the future come with unknowns about career and family aspects. We see how these questions connect people in different and unexpected ways.

[MAP]

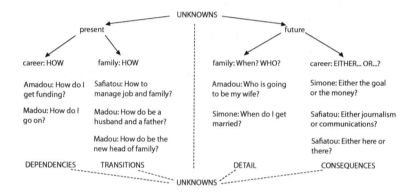

KNOWING THE UNKNOWN in the present.

The unknowns presented in this section are rooted in the present as graduates deal with questions about how to deal with a current situation related to their careers or family lives. Depending on the present situation, they know what they do not know.

Career unknown: DEPENDENCIES.

Overall, crucial questions concern the when and how of a situation. Since the question of when is answered here in the now of the present moment, the how is what is remaining, i.e. how to proceed from a road blocked either due to an ongoing lack of funding or an emerging political crisis.

Family unknown: TRANSITIONS.

With regards to their emerging family life, both Safiatou and Madou are figuring out a situation yet unfamiliar to them. Here, their questions concern them being and becoming a part of their own family. Whereas Safi is concerned with managing both her career and family, Madou deals with questions about responsibility for the family he was born into, him being a husband and soon to be a father.

Both unknown dependencies and transitions are rooted in the present situation, which is either unknown due to external factors graduates are suddenly and temporarily (see Madou and the coup) or naturally (see Amadou and his clients) currently unable to account for. Both find themselves in situations in which they do not know: Facing everyday dependencies, Amadou knows what he knows and what he does not know and will not be able to know; Madou facing sudden change requiring knowledge on an everyday basis, which is new to him. Knowledge that will ultimately allow him to distinguish between what he knows he knows and knows he does not know.

Or due to recent voluntary decisions (getting married) or sudden events (death of the father) leading to new situations, which comes along with new questions and demands and, therefore, requires new knowledge and routines. Moreover, these situations challenge graduates to take on a new becoming: a business woman and wife to become a mother and a bachelor to become a husband.

CAREER: HOW?

Amadou: How do I get funding?

In 2013, four years after his graduation, he has abandoned the telephone cabin, because it does not pay anymore. He accepted a fixed employment at his aunts' cafeteria, where he operates as her representative: he supervises the staff, purchases food, takes care of customers and negotiates with clients. Every day, he leaves the house at six in the morning and comes after dinner has been served. He goes jogging, because he has gained some weight and he is aware of the fact that women regard fat men as being lazy and not attractive. He goes to bed around one 'o clock in the morning. Before that, he

2 Graduates | Situating *La Chance* in Graduates' Everyday Lives.

quickly takes a shower after coming home and leaves for his *grin*[1] behind his house, where he has his three rounds of tea, launches into lively discussions on almost every topic and takes some extensive naps. For more than a year now, this is his daily routine – not even one day of vacation. "Some people say that I can't do this job every day without any rest. But their limits are not mine! I force myself to do that and I know that I'm strong." Amadou has a lot of projects in his mind, but he feels like he has got to give something back to his aunt, where he has been living for years. It seems as if he has abandoned his former aim of becoming a diplomat in favor of becoming a famous and generous businessman. He has read everything about Steve Jobs and Bill Gates – once derided mavericks, now among the best-known and most respected people in the world. If you want to be a successful businessman, "*il faut voler la conscience des gens*" ("It's all about stealing people's conscience."). It really does not matter whether you offer the best product or the best price, it is really all about convincing people. He feels that this is what he is learning in the cafeteria right now; that is his benefit. To him, the job is not waiting, but a sacrifice for his aunt and preparation for his own future career.

Africa can only advance if it recognizes its own realities and strengths, Amadou argues. His analysis debunks the false belief that everything associated with Europe is better; this is what paralyzes his generation. Africa's main issue is that people have just adapted to European ideas, definitions and also to European dreams. "I studied law, but hardly anyone in Mali can afford a lawyer" (conversation with Amadou 2014). His cleaning business idea responds to an African problem, and it has got the capability to revolutionize the continent, he assures. His business idea is cleaning households, offices, government buildings and whole neighborhoods. The city is dirty and no one likes the dirt, he says. The dirt makes people uncomfortable and it causes disease. Things and places will always get dirty again, he says, and people will recognize the beauty and the advantages of cleanliness, which assures future demand for his business. Amadou already presented his project to government officials and businessmen. Both parties told him that he needs to finance his service in advance. The government pays well, but only after prolonged waiting periods, which easily destroys young enterprises. Amadou has the capacity and a promising idea, but no seed money.

---

1 grin, le: (French) tea circle. For further information on the shared practice of drinking tea in West Africa, see (Ralph 2008) and (Masquelier 2013, 2019).

He knows that it is going to be tough again, but here is no respect for people who had an easy way to the top. Only fighters get respect, he says, and he will fight. He wants to taste success and he is convinced that it is going to taste better to him than to any son of a millionaire.

Madou: How do I go on?

On 21 March 2012, military forces under the leadership of Captain Amadou Sanogo conducted a coup d'état in Mali (Whitehouse 2017). Amadou Toumani Toure, the reigning president, was ousted and left the country. Initially, the intention was to end the current regime's disrespect for the national military's needs, especially in the northern part of the country. Within a month after the coup, an interim government was put in place in Bamako. Meanwhile, benefiting from the absence of the Malian military in the North, separatist and jihadist groups took over and occupied Timbuktu, Gao, and Kidal. They increasingly gained territory towards the south of the country, which resulted in French military intervention (Operation Serval) in December that same year. For years,[2] UN-troops (MINUSMA) continue their peace-keeping mission in Mali. The event and its close aftermath constituted a sudden rupture for Malian society. Here is how it affected Madou's life.

> So, he (physics professor at a university in Germany) sent me an invitation letter saying that he would supervise me during my Master's and later on for the PhD... But then there was the Coup d'état here in Mali. So, that kind of messed up things. (My translation, interview, 2013, with Madou, graduated in Physics.)

After his graduation in 2010, Madou did not want to continue studies in Mali. This would have meant studying either at ENI in order to become an engineer or at ENSUP in order to become a professor. Madou did not aspire for either, nor did he want to start anew. He wanted to continue with his studies, and since there were no consecutive study programs offered in Mali during that time, he needed to go to another country, which he did. In 2011, Madou spent his summer vacation at a friend's house in Germany. At the local university, he approached a professor at the physics department who appreciated his talents. Ultimately, he received a PhD scholarship which was supposed to

---

2 For further information on the aftermath of the coup d'état see Moseley, 2017.

start in April 2012. In January though, the coup d'état took place and made it impossible for him to leave the country.

A little more than a year later, Madou had already passed all his exams at a private university and signed a contract at Orange in January, where he is now working as a financial analyst. He also started studying a business master he pays for himself. Orange is big in his life now. He shares the whole story with me: He started out at the company as an intern and later worked on his first limited contract in the archives, then in the back-office, then as assistant operation support. There was a new position for which he had the experience, but not the qualification, so he went for the master. This assured him a new promised contract. He is happy all round with his new job for which he worked hard and he is motivated. It was difficult, he says, but a nice experience. He likes working for Orange, because they give him responsibility, money and respect. *"C'est l'entreprise ideal pour les jeunes."* – "It's the perfect company for young people." Basically, because they prioritize experience and competence over age, he says. His father died six months ago, but with this job, he says, he is able to support his mother and family, and is going to be able to found and support a family in the near future.

He still wants to become a researcher. There is a "disponibilité" program at Orange. He will soon ask for that. So, it is still totally possible for him to go, leave the country in order to do research. He likes physics, if he did research and his Phd, this would really not be for the money. Sometimes, when he is working night shifts and there is not a lot of work, he would do research on his office computer. But right now, he cannot, because he is way too exhausted for that. "I just want to get distracted", he says. It's been three years without vacation. But this is on him, he admits. He prefers to not go on vacation if he knows he is going to stay in Mali for his whole time off. Otherwise it's no real vacation, because people call him all the time.

How come he is so confident in his ability to accomplish all the things he would like to do? It is that easy: "On peut faire les deux." – "You can do both." He can both be employed at Orange and do his PhD research; he would only have to take a year off for his research, but with the guarantee to get his job back after that. And he finds solutions to make that possible.

Unknown: DEPENDENCIES.

Dependence on external factors: sudden political change.

To Madou, the coup d'état constituted a moment in which his "seemingly established future" (Johnson-Hanks 2002, 878) of becoming a researcher was suddenly blocked. Caused by a sudden rupture, Madou was forced to reorient and look for other perspectives he might not have thought of before. New questions arose; new knowledge was required. The coup came along with immediate consequences for Madou, which would not necessarily have to be a foregone conclusion. For his younger brother Mohamed, the situation was different. When the coup occurred, he was still a student. Due to the circumstances, the university was closed for a couple of weeks, and it was difficult to anticipate the political and social consequences of the coup. However, the coup did not immediately make him question his own situation as a student. In 2014, however, Mohamed, too, recognizes the impact of the coup:

> "The crisis slowed down a lot of things. Maybe our former president would have put many young people into the administration, maybe he could have done that. The coup d'état... I mean, compared to other countries... it's not good, because it slowed down our economy and put the country behind. When you're behind, it's like standing still. It's been shocking, but now we're trying to forget about that little by little."

Noticeably, Mohamed refers to the coup as something that has turned into a long-term, tangible crisis on a broad societal level. He does not explicitly relate this to his personal situation.

Dependence on external factors: business.

Amadou is an entrepreneur and knows that his everyday business is dependent on external factors. He knows what he knows and does not know. He does not know if there will be clients today or business partners and investments tomorrow. During his days as a telephone stall owner, he depended on the demand of his customers. He tried to balance that out by being on standby for as long as he could every day. In the end, the demand declined to a point that he could no longer justify his time spent there. Later, and by virtue of his need to give back to his aunt, he is entirely dependent on her and her business's schedule. Though he knows that he will not do this forever, there is still no tangible alternative yet. While he does have a business idea, its success is dependent on business partners' liquidity or his family member's willingness to invest. Amadou is convinced he will succeed in business one day. However, today, his employment opportunities are dependent on external factors such as clients, bosses and business partners.

FAMILY: HOW?

Safi: How to manage job and family?

Every morning at eight, Abba gives her a ride to her workplace. At five, she takes a taxi back home and starts preparing dinner for her in-laws. On the weekends, she visits her mother and spends time with her friends and her husband. She lives with her husband at his parents' house now. "C'est le changement totale" – "Everything has changed". On her facebook page, she posts *"En train de vivre les plus beaux moments et importantes de ma vie... Yessss a cette transition Hamdoullah tellement fière de tout ça"* (Safiatou 2013). While she looks forward to becoming a mother, her pregnancy is exhausting. Nevertheless, she will not let that affect her professional duties. She works full time until the week before her first baby, a son, arrives.

"Marriage is one of the steps in a woman's life"[3] – just like giving birth to children and getting a job, Safiatou says. "This is every girl's dream in Mali," she once said. Safiatou is happy to be with a man she loves and with whom she shares the same values. She appreciates hanging out with him, doing business with him, and cooking dinner for him and his family. She is aware of her responsibilities at home, and she contributes to the family's well-being with both recipes from her mother and the salary from the communications agency. At the same time, new uncertainties arise out of the very fact of being married, such as acclimating to the role of being a wife, daughter-in-law, and mother. In other words, while marriage puts an end to some uncertainties in life, new uncertainties are attached to it. The new situation raises new questions, which, consequently, demand new answers: how do I manage to be both a good copy writer and a good wife and a good daughter-

---

3 Whitehouse summarizes and discusses current common Malian discourse on marriage (Whitehouse 2016).

in-law? Should I keep the job that needs me to commute two hours a day or should I look for another one that is closer to home?

Madou: how to be a husband and a father?

Madou is a tall man. As always, he dresses up, but his style has changed from urban cool to business. Rather than baggy pants and t-shirts, he now wears suit pants and button-up shirts, and sometimes a sack coat. He is also comfortable in Boubou, on Fridays at least, and he still buys random soccer clothes, which he wears in his free time. Madou likes women, and he knows that women like men who work for large companies like he does. He emphasizes that he has become serious now, which means he does not play around with various partners and is committed to one relationship and is faithful to his future wife. Since he works on an unlimited contract, he is finally able to save money for his wedding, which is scheduled for next year. Also, there is a woman in his life, Sara. She is pretty, listens to his problems, gives advice, and is always interested. In 2015, he is engaged to a different woman; her name is Bintou. They are the same age and they studied physics together at the university. She is "pretty, slim and a good Muslim," he says. Of course, he is going to provide for his little family, but "she's going to help me, too." Married life is going to be a new situation for Madou. He will be responsible for his own family and not only for himself and his mother's household anymore. To him, responsibility in marriage means to provide and to be faithful. The financial aspect is not an issue, but being faithful causes uncertainty. He used to go out with several partners at a time; now, he is going to spend the rest of his life with just one. He fasts two days a week now, because that increases his wisdom and decreases his sexual appetite. Just as fast as Madou gets excited about things, he gets bored by them as well. He wants to have kids soon, because they help keep things exciting, he says.

He is engaged now, not to the woman we talked about last year. He feels ready to get married now: "*Maintenant, il y a beaucoup de responsabilités, j'ai grandi et j'ai un travail et je peux m'occuper d'une famille maintenant*". Even though he loves and appreciates his future wife, he does not know what marriage is going to be like and what is going to happen. He would like to have kids fast, because kids mean change and it is by change that things stay exciting. Of course, he is going to provide for his future family, but his wife is going to work as well. "Elle va m'aider, quoi." – "She is going to help me, you know." Right now, the house gets a makeover in order to be nice for the newlyweds. He does that for his wife, not because he thinks it is necessary. He likes it the way it is.

Madou: how to be the new head of my family?

In fall 2013, Madou experienced a sudden rupture with the death of their father. I regard this event as a context of uncertainty, which requires for him to figure out how to deal with this new situation.

> You know, I've lost my father. So, as the first son, I am supposed to take over his position in the family here. [...] I have to support the family and make sure they are happy... just like my father would have done. That's it. (My translation, interview, 2014, with Madou, graduated in Physics.)

With his father's death, Madou's position in the family immediately changes. As the first son, Madou is supposed to be a role model for his brother and sisters, and now, he is the new head of the family. Previously, Madou had always contributed some money to the family's household voluntarily, but now it is his duty to do so. He is responsible for paying the electricity and doctor's bills; he also gives money to his younger sisters for gas and food. That hurts, he says jokingly. "I just have to improve managing my money... avoid wasting it." But there are a lot of things you cannot foresee. "Il y a beaucoup d'imprévues." Of course, you can save money for something, but then someone gets sick and the money is gone, he says. He has to manage his money even better and avoid wasting it. "Instead of taking advantage of my youth, I have to grow up now," he says. Saving money or dealing with money responsibly is associated with being grown up, whereas youth is associated with wasting money. If his father were not dead, he could do everything he wanted with the money he is earning. With his father dead, he takes over responsibility – not necessarily, because his family forces him to, but because he feels like doing it. Additionally, his employment enables him to do so. Madou sets the rules that enable him to present himself as a responsible person, he says. In this sense, a responsible person is someone that knows how to deal with money, or even better, how to evaluate between different expenses. He says, if there is a problem and he does not have money, "C'est grave" – "It's bad". In case of unexpected problems, he must be able to provide money. To prepare for this, Madou saves money he would usually spend on travel, go out at night, probably for dinner and dancing. In either case, while problems themselves cannot be avoided, the possibility that a problem may become "grave" can be avoided, by growing up and saving money. It is this kind of thinking and realizing the connection that made him become a more responsible person.

Unknown: TRANSITIONS.

Being a businesswoman and wife and becoming a mother.

Safiatou loves her job, but she needs to find another agency, she says in 2015. Her workplace is an hour's drive away from home. This is precious time she could spend with her son, who has now begun to speak little by little. One of the words he uses most often is "Marietou," which is the name of the housemaid who carries him around all day, while Safiatou is at work. Safiatou knows that she has all the support she needs from her family in order to manage both her career and her home life, but the fact she only sees her son for half an hour in the morning and about an hour in the evening makes her sad. All in all, Safiatou realizes that it is no longer possible for her to simultaneously work her job and care for her baby to her satisfaction. It is a challenging situation, which requires new knowledge on how to arrange the new situation. In Safiatou's case, uncertainty is more a matter of decision-making and dealing with the consequences, of getting used to and developing new routines rather than a matter of not being able to predict consequences. Realizing that it is a true challenge to satisfy both her ambitions at work and at home is new to her, making her call a seemingly established future into question. It is a different situation with a kid – a situation that requires re-evaluation of priorities, new routines, new knowledge.

Being a bachelor and becoming husband and father.

Madou, too, wonders about how to be a good husband and a father, which is a new situation. In contrast to Safiatou, that he keeps working at the telecommunications agency is not a question at all; in fact, it is his responsibility as the provider in the family.

Being a son and becoming the head of the family.

Whereas the first two new and unfamiliar situations are result of the voluntary decisions the respective graduates took by themselves, the death of Madou's father constitutes a personal loss and rupture he certainly did not welcome. The death of his father opened up a new situation for Madou, which required new knowledge. Up until that moment, Madou did not experience the responsibilities of being a head of a family. Even though he knows very well what he is expected to do in general, his questions are answered as he becomes familiar with his new position.

KNOWING THE UNKNOWN in the future.

The unknowns presented are pointing towards the future as graduates deal with questions about when particular events related to family lives or careers are going to take place. With regard to the future, graduates know what exactly they do not know about it.

Family unknown: DETAIL.

Graduates know they are going to get married. However, there are details such as time and partner, which are unknown. Yet, this does not only apply to marriage, but also to career questions. We saw that both women, for instance, know they are going to succeed in their careers, just not in which exact domain or based on which exact contract. They do not know when they will know about these details, but they do know that they will. They know about the fact itself, they do not know about the details of the parameters that make these facts come into existence.

Career unknown: CONSEQUENCES.

The difference between transitions in the present and consequences in the future is connected to the decision itself. Both unknown transitions (present) and unknown consequences (future) are connected to decisions. The difference is that the situation of an unknown transition in the present is characterized by the consequences of a decision already taken. So, whereas the decision itself is located in the past, the present outcome of the decision is constituted by a new situation. The situation of unknown consequences in the future relates to a decision under evaluation in the present. Therefore, the decision is located in the future, in which the currently unknown outcome of a decision will present itself.

FAMILY: WHEN? WHO?

Amadou: Who is going to be my wife?

We're sitting in front of the cabin. Issiaka, Madou, Amadou and me. Amadou is preparing tea for us. Issiaka starts teasing Amadou: "Look at him, he's just sitting there, waiting to get money." Two years ago, Amadou had finished studying and ever since he has been working two jobs, three months each. Issiaka says that Amadou has a girlfriend, but he refuses to marry her, because he can't afford to buy her anything. He grabs his shoulder, laughs. Amadou is obviously not interested in what Issiaka is saying. Since I've never seen Amadou with a girl and I know Issiaka's provocations, I don't engage in the discussion, but listen closely. Issiaka continues with his teasing. Ignoring him does not work, so I finally decide to react to it with an ambitious "Ah bon!" Amadou instantly responds. "Mais c'est vrai." – "But it's true." And continues repeating what Issiaka just said: "I don't have any money to pay neither for the wedding nor for a house or a car". (Field notes 2009)

On a Friday in March 2015, Amadou arrives from Segou. He's doing fine. He looks good – "en forme". He's set up his own business which serves as a kind of mediator for Orange Money. Not directly Orange Money though. It's Orange Money that pays his business, but not him. In fact, Orange Money needs his business in order to gain access to more rural areas like Segou. He calls it "ma boîte" – "his company". Tonton Hamidou, who lives in the United States as a manager, invested in Amadou's company. He came up with the idea. When he tells me about it, he speaks softly and quietly and does not look me in the eye. He's telling me the truth though. I know that it was Hamidou's idea. He believes in Amadou and his talents. He told me it hurts him to see Amadou's talents getting wasted in the cafeteria. Amadou later talks about how his business is advancing: he talks about how he manages millions of Francs CFA, transfers them from one account to another – easily. He stands in front of me like a professional boxer only minutes before a fight. His head up high, I can see where his chin beard ends. He feels good about it, obviously. I always felt like he brightened up his duty in the cafeteria and I'm happy he doesn't have to do that anymore. He came to Bamako only for the weekend, because he needs to take care of his future marriage. He doesn't do that because he wants it, but because his mother does, he says. She found him a future

> wife. He doesn't love her yet, but she's educated and is working in journalism. The two of them met some time ago and now things are getting serious. He says, he can feel the pressure and he doesn't want to disappoint his mother. You can't ignore your mothers request, he explains, especially because he's getting paid big time now, so no one believes anymore he's unable to found a family in terms of finances. Anyway, he's going to do it. He adapts easily, he says, he's simple and if there is one thing he can do it's make things work. "Bon, c'est la famille maintenant, hein?", I comment. "C'est ça même la vie. Devenir independant et puis fonder une famille." – "That's what life is: you become independent, then you found a family", he responds with his serious thinker face eyebrows far apart from his eyes that are focusing me, "hein? T'as compris, non?". (Field notes, March 2015.)

Six years lie between these two vignettes. One might assume that this new context creates uncertainty, but it does not seem to do so. Amadou knows everything he needs to know for this marriage to work out: he earns enough money, his mother suggested the woman, and the woman is educated. Now, they just have to get along, which he knows they will, because, to him, getting along depends solely on his own mindset.

Simone: When do I get married?

C'est ton rêve!

> Simone's hair is tightly attached to her scalp; her bun explodes on top of her head. She wears make-up, just a little, so that no one sees that she's tired. I first met her in 2009, when I was doing an internship at national TV. She sat in the conference room focused on her writing, but participating in the joking that happened around her. She was the "wife" to a lot of men there.[4] "That's Simone, my wife! Isn't she pretty?", says a sports journalist, introducing her with his arm around her shoulder. She laughs about it and gets rid of his arm. With her back straight, her arm firmly against her chest, and her head up, she says: "C'est ton rêve, petit!" (Field notes, April 2009.)

---

4 For studies on joking in relationships see, for instance Jones 2007.

As a single woman in her twenties, marriage is a topic in Simone's life as well. "2015 is going to be my year," she says. "I will get married and pregnant!" Simone became engaged to a Malian living in France when she was still a student. When her father got sick, she took care of him, which made her fiancé feel neglected. So, "je l'ai abandonné" – "I abandoned him", she says. For quite some time, she is in love with an older man. "C'est un papa cool pour moi" – "He's a cool daddy for me", she says and laughs. Yet, she breaks up with him, because he is simply too old. Religion is also an issue: He is Muslim and she is Christian, and he is married.

Simone is 25 years old and not yet married. She broke up with her boyfriend, whom she loved, because she knew they would never get married. Over the years, she learned that falling in love with a man does not necessarily lead to an engagement, nor does an engagement lead to marriage. "I'm getting older; I'm not in a hurry though," she says. She is confident that she will get married and have kids; it is the fact that she has not met her future husband yet and the fact that she is getting older that increases her feeling of urgency, but not of uncertainty: she will marry this year.[5] She knows she needs to find her future husband soon. She is not uncertain; there are no questions. And that is based on everything she knows about her circumstances and marriage in Mali.

Unknown: DETAIL.

Future marriage is not questioned. Graduates know they are going to get married. Just that important details such as time and partner are unknown.

CAREER: EITHER... OR...?

Simone: The goal or the money?

VIGNETTE: At work.

> Simone is working on her paper. It's about mobile phones, because today is the International Day of Mobile Phones. She has conducted interviews, which are all quite alike. She records her commentary, then we have to wait quite

---

5 She did get married in December 2015.

2 Graduates | Situating *La Chance* in Graduates' Everyday Lives.

some time for a cutter to finish up her clip. Meanwhile, the place becomes noisy to a point where it becomes difficult to follow the conversation. "C'est pas un marché ici" – "This is not a market right here", Simone shouts in French, not in Bambara. Everyone is quiet.

40 Minutes after my arrival, we are off looking for a quiet place in order to conduct the interview. We walk around the station and say hello to everyone. Today, Simone is wearing a dress with dices on it; they show the numbers one and six. The dress's cut is in style, it is tight with puffed sleeves. She is carrying two Ray Ban – Originals from Morocco. We end up in Cheick's office; he actually quits his office and hands his keys over to Simone. He is the news director of Mali's national television. Here we are in his office. Simone puts her phone on silent mode, stretches her back and takes a deep breath: "Alright, I'm ready, let's go!" [...]

Straight after the interview, we're taking a taxi to a communications agency in Missira, where she's been working for quite a while. So that's what she does after work. TM2 is not about the money, but about the job, but still, she needs money to eat. She sometimes finds money "sur le terrain" when she is doing research in the city. Sometimes people, especially government institutions would give journalists some money for their efforts. The agency produces shows for TM2. They have expensive stuff and technological expertise, but no journalists around. Simone knocks at the front and the backdoor – the place looks closed and empty. She has to call someone on the phone before we can finally enter. There is an office with wooden walls inside a big room, no windows, no nothing. The walls are covered in blankets. Simone says hi to three people and sits down on a couch comfortably and checks Facebook. She's tired, exhausted and has a headache, she told me before. After 20 minutes, she's annoyed and says that she's going to leave. Nothing has happened so far. The boss of the group now seems to get out of his chill mode, grabs a piece of paper, a pen and starts talking about what's going to happen at "Le monde des enfants", the new TV format. Simone suddenly puts her phone away. Focus! No more signs of tiredness in her face.

Her boss suggests having something like kids news in the middle of the show: Every week there should be a portrait of a good and interesting student... just like they've been doing it sometime else. Simone says, she saw that story the other day and "this was not a portrait!" She's talking with a strong and dominant voice. Everybody listens. She tells them what journalism is, how questions are asked, which images it needs and which topics are interesting. She makes them understand that they really got the facilities and all, but it's her expertise they'll need in order to succeed. Whenever the conversation stops, she gets back to her bored face asking "That's it? May I leave now?" At 7 p.m., she says she's got to leave now, because she's obligated to watch the news tonight, otherwise people would give her a hard time at work tomorrow. She doesn't leave to watch it, but she keeps repeating she relinquished. Around 9 p.m., Adama, one of the guys, gives her a ride home. Sitting in the car, Simone instantly falls asleep. Her boyfriend is going to come see her tonight, too. Maybe not. He's still at the TV station. And she's got to rest, she's still having that headache and she has to be ready to perform tomorrow – as chef d'édition. (Field notes, February 2014.)

Simone: What am I going to do?

In 2014, Simone is working as an intern at Mali's new, second TV channel. She has been working there since 2009. She started off as an intern, accompanying journalists and realizing her first reports on the radio. She did her Masters in journalism and spent every semester break at the station. Today, everybody knows her at the station; she is allowed to use one of the directors' offices for private purposes, as she did during our interview. She works on her own reports and supervises the evening news. She is one of the few people working for the new TV channel. However, she is still working there with the status of an intern: full time and for free. "Je suis jeune. Je peux faire ça" – "I'm young. I can do that," she repeats. For nearly five years, she has been told that she would get a contract as a journalist. This promise has been changed from "one day, you'll get a contract" to "once you have a degree" to "once we employ new staff" to "next time, you'll get a contract." It is always so close. In August 2014, she says the officials told her the station would contract new employees "on January 5th 2015." Soon. "Reaching goals is more important than money," she said, reflecting on her status as an intern with the goal to become a journalist.

Dans trois ans, je me vois sur Africa24 où France24. On ne fait que souhaiter le meilleur. (Rire) Donc, je souhaite le meilleur pour moi. Et c'est mon rêve d'aller présenter un jour où entendre ma voix sur France24 où correspondante de RFI au Mali. C'est un rêve. (Simone 2014)

In this situation, Simone was promised a contract, which she has not yet been given. Though she may get it in the future, here is what she knows for now: after five years and everything she has accomplished so far in journalism, it is supposed to be her turn. Her professional future depends on the station's decision. So, the discrepancy between what is being promised, along with her continuous engagement and being repeatedly disappointed, constitutes her uncertainty. Now, based on what she knows about that situation, Simone evaluates her options. For the time being, she decides to stay with the station as an intern without a promised contract.

By the end of 2014, Simone starts working mostly at night at the International Airport Bamako-Senou as an airline assistant. Her uncle called her attention to this job and since her father has gotten sick, she felt like she needed to support the family financially, so she decided to apply for the job and got it. She left TM2, because "c'était juste des promesses… pas de contrat", she explains. Nevertheless, she has found an opportunity to continue with her journalist activities as she also works temporarily as chief editor at sahelien.com, a website that informs mostly on politics from the region. Its reporters are locals that have been trained by BBC, RFI and Reuters journalists.

Safiatou: What is best?

Journalism or communications?

Back in Mali in 2013, Safiatou starts working as a copy writer at one of the world's largest marketing agencies. She receives this opportunity by using her networks – "j'ai joué sur mes relations". Her contacts at national TV, where she had her first working experiences, provided her this job in marketing communication. Safiatou loves writing. To her, the beauty of journalism is not about information, but about words – as is the case with marketing. Plus, she argues, journalism is poorly paid and time consuming, which makes it impossible to do any other business along the way. She is better off with communications, which offers advantageous working conditions. She supervises the production of television ads for Malitel and Diago. She is building up experience for her own communications agency, which she plans to set up in a couple of years. She still admires journalists, but she understands that it's difficult to make money in that sector. She says that in the end, the only difference between a copy writer and a journalist is fame. Safiatou does not want to become famous, but a successful businesswoman.

Here or there?

Five months before the baby arrives, Safiatou and I meet again. At that time, the newlyweds are planning to move to the United States of America. Abba needs to get his Master's degree and their baby, once born in the States, will get the US as well as the Malian citizenship. That will facilitate traveling, studying and even living for their baby. They both prefer to stay in Mali, but since they will become parents soon, they cannot continue to think about themselves only and moving is just the most responsible way to go, she explains. They are both still young, but they have to think about their future, about a better life than this, she says. She is well aware of the fact that their chances to get the visa for the USA are low, but they won't pass up any opportunity. Her pregnancy is exhausting and she can hardly live with the fact that she cannot work with the same energy and enthusiasm as she did before. She does not want to be seen as a pregnant woman, but as a business woman, who is also expecting a baby.

Unknown: CONSEQUENCES.

Safiatou and Simone are best friends. They received the same education in journalism, and though they face the same challenges in the same profession, they deal with them differently. While both women were committed to journalism, Simone sticks with journalism, Safiatou has decided to switch jobs. They knew at a young age they wanted to pursue this goal, which they did as they studied abroad, acquired four diplomas, and engaged in various internships. Realizing that the qualifications they had acquired and, more importantly, they had dedicated themselves to for years, are likely to not pay off, creates uncertainty – it "calls a seemingly established future into question" (Johnson-Hanks 2002, 878). It raises questions about evaluation and priorities. They both possess similar professional qualifications, but they evaluated their choices in accordance with their individual, differing priorities. Recognizing the difficulty of becoming a journalist in Mali, Simone continued moving forward, while Safiatou reoriented her course. To Simone, journalism was about delivering the news and the fame. She does not know when she will get her contract – which depends on her boss' decision (external factor see unknown: DEPENDENCIES) – but she believes that she will get one. To Safiatou though, journalism was about writing and the excitement that comes with it. Ultimately, she knew that copy writing has the same traits plus a bigger salary, so she changed professional directions. In both cases questions are raised which are evaluated based on current experience and knowledge, followed by a decision: Simone sticks with her current employer and stays in her situation, which is highly dependent on other peoples' decisions – 'social contingencies' (Whyte 2015). Safiatou accepts another job, which creates a new uncertain situation requiring new knowledge.

Summary.

To sum up, I chose to focus on individuals' biographies first, before I continued to present in detail the questions they are concerned with in their everyday lives in relation to knowledge. Based on graduates' everyday experiences, I extracted present and future unknowns. The unknowns rooted in the present indicate dependencies and transitions. There are everyday external dependencies, such as social contingencies, and dependencies, which suddenly become apparent. Whereas everyday dependencies are known to be unknown, sudden dependencies open up a new unknown, which requires new knowledge. Another unknown originates in transitions, which follow decisions or events and require an individual to become what is yet an unknown to them. Transitions raise new questions and require new knowledge. The unknowns rooted in the future draw from present knowns about the future, but contain unknown details, i.e. the exact time, person or condition) and there are also known unknowns concerning the overall future outcome of present decisions. Ultimately, these findings sketch out the intersection between the known and the unknown, which is the foundation for the phenomenon of *la chance*. Let me explain:

Graduates' everyday uncertainties vary in their relationship with knowledge: everyday uncertainties describe situations in which current knowledge is evaluated, part of that knowledge is the awareness of conditions which are impossible to know. Immediate uncertainties are triggered by ruptures or new situations, which require new knowledge. Situations with no uncertainty are defined by a present which is sufficiently known. Contexts of uncertainty are characterized by the unknown; *la chance* – once identified – puts an end to the unknown. *La chance* appears in uncertain situations as knowledge and difficult situations as a solution. More explicitly, contexts of uncertainty are contexts of *la chance* in two manners: first of all, contexts of uncertainty (e.g. job situation for Simone and Safiatou, coup d'état for Madou) open up space for *la chance*; meanwhile, contexts of no uncertainty (e.g. Amadou: marriage, Simone: marriage, Mohamed: coup d'état) are characterized by *la chance* as well, but in a different sense. Whereas contexts of uncertainty offer potential for *la chance* to appear, contexts of no uncertainty are predicated by *la chance*. This distinction is crucial and indicates the need for a more detailed analysis of *la chance*, which I offer in part two.

Part 2: Assemblage of *la chance*

3 A Manual

VIGNETTE: Dieu donne *la chance*, mais toi aussi tu peux t'ouvrir *la chance*.

> He sat in one of these metal chairs with seats made out of plastic strings; he did not lean back comfortably, but he sat there with one of the armrests between his knees, legs squatting and wide open, his upper body leaned forward, his elbows on his knees, his hands and forearms moving, sometimes meeting for a quick and concluding hand clap. He said: "Dieu donne *la chance*, mais toi aussi tu peux t'ouvrir *la chance*. Ou bien?!" – "God provides *la chance*, but you can open up *la chance* yourself as well. Right?!" (Field notes, May 2014.)

With reference to *la chance*, university graduates make sense of their situation and they play with it. Examining graduates' knowledge about their situation, we see that *la chance* is so much more than its translation "luck" reveals. Throughout this second part of the book, we see how *la chance* emerges at the intersection between what graduates know and what they know they don't know. *La chance* makes sense. *La chance* is known to make a difference between those who get employed and those who do not. However, *la chance* is elusive in a sense that it appears to be indexical in concrete contexts, but it escapes our grasp as soon as we try to approach its essence.

The chapters four and five are based on graduates' knowledge accessed through narrative interviews. Whereas layer one sets out to analyze the empirical phenomenon of *la chance* as referred to by university graduates in Bamako, layer two continues to develop a conceptual framework of *la chance*, which is disembedded from the particular Malian context. The assemblage style of the following chapters helps me keep these two layers separate and at the same time put them in relation.

INVITATION: Dear Reader,...

There are different ways of reading a book: reading for an argument, which means focusing on all the details and examples, reading for a particular quote, reading with the purpose of finding inspiration... Exploration is usually conducted in a superficial way, jumping across sections and sticking with whatever catches our interest, diving in deep and resurfacing above sea level again. Exploration comes along with the connotation of incompleteness. However, the idea of incompleteness only works when opposed to the idea of completeness, and the assemblage does not claim to be complete. Of course, you can read the entire assemblage provided here, but I would not recommend it. It is repetitive at times and always incomplete. An assemblage always remains incomplete, and thus, it allows for something to emerge within it.

The ideas which emerged through my engagement with the extracts in the assemblage are presented in the summaries in chapter four, i.e. *la chance* as prerequisites, sprouts, outcomes as well as the emergence and the summaries in chapter five, i.e. the practice of opening up *la chance* as preparation, identification, transformation as well as the game of *la chance*. You might see other things emerge, you most likely will, you might also see redundancies or feel like I missed important aspects and you might want to argue with me or add something, and that is exactly what the explorative reading experience is supposed to be.

SO,

You can read the following chapters in a linear way (layer one in its entirety, thus, skipping layer two and the other way around) and read about my journey of discovering *la chance* in the documentation of my research process. I went on this journey twice so far: the first time looking at *la chance* as a members' phenomenon, wearing an ethnomethodologist's glasses (see layer 1), and the second time looking for conceptual clues on *la chance* (see layer 2).

You can also read it in a fragmented way to explore and experience both la *chance* and *la chance* on your own: read a bit and stop, continue reading a few pages later, jumping back and forth. Do it. Allow for *la chance* to emerge. Confusion is part of the process. Enjoy the ride!

Imagine this part of the book like a road trip on which you can follow my traces or decide on your own where you want to stop and if you want to stop at all. There might be traffic jams, you might want to roll down the window, listen to the radio and be reminded of the past, be present in the moment or fabulate about the future. Trust that you will recognize your destination when you get there. Until then, just keep moving. A road trip is about the journey.

So, if you have a hard copy of this book, please do not be shy to make effective use of its haptics and thumb through the pages, skim it, skip some pages, stick with some thoughts and let go of others.

If you have a digital version of the book, use it like an instagram feed: scroll. Trust that there will be thumb nails catching your attention and you might want to think about leaving a comment in the section below and it's alright if other posts fail to grasp your attention. Just keep scrolling.

Now, if...

... 1 you chose the linear option, please just keep reading. But if you chose the fragmented one, jump straight to chapter four. The is a map on the next page, if you like one.

...2 you would like to know more about the assemblage style before diving into it, please finish reading this chapter first.

[MAP]

If you are looking to explore *la chance* for yourself,

please explore the accounts on *la chance* in the assemblage by skipping, imagining, interpreting, skimming, comparing, stopping, reading closely... read however you like and allow for *la chance* to emerge.

If you are looking for a (1) structured assemblage of (2) graduates' accounts on *la chance* as well as the (3) findings and the (4) argumentative tracings I derived from them,

please follow my directions by reading along through sections (1) to (4):

(1) the major sections,

> e.g. "*La chance* is a prerequisite".

(2) the accounts,

> e.g. the code in layer one "L1: predicate\prerequisite\companion" plus the following clue in layer two "L2: *La chance* is having what you want".

(3) the findings from that,

> e.g. "PREREQUISITES"

(4) my tracings to layer one (L1) and layer 2 (L2),

> e.g. "Tracing L1: prerequisites, sprouts, outcomes" and "Tracing L2: clues on *la chance*".

What is *la chance*?

The Discovery: *La chance*.

During my second field trip in 2014, I had a conversation with my friend Sekou. It was dark outside already, and we sat in front of the house, drinking tea and watching the busy but calm street scenery in front of us. We talked about *la chance*. I vividly remember this encounter and especially him saying: *"God provides la chance, but you can open up la chance yourself as well. Right?!"* I was hooked. All of a sudden, I knew *this* was what I was looking for and what I had been looking at all along: *la chance*. The next day, I went through my previously transcribed and coded interview data from 2013 with MAXQDA. I did a quick in-vivo coding (189), in which *la chance* was mentioned 164 times. *La chance* appeared in graduates' accounts of the past, the present, and the future. It was referred to as both cause and effect of either a state in time or a transition of times. Approaching the idea of *la chance* analytically in the interviews, I looked at the various contexts in which informants mentioned *la chance*, i.e. in three different contexts: first, in fixed expressions such as "bonne chance" – "good luck" or "tenter *la chance*" "challenge one's luck." The second context centers on the description of *la chance*, either abstract "avoir l'opportunité de faire qc" – "to have the opportunity of doing something" or concrete "travailler dans les ONGs" – "work for an NGO" or "faire un stage" – "do an internship". Generally, *la chance* refers to *doing something*, whether professional (create, manage, realize) or non-professional (live, love, play), and it is also *to have* (diploma, opportunity, employment) or *to be something* (chosen, lucky, accepted). The third context in which *la chance* is mentioned problematizes how it can be accessed, which is either actively "se battre" – "fight," "prendre ta vie en main" – "take control of life" or passive "Dieu donne *la chance*" – "God provides *la chance*."

The Challenge: Access.

Though *la chance* emerged from the interviews, I could not observe it. The German anthropologist Gerd Spittler, for instance, dealt with an opposite challenge researching the Tuareg in Northern Mali. Asking them questions about their everyday activities did not reveal much information. The Tuareg execute their work on an everyday basis; it is familiar to the extent that it becomes hard for them to describe – Polanyi calls that tacit knowledge (Polanyi 1973 in Spittler,

2001). Spittler overcame that problem by accompanying his informants and asking them questions with reference to what he had observed in the first place. He calls this combination of observation and naturally occurring conversation "deep participation" (ibid. 6). Graduates' knowledge about the phenomenon of *la chance* is tacit knowledge as well, yet the challenge is different. Whereas Spittler dealt with the challenge of researching an everyday activity that was difficult to grasp by talk alone, but approachable by observation, my challenge is to research a phenomenon which is difficult to observe in action, but appeared frequently in how graduates talk about their everyday life and imagined futures. So, I did the opposite of what Spittler did and started asking specifically for *la chance*: What is *la chance*? What is *la chance* to you? Are there moments in your life in which you encountered *la chance*?

The Approach: Ethnomethodology.

> "God provides *la chance*, but you can open up *la chance* yourself as well". Drawing from this quote, you notice that I could have based my work on concepts around religion, the idea of youthful agency, or on the ambiguity of the concept of *la chance*. And this certainly is how *la chance* presents itself to me at first sight. To graduates I talked to though, *la chance* is a social fact and, therefore, "known in common without saying" (Garfinkel et al. 1988, 146 in Pollner 2007, 125).

Ethnomethodology encourages researchers to investigate what members take for granted as "unalterably 'factual', that is, what they unthinkingly, naturally, unreflectively see/experience as part of the normal order of things" (Pollner 2007, 125). One central point of ethnomethodological research reveals how the taken-for-granted is produced by members. *La chance* was familiar to the graduates with whom I talked, but it seemed strange to me after a first inspection. So, I took my curiosity about *la chance* as a point of departure and selected related data "to see what can be discovered in and from them" (Hester 1997, 1). The analytical tool I applied to my data is Membership Categorization, which originates in ethnomethodological thinking.

The assumption.

In order to explore the phenomenon of *la chance* in graduates' accounts, I accepted 'An Invitation to Ethnomethodology' (Francis 2004) and analyzed their talk conducting Membership Categorization Analysis (MCA). MCA "is concerned with the organization of common-sense knowledge in terms of the categories members employ in accomplishing their activities in and through talk" (Francis 2004, 21). Graduates are members. And yes, "graduate" is a categorization I made by selecting them as part of my research sample. In conversation with me, graduates (or members) share ideas about themselves in context, about their past, their present and their future. In doing so, they establish relationships between the categories they use and thereby reveal their knowledge and understanding of the world. I analyze this knowledge with a particular focus on the phenomenon of *la chance*.

> One of the core ideas is that "social facts are treated as accomplishments" (Have 2004), which are produced by the members of a social setting. Ethnomethodology aims at examining the constitution of these accomplishments, not at their explanation (Francis 2004, 207). Considering individuals "as members" of a society producing social facts serves ethnomethodology's focus on practical accomplishments (Have 2004, 20). Members are "conceived as practical actors who are themselves (1) practical analysts of, and inquirers into, the world, (2) using whatever materials there are to hand to get done the tasks and business they are engaged in" (Hester 1997, 1f.).

Let me explain:
The Tool: membership categorization analysis (MCA).

MCA is about the identification of membership categorization devices, which are a collection of membership categories and their rules of application. Here is a popular example: "The baby cries. The mommy picks it up." The 'baby' and the 'mommy' are so-called categories. Now, there are rules of application such as category-bound activities, which refer to activities connected with a category (e.g. 'crying' as a category-bound activity of the 'baby' or 'picking up' for the 'mommy') (Stokoe 2012, 281). In other words, category-bound activities give information about what a certain category ('baby', 'mommy') does. Another rule of application pertinent to this case is category-tied predicates, which refer to characteristics connected with a category (e.g. 'demanding' as a category tied predicate of the 'baby' or 'caring' for the 'mommy').

Baby – mommy. → Graduate – la chance.

In our case, "graduate" can either be a collective category (a device) or an individual category depending on the way it is applied. For example, graduate is a device in case it subsumes the categories "sociology graduate," "physics graduate," "graduate from 2013, 2012 or 2015" and "female or male graduate," but it might as well be a category of "youth" or "society." In my analysis, I operationalize "the graduate" as a category because this enables me to explore the relationship to *la chance*. What does that mean? Again, "the baby cried; the mommy picked it up." There is nothing strange about this phrase, right? Vice versa though, it becomes irritating: "The mommy cried. The baby picked her up." This simple twist of words makes the familiar strange and thereby reveals what we take for granted: the mommy picks up the baby and not vice versa. However, when it comes to the phenomenon of *la chance*, both versions are accurate: "*La chance* called. The graduate picked it up." (In other words, *la chance* appeared and the graduate took it.) And vice versa: "The graduate cried. *La chance* picked her/him up." (The graduate was searching and *la chance* appeared.) At first, the relation between *la chance* and the graduate presents itself as ambiguous. "La chance" and "graduate" constitute what MCA calls a standardized relational pair, but it is not a unique pair: "la chance" is not constituted by "graduate," and "graduate" does not constitute "la chance." *La chance* exists without the graduate, and the graduate still exists without *la chance*. However, the relationship between the two is crucial because "la chance" defines "graduate" and "graduate" identifies "la chance." Membership categorization analysis has been a useful tool for me to disentangle the nature of *la chance*, first by itemizing informants' common-sense meanings of *la chance* and second, by systematizing different types of *la chance*. Rather than members' descriptions of persons (e.g. "baby," "mommy"), I was interested in their descriptions of a phenomenon, specifically, university graduates' descriptions of *la chance*.

To sum up,

ethnomethodology promotes the investigation of members' phenomena and their production. *La chance* is a relevant phenomenon to university graduates – it is a members' phenomenon. I will start my analysis in the first layer by presenting the accounts, which I will then contextualize.

"MCA focuses on 'members' methodical practices in describing *the world*, and displaying their understanding of *the world* and of the *commonsense* routine workings of *society*' (Fitzgerald et al. 2009, 47; emphasis added)" (Stokoe 2012, 278). In other words, instead of analyst categories, e.g. luck, chance, fate, MCA offers the opportunity to take members' categories (Stokoe 2012, 278) seriously, i.e. graduates' categories. Being interested in graduates' categorizations of *la chance*, I coded for devices of *la chance* as used by graduates.

What is la chance? Category-tied predicates (chapter 4: Emergence)

AND

What does la chance do? Category-bound activities (chapter 5: Encounter)

I focus on two aspects of these devices: category-tied predicates, which represent characteristics of the category coded, and category-bound activities, which represent practices attached to the category. In chapter four, "Emergence", I present the result of my coding for category-tied predicates of *la chance*, which helped me approach the question of what *la chance* is. In that same manner, in chapter five, "Encounter", I introduce my coding for category-bound activities of *la chance*, which represent graduates' practices of approaching *la chance*.

In the next section, I examine the knowledge on which the accounts are based in order to ultimately elaborate a systematics of the phenomenon *la chance*.

What is *la chance* – yet, again?

Having revisited my previous research, another puzzle emerges: how come la chance is so much more, yet again?

Vignette: A note to myself Why didn't I see this before?

> So, I started looking for clues, I found plenty and most of them seemed new to me. I started analyzing graduates' accounts on *la chance* again. First, I thought this would help refresh my sense of the details of *la chance*. (...) Now, I am in the process of going through the individual accounts again and I realize that I am still surprised by some of them. I am still able to find something new in them. Why didn't I see this before? (Note, May 2020)

This reflective jotting-down impacts the following chapters in two ways:

1. Naturally, you, the reader, might not agree with what I am saying. I do not shy away from saying what I think of it, of my own interpretation of it, but I allow the reader to do just the same thing, to disagree with me, and more importantly, access *la chance* in her or his own way and in doing so contributing to the concept of *la chance*. It is not a fixed concept, neither to the graduates, nor to me as a researcher, nor to you – the readers.

So, because graduates' accounts are more than my interpretation, I included their accounts.

2. That elusiveness is what *la chance* does. And that is what concepts do. It is precisely why this experience and the problematization of it is so valuable to conceptual work in African Studies.

So, because the result of my analysis changes depending on the way I look at it, I included my account of their accounts.

Now, I put these two layers together.

So, whereas in layer one, I focus on *la chance* as an empirical phenomenon situated in graduates' contexts in Bamako in order to capture a systematization of *la chance*, in layer two, I focus on the content level only, this time disembedded from the empirical context in order to extract conceptual clues, which I later relate back to the empirical level.

The idea of an assemblage helps me do that.

At the end of the chapters four and five, there are tracings which summarize my findings and abstract from them. I use the word tracing because I understand that the map allows for more connections in addition to the ones I see. And it is on you, the reader, to add to the assemblage.

In an assemblage.

What we see: A perceived idea of *la chance*.

We do seem to have a very clear idea of what *la chance* is from the very beginning. Hearing *la chance* we think of chance, luck, opportunity, for instance. If we hear about *la chance* in the Malian context, we associate it with Muslim religion, humbleness, an explanation. In that sense, *la chance* is very much what Flaubert refers to as a "received idea", which is an "idea so well understood, it no longer bears thinking about it in a critical way" (Buchanan, 3). Doing research on graduates in Mali challenged my reception of *la chance*, which is why I prefer to stick with the emic term "la chance" in order to allow for the concept to reveal its own meanings throughout the process of analysis. So, rather than finding a different word for *la chance* or altering its translation, I decided to problematize *la chance* and in doing so open up the received idea of *la chance* for complication (Buchanan, 18).

In the following part of the book, we deal exclusively with graduates' narrative accounts of *la chance*, in which they describe *la chance*. Following ethnomethodology, we account for these descriptions as a practice, as something members do. Therefore, *la chance* is not simply out there, on the contrary, *la chance* is done by graduates, i.e. in their narrative accounts. So, we get to listen and explore their descriptions, rather than our own assumptions. As we try to grasp the phenomenon of *la chance*, we have to acknowledge that we cannot see it if we have not already seen it.

What an assemblage allows me to do: from a perceived idea to a systematics of the unknown.

Content and Form.

An assemblage does not work in a mechanical fashion; an assemblage works as a piece of art. It works by creating an association, a new kind of relation (Buchanan 21). Therefore, the question guiding Deleuze and Guattari's work on the assemblage is not "how does it work?" (that is what Delanda is trying to grasp with his assemblage theory though), but "why is it happening?" (Buchanan 12). Dealing with *la chance*, I approach both questions: How does *la chance* work? And why is it happening?

Logic: open.

An assemblage has a general logic, but it is an open system (Buchanan 15). So, the concept of an assemblage helps me to grasp the general logic of *la chance*, but also to keep it open. Specifically, assemblage relates to the book with regards to form, content and connection: First off, assemblage accounts for the way in which the chapters in this second part of the book are organized as well as how I present and describe the data I use. This assemblage shape further informs the assemblage content, i.e layer one, the systematization of *la chance* and layer two, the destabilization of layer one. Both layers ultimately allow for new connections and relations between the layers to emerge.

Form: An assemblage allows for the possibility to enter it at any point.

The assemblage shape and form of the following chapters helps me keep these two layers separate and put them in relation. It helps getting rid of the idea of providing a linear text within which one coding transitions smoothly into another. This also actively engages the reader in the experience of exploration. Of course, I provide my interpretation and my analysis with the codings, but at the same time I offer the possibility for you to explore on your own. Using the coding schemes and the clues for orientation, you will be able to move around in the book, not reading it in a linear fashion, but depending on what you would like to read about. Really exploring things. Jumping around, moving through parts of the book at your own pace. For orientation, I provide a map.

Avoiding presuppositions and unsettling stabilities.

Developed by Deleuze and Guattari, the assemblage remains an incomplete project. However, it has principles and one of them is the elimination of presuppositions, which means "to not know what everybody knows" and "to not recognize what everybody is supposed to recognize" (Buchanan).

In other words, an assemblage as an epistemological tool. It offers a way of looking at the world by avoiding presuppositions and, therefore, seeing the world differently.

I use the assemblage as "a mode of discovery" (Aneesh 2017, 129), a method which allows me to focus on a phenomenon hardly visible and seemingly ambiguous. It further is a reminder to keep questioning not only my own presuppositions prior to doing research, but also the very findings of my research. In that sense it is a reminder to actively destabilize what is already established (ibid.).

Systematization:
Grasping emergence within relations.

Drawing from Deleuze and Guattari's work, Delanda establishes the assemblage as a system for researchers to be used as a theory and method to account for empirical realities. According to him, an assemblage is a whole constituted by parts building relations, and within these relations something new emerges. That emergence is immanent to the parts, but only actualized in relation, which is why assemblages are decomposable and irreducible. Therefore, an assemblage can only be understood as a whole, including all its parts and relations.

Here is an example: A warrior is an assemblage (Delanda). A warrior is more than a woman plus a horse plus a weapon. The warrior emerges in the relationship between the components interacting with each other. If there is no interaction between the parts, we are dealing with a collection. The components have the capacity to build a warrior. Looking at a warrior as an assemblage, we see that the properties of the whole are irreducible to the properties of its parts. In other words, assemblages build connections within which properties emerge. An emergent property comes into existence when parts interact and in doing so exercise their capacities. Something novel emerges only in relation, but inherent to the part. In other words, for these properties to emerge, the parts need to interact. Assemblages are decomposable, but they are not reducible. In assemblages, the parts' capacities are defined by their interaction with each other. Capacity is important here. A capacity is not a property. A capacity is actualized in relation.

Just like the warrior emerging within an assemblage of a woman, a horse and a weapon, *la chance* emerges in assemblages of heterogeneous units. *La chance* emerges in an assemblage and *la chance* is the assemblage. At least that is how we look at *la chance* here in this book. So, let me be very clear: People themselves do not become *la chance* like a woman can become a warrior in interaction with a weapon and a horse, but *la chance* comes into being within that assemblage. Put differently, *la chance* is the warrior itself. *La chance*, just like the warrior is decomposable, yet, not reducible to its parts.

Phases.

The nature of an assemblage varies between fixed and fluid, between closed and open according to Manuel Delanda (2006, 253). Depending on the parameters, the assemblage changes in its phases which emerge between sharp distinctions at the edges. These phases account for types immanent to the assemblage. For instance, water emerges as a type between the sharp edges of gas and ice. Water is immanent to the assemblage of H2O, just like gas and ice. The point here is not to carve out binaries and boundaries, but to work with them. Just like Deleuze and Guattari talk about trees and rhizomes, the tree has the capacity to become a rhizome and vice versa. One is immanent in the other.

I draw inspiration from these phases in the sense that I present a systematics of *la chance* that shows how *la chance* emerges in different phases (prerequisites, sprouts and outcomes).

Immanence.

Contrary to Delanda, Buchanan argues that phenomena in assemblages do not change incrementally, i.e. in phases, but they emerge all at the same time (Buchanan 2021, 18). Being more than the sum of its parts, an assemblage itself is about emergence. The stages are not progressing, but emerging. Similarly, *la chance* is not developing in stages, but rather in accordance with properties already immanent to its parts. *La chance* emerges in relations immanent (yet, not necessarily actualized) to the parts that constitute the world around us (yet, not in a linear fashion). In other words, even though there are multiple types of *la chance*, one type does not necessarily lead to another. In their potential, all phases exist simultaneously.

Destabilization:
Emergence of new kinds of relations.

For instance, prerequisites, sprouts and outcomes, or — to use Delanda's term — the phases of *la chance*, are one tracing I find in the assemblage. This layer is an offer I am able to make based on my analysis and interpretation, but I leave it to the reader to make sense of it in a different way. And in fact, I did the same, as you can see in layer two, with a second attempt to approach *la chance* via an explorative content analysis directed towards clues that speak to me rather than members' categories. This second layer is not me dismissing what I first did in layer one, rather I destabilize and rework the initial result of my analysis. Both layers are useful in their own terms, yet, together they inform each other and again allow for new relations to be made and new phenomena to emerge.

4   *La chance* | Emergence.

Layer 1. Members predicates: *La chance* appears.

The first layer (L1) is about the phenomenon of *la chance* as categorized by university graduates. The questions raised in this chapter are: What do the graduates categorize as *la chance* and what do they know about *la chance*? In order to find out how *la chance* was experienced by graduates in the past, we will explore university graduates' stories about their lives through their own narrated autobiographies.

Now, this is where the description gets a bit technical:

Guided by the question "What is *la chance*?" I coded the interview transcripts for category-tied predicates of *la chance* applied by my informants. The category I focused on was *la chance*; and within that members' category, I focused on the devices which categorize *la chance*. Overall, I coded 244 accounts in which graduates related to *la chance* and came up with 17 predicates of *la chance*. By virtue of that first round of coding, I came up with the following devices: "companion", "social context", "means", "networks", "opportunity", "special" and "possession", for instance. To put this very simply, *la chance* categorized with the device "social context" means that "*la chance* is social context" and likewise, "*la chance* is networks", "*la chance* is special" and so on. In the second-cycle coding I refined the devices I categorized in my initial coding by splitting (Dey 2003, 139), for instance, "networks" into family, friendship and professional networks. Similarly, I distinguished "opportunities" as a result of previous "choices", as a "reward" for previous action or as "success". For instance, "*la chance* is an opportunity resulting from previous choices". More importantly though, by comparing and combining the devices resulting from my first-cycle coding, I identified patterns shared by some of them and spliced them accordingly (Dey 2003, 139). For instance, I realized the devices "means", "networks" and "social context" were perceived as a given "privilege" by graduates, whereas "possession", "possibility" and "access" are attributed to a personal "achievement". Quite unlike these groups, "opportunity" and "special" share the commonality of being manifested in a unique "moment" of time. Accordingly, on this level "*la chance* is a privilege", "*la chance* is a moment" and "*la chance* is an achievement". Abstracting from these overarching categories, which are based on the category-tied predicates of *la chance*, I developed the constituent parts of *la chance*, namely "prerequisites of *la chance*", "sprouts of *la chance*" and "outcomes of *la chance*".

All in all, the examination of *la chance* as a category resulted in a differentiation of the phenomenon into prerequisites, sprouts, and outcomes. I chose these terms as representative for the kind of *la chance* to which they refer. In that sense, *la chance* might as well be considered a collective category – a membership categorization device consisting of these three categories each featuring different predicates. At first, these categories (prerequisites, sprouts, and outcomes) were invisible; they represent graduates' taken-for-granted knowledge of the features of *la chance*.

Layer 2. Clues: *La chance* emerges.

The second layer (L2) contains clues extracted from graduates' narrative accounts that indicate (I) how *la chance* emerges in particular situations and (II) how *la chance* operates in general instances.

I What is *la chance*?

We will see that:

(1) *La chance* is possession. *La chance* is ability.
Within the relations between *la chance* and work, *la chance* and education, *la chance* and money as well as *la chance* and employment, we will see how *la chance* emerges as a possession, namely, something people have and as an ability, which refers to a person's potential of having something like employment or money, for instance.

(2) *La chance* is connected to and different from "not *la chance*" and "*la malchance*".

Example.

Original Interview Extract in French.

Susann: Est-ce que tu penses que tu auras besoin de (la) chance pour réussir?

Mamadi: Ça c'est clair, même si tu es diplômé avec un doctorat, si tu n'as pas la chance tu restes toujours à la maison. La chance aussi a un impact

Layer 1: Coding Scheme.

L1: predicate\prerequisite\companion

Susann: Do you think you need la chance in order to succeed?
Mamadi: Of course I do! Even if you have a PhD, if you dont have la chance, you're going to stay at home. La chance does have an impact as well. (My translation, interview, 2015, with Mamadi, graduated in Sociology.)

Narrative Interview Account.

La chance is impactful and necessary in ensuring success, which is, in other words, "to not stay at home". Even having a PhD does not ensure success in this endeavor, not like la chance does. The equation is simple: with a PhD you stay at home, but with a PhD in combination with la chance, you will not. Mamadi does not quantify la chance's impact; la chance seems to be binary. One either has la chance, or one does not – the possession of a PhD does not equate to the presence or absence of la chance. In other words, la chance is like a companion.

Interpretation 1: Membership Categorization Analysis focusing on predicates (chapter 4) and activities (chapter 5) of "la chance" as an empirical phenomenon.

Layer 2: Clue.

L2: La chance is having what you want.

I specifically ask for the causal relationship between la chance and success. Without la chance, you stay at home, which is something you do not want. The exceptional qualification of a PhD is not enough to get you out of the home - and into a job. You do need la chance in order to get a job, which does not mean that it is enough to have la chance.
A PhD is not la chance. La chance is to get out of the home and into a job.

Interpretation 2: Explorative Content Analysis focusing on predicates (chapter 4) and activities (chapter 5) of la chance as a concept.

II How does *la chance* operate?

We will see that:

(1) *La chance* is a process and a product.
La chance emerges within a combination of structural and agentive factors and it becomes visible through its particular distribution among university graduates.

(2) *La chance* is distributed, thus, *la chance* distinguishes.
La chance is distributed in different ways. Therefore, *la chance* is special and not taken for granted by those who have *la chance*. Furthermore, *la chance* is relative, i.e. a matter of consideration – relative to oneself and relative to others.

Assemblage: *la chance.*

La chance is a prerequisite.

Susann: Est-ce que tu penses que tu auras besoin de (la) chance pour réussir?

Mamadi: Ça c'est clair, même si tu es diplômé avec un doctorat, si tu n'as pas *la chance* tu restes toujours à la maison. *La chance* aussi a un impact.

L1: predicate\prerequisite\companion

Susann: Do you think you need *la chance* in order to succeed?

Mamadi: Of course I do! Even if you have a PhD, if you don't have *la chance*, you're going to stay at home. *La chance* does have an impact as well.

(My translation, interview, 2015, with Mamadi, graduated in Sociology.)

La chance is impactful and necessary in ensuring success, which is, in other words, "to not stay at home". Even having a PhD does not ensure success in this endeavor, not like *la chance* does. The equation is simple: with a PhD you stay at home, but with a PhD in combination with *la chance*, you will not. Mamadi does not quantify *la chance*'s impact; *la chance* seems to be binary. One either has *la chance*, or one does not – the possession of a PhD does not equate to the presence or absence of *la chance*. In other words, *la chance* is like a companion.

L2: *La chance* is having what you want.

I specifically ask for the causal relationship between *la chance* and success.

Without *la chance*, you stay at home, which is something you do not want.

The exceptional qualification of a PhD is not enough to get you out of the home – and into a job. You do need *la chance* in order to get a job, which does not mean that it is enough to have *la chance*.

A PhD is not *la chance*. *La chance* is to get out of the home and into a job.

Susann Ludwig: *La chance*

Susann: Tu as dit que tu aimais travailler dans un bureau, pourquoi ?

Ibrahim: J'ai envie de travailler dans un bureau et je voulais toujours travailler dans un bureau, et puis pourquoi? Parce que j'ai dit que si tu as pu étudier, ce n'est pas obligatoirement pour travailler dans un bureau. Chacun a sa chance dans la vie. Mais quand même, moi j'ai merais travailler dans un bureau. Pourquoi ? Si tu travailles dans un service, c'est comme si tu avais beaucoup d'assurance.

L1: predicate\prerequisite\companion

Susann: You said you like working in an office, how come?

Ibrahim: I like working in an office and I always wanted to work in an office. Because having graduated doesn't necessarily mean that you're going to work in an office. Everybody has his/her *la chance* in life. Anyway, I wanted to work in an office, because if you work in an office, you've got some guarantees.

(My translation, interview, 2013, with Ibrahim, graduated in Law.)

Again, graduation does not necessarily guarantee an office job; it results from a degree plus *la chance*. Ibrahim's office job represents what he likes and has always wanted, because it comes with guarantees, which seems to be an advantage. The difference between those who do have an office job and those who do not is not the acquisition of a degree, but *la chance*. Everybody is provided with *la chance* individually. Again, *la chance* is not quantified; it is either about having *la chance* and therefore, the office job, or not. You only know you have it, if you have something. Ibrahim knows that he has *la chance* in his life, because he works in an office.

L2: *La chance* is dependent on the person having it.

Graduation from university does not necessarily lead to an office job.

An office job, his office job, comes with specific traits, i.e. it is guaranteed in general and it is desired by him in particular. An office job is a guaranteed job. A guaranteed job is not for everyone who has graduated. An office job is *la chance*. *La chance* is personalized to an individual's life. Some individual's do have *la chance* to work an office job, others do not. The distinguishing factor between those graduates who do have guaranteed employment and those who do not is *la chance*.

Susann: Est-ce-que tu penses que c'est Dieu qui nous a fait rencontrer ?

Siaka: Ah, non. C'est une coïncidence. Tu sais, chez nous, quand on parle de Dieu seulement, c'est la religion qui est là. Ça c'est une coïncidence, donc le fait que nous étions presque dans le même carré, c'est une coïncidence qu'on s'est rencontrés. L'être humain, il n'est rien s'il n'est pas dans le milieu, je veux parler du milieu, quoi en fait. Il y a certains quartiers à Bamako où tu ne vois pas les Blancs. Oui, ça, c'est ma chance, je t'ai rencontrée.

L1: predicate\prerequisite\social context

Susann: Do you think that God made us meet in the first place?

Siaka: Ah, no. That was a coincidence. You know, if we talk about God here, it's all about religion. But this is really a coincidence. So, the fact that we were almost neighbors. It's a coincidence that we met. [...] Human beings are shaped by their environment. So, I'd say that it's the environment. There are areas in Bamako where you'd never meet a white person. And yeah, that was ma chance.

(My translation, interview, 2015, with Siaka, graduated in English.)

University graduates do not consider *la chance* as a part of their personal achievement; they are provided with it. Mostly, prerequisites are attributed to external circumstances. The previous example demonstrates a clear distinction between the two: God is religion; coincidence is different. Yet, both provide *la chance*.

La chance is the reason that Siaka and I met. He knows there are no white people in some areas of Bamako. Siaka lives in a middle-class neighborhood about forty minutes away from the city center, and he met a white person in his own neighborhood. That was a coincidence; to him, that was his *la chance*.[1] The environment is important when it comes to *la chance*. Living in the same area and getting to know each other are coincidences, and living in the right environment makes it more likely to find *la chance*, even if one is not looking

---

1 Siaka, my field assistant, described the fact that we met as *la chance* because it later lead to employment for him.

for it. To him, the area in which he lives is a prerequisite; and this is *la chance* in the sense that it predestined us to meet each other. Coincidence is *la chance*.[2]

L2: *La chance* has nothing to do with religion.

God? No!
La chance has nothing to do with religion.
This is really the clue here. And he argues for that as well.
How come we met? I ask explicitly about God.
God did not make us meet.
God is religion and both is NOT coincidence.
Our first encounter is coincidence.
He and I are neighbors.
We met.
We are shaped by our environment. We are shaped by our neighborhood.
I am a white. I live in Faladie. Faladie is not a neighborhood where you'd never meet a white person.
With regard to our first encounter, to him, *la chance* was to live in Faladie.
The environment made us meet. The environment is *la chance*.

If I take all these accounts and analyze them like that, it is almost as if I were putting together a profile of a potential perpetrator in a legal case. I collect all the accounts and check them for clues. Is that exciting? I take three things away from this extract: *La chance* has nothing to do with religion. *La chance* is coincidence. *La chance* makes people meet in certain environments.

---

2 Furthermore, he makes a distinction saying that God is religion and not *la chance*; instead, coincidence is *la chance*. I will go into more detail about this later when elaborating on the standardized relational pair: *la chance* and God.

J'ai eu *la chance* d'être allée à l'école, il n'y a pas beaucoup de filles... Certains n'ont pas eu cette chance-là, qui sont dans les rues. Des filles et des garçons. (...) Les parents ont des problèmes pour payer la mensualité des enfants. (...) Donc, moi je trouve qu'aller à l'école, c'est une chance. Être instruite, être intellectuelle c'est une chance, parce que tout le monde n'est pas intellectuel, tout le monde n'a pas eu *la chance* d'aller à l'école. Moi, je dirais que j'ai eu cette chance-là, ça c'est la première chance que j'ai eue dans cette vie.

L1: predicate\prerequisite\means

Going to school as a kid was *ma chance* to me. There are a lot of girls and also boys that do not have this *la chance* and they are on the streets today. [...] It's because their parents did not have the means to send them to school. [...] I'd say school is *la chance* for me... being literate, being intellectual. That is *la chance*. Not everyone is an intellectual, because not everyone had *la chance* to go to school. I'd say I've had that *la chance*, that's the first *la chance* I've had in this life. (My translation, interview, 2015, with Rokiatou, graduated in Sociology.)

Graduates are aware of their privilege of education. *La chance* is going to school. Rokiatou is aware of the fact that a lot of kids did not go to school and that many Malians cannot read or write. She also knows that there are not a lot of intellectuals. She is one of the few that has been able to go to school and even graduate from university. The difference between her and those who did not go to school is their parents' means. Since her parents did have the means to send their daughter to school, Rokiatou is part of the country's educational elite. To her, this is *la chance*.

L2: *La chance* is not taken for granted.

Going to school is a person's *la chance*. Going to school is not a taken-for-granted for boys, but especially for girls. The reason why some kids do not go to school is because of their family's lack of means. The consequence of not going to school is being out on the streets. To her, going to school has been *la chance*. Having been able to go to school not only kept her off the streets, but it also made her become an intellectual. Being an intellectual is preconditioned by the capability of going to school rather than the intellectual capacity of an individual. Being on or off the streets starts here in school. Being an intellectual is not primarily about an individual's mental capacity, but more about an individual's preconditions, i.e. sometimes gender (girls, but also boys) and the family's means.

Moi j'ai eu *la chance* de la génération qui a eu beaucoup de performance en fait, mais j'ai étudié dans la sérénité, c'est-à-dire que les maitres étaient sévères en fait. Je sais quand j'ai eu ce courage d'apprendre, je peux même dire qu'on n'avait même pas besoin d'être dans les écoles privées pour étudier en ce moment parce que les maitres étaient rigoureux. (...) J'ai bénéficié même plus qu'un élève d'une école privée, donc je peux dire que j'ai eu *la chance*, c'est une chance pour moi aussi parce que c'est l'école publique : quand on est là, on ne paye pas, ici au Mali.

L1: predicate\prerequisite\societal context

I've had *la chance* to be part of a very performant generation, really. I studied seriously, which means that our teachers were strict. I know that they were the ones to encourage me to study. There was no need for me to go to a private school because they were really rigorous. [...] I benefited from that even more than most students at private schools did. So, I can say that I've had *la chance*. This was *la chance* for me, also because public school is free of charge in Mali. (My translation, interview, 2015, with Amadou, graduated in International Law.)

Amadou emphasizes *la chance* in connection with his education as well, except that he locates *la chance* within a specific period in time that was especially advantageous to him. It was *la chance* that he went to public schools at a time when they were still performant and teachers were still rigorous. At that time, public school was free and he did not need to go to a private school. That was *la chance*, too. He knows that this has since changed, and today, public schools are still free of charge, but their educational quality is highly contested. Private schools are expensive, which is why it is assumed they offer better education. Amadou, however, had the advantage of receiving his education at a time when public schooling was free of charge and still associated with quality – this was *la chance* to him. Both graduates who attended private schools and graduates who attended public schools consider their schooling as *la chance*. The private students, Safiatou, Simone and Boubacar, emphasize the advantage of small class sizes and better learning conditions, and are thankful for their parent's decision to pay expensive fees. The public school students, Amadou and Oumar, instead emphasize the privilege of getting high quality education provided by the state; their parents never could have afforded it. *La chance* makes the difference between those who live in a certain area, and those who do not, between those whose parents are able to pay for education and those whose parents cannot, or between those who grew up during a certain period in time and those who grew up later. In other words, *la chance* exists in a state of relativity. Graduates recognize their own prerequisites in respect to *la chance* as they compare their circumstances with others' and at the same time, they identify their advantageous position.

L2: *La chance* is coincidence.
La chance is to coincidentally be part of a particular group of people, in this case of a performant generation. He went to a public school free of charge and high in quality of education provided by strict, rigorous teachers who made him understand the value of studying. He distinguishes generations, i.e. his generation from other generations as well as schools, i.e. public and private schools, which are different in terms of fees and education. He contrasts his public school experience with private school students who receive quality education for money. His education was high quality, but for free. His parents would not have been able to pay for his education, so, it was *la chance* to him to receive it despite the odds. He found the traits of a private school in his public school.

J'ai eu *la chance* de voyager, aucun membre de ma famille, de ma vraie famille, de mes descendants n'ont eu *la chance* d'aller à l'extérieur pour avoir un bon diplôme. Je remercie Dieu pour ça. J'ai eu *la chance* après mes études ou bien avant mes études d'intégrer un milieu que je ne pensais pas intégrer. J'ai eu *la chance* de faire des grands reportages avec les personnalités de ce pays alors que je ne pensais pas que j'aurais pu avoir des contacts avec eux ou créer un lien d'amitié avec eux ; j'ai eu *la chance*. (...) J'ai eu *la chance* d'avoir des parents merveilleux, j'ai eu *la chance* d'être issue d'une famille mixte où chrétiens et musulmans vivent dans l'harmonie sans contrainte, j'ai eu beaucoup de chances dans la vie. (...) j'ai eu beaucoup de chances dans la vie. J'ai eu *la chance* d'être en bonne santé.

L1: predicate\prerequisite\means

I've had *la chance* to travel. No one in my family had *la chance* to travel abroad before. I did my university degree (Master's) abroad. I thank God for that. I also never thought of integrating professionally that fast. That was *la chance*. [...] I also had *la chance* to have wonderful parents. I grew up in a family with different religious beliefs in harmony. I have a lot of *la chance*. [...] I have *la chance* to be healthy. (My translation, interview, 2015, with Simone, graduated in Law.)

Traveling is *la chance* to Simone. She knows that she was the first person in her family to travel and even study abroad. Simone recognizes her personal circumstances as exceptional in relation to the rest of her family – and that is what makes her think of *la chance*. In contrast to many other graduates, Simone also quickly received an offer of employment. She lists numerous examples of what *la chance* signifies to her: her opportunities, her job, her family, and her health. She expresses gratitude for these many instances of *la chance*. She had a lot of *la chance*, she says, and attributes her *la chance* to her family and to God. Now, to Simone, *la chance* is that the family she was born into made her become an exception.

L2: La chance is something unlikely.

Having *la chance*:
Travels. First one in the family.
University degree abroad.
Thankful to God.
Getting a job fast.

Parents. Harmony against the odds.

Health.

Different religious beliefs in one family come along with potential conflict.

Harmony in her family.

La chance is things she does not take for granted and are exceptional relative to others in her family or the situation in Mali.

Two important lessons here:

To have *la chance* is to be able to do x when it is more likely to do y. X is something to be thankful for.

Being thankful to God for *la chance*, which does not necessarily mean that *la chance* originates in God.

La chance makes you an exception.

When you are the exception, you know it is *la chance*.

Is there a difference

Oumar: C'est ce fait-là, seulement, quand je vois les gens que j'ai comme amis, comme compagnons de tous les jours, vraiment je me dis que j'ai beaucoup de chance, voilà. *La chance*, elle peut venir aussi comme ça.

Susann: Donc, ce n'est pas que tu as reçu le boulot?

Oumar: Non, non, parce que le boulot que j'ai eu, c'est grâce à Adama, voilà, c'est *la chance* que j'ai eue, c'est *la chance* que j'ai eue d'ailleurs d'avoir Adama comme ami, qui m'a permis d'avoir le boulot à l'Orange. Et c'est la même chose : quand j'ai fait les études, oui bon, pendant mes études, très souvent il payait mon transport pour aller à l'école - je t'avais dit ça, non ? Pour moi quoi, donc c'est *la chance* que j'ai eue de le rencontrer qui fait qu'on est là aujourd'hui.

L1: predicate\prerequisite\friendship

Oumar: I've always met amazing people in my life. I consider that to be *la chance*. But it wasn't me who provoked it. [...]

Susann: So, receiving your job is not?

Oumar: No, no. [...] It's because of Adama that I got that job today. So, *la chance* that I have is to have Adama as a friend. At university, it was the same... he often paid for my transport to school because I couldn't afford it. [...] It is *la chance* that I met him and the reason why I am where I am today.

(My translation, interview, 2015, with Oumar, graduated in Economics.)

To him, *la chance* is his friendship with Adama, which he did not enforce. How come their friendship is *la chance* to him? Oumar attributes the fact that he was able to finish his studies and find employment to his friend Adama, who has always been supportive. Oumar's father lost his government job and ever since his family has been struggling with money. Oumar was not able to pay his transport to school. His situation seemed predetermined to Oumar, yet, his friend helped him out and changed everything. Overcoming this predetermination makes Oumar speak of *la chance*. In this case, friendship prerequisites access to a job and money.

L2: *La chance* is a matter of consideration.

Meeting amazing people is *la chance*, he considers. *La chance* is a matter of consideration. Meeting people is not something you can provoke. (It is probably coincidence.) Siaka. *La chance* is found in the encounter.

I ask for the job. Was that *la chance*? No. He got the job because of Adama, a person he met in his life and who became a friend. *La chance* is having Adama as a friend. Adama did not only get him the job, but he also contributed to him qualifying for the job in the first place. Meeting Adama was *la chance*.

There is *la chance* you can provoke, and there is *la chance* you cannot provoke.

La situation du travail c'est insupportable. Si tu n'as pas de relations, tu penses que tu ne seras pas engagé quelque part. Sauf si tu as *la chance*, et cette chance est provoquée par quelqu'un que tu connais. Si tu ne connais personne, qui va t'engager ?

L1: predicate\prerequisite\networks

The labor market situation in Mali is untenable. If you don't know people who might employ you some place... unless you've got *la chance*. But who's the one to provoke *la chance* in this case? Somebody you know. But if you don't know anyone, who's going to employ you? (My translation, interview, 2015, with Amadou, graduated in International Law.)

Amadou connects job access to *la chance*: *La chance* is to get employed, according to Amadou. This is based on his knowledge about the employment situation in Mali: he knows that the labor market is unstable and unemployment rates are high. He also knows that people tend to employ people they know. Put differently, people you know might provoke *la chance* for you. Now, if you get an employment, it is *la chance* either because it is rare to get a job due to the unstable situation, or because of networks of people who support you. Amadou connects *la chance* with networks and employment. Knowing people is *la chance*, because this leads to employment. *La chance* opens up for you with the people you know. In knowing people, you have and you will have *la chance*. And vice versa: if you don't know people, you don't have and you won't have *la chance*. Relations are presented as *la chance* in a sense of prerequisites. In fact, those prerequisites act for individuals as they look for someone's *la chance* and provide them with a sprout of *la chance*. These prerequisites accumulate *la chance* further; they are a sure-fire success. Amadou presents relations as not subject to change, one either has or does not have relations. And since he doesn't have relations, there is nothing he can do about his unemployment.

L2: *La chance* depends on the context.

Due to the conditions of Mali's labor market, employment is *la chance*. It is specific to that untenable situation. Employment is not *la chance* in general, but against the background of the labor market situation in Mali, knowing people and having *la chance* is the same thing when it comes to employment.

People provoke *la chance* for you. You cannot provoke *la chance* of being employed on your own. You need *la chance* to know particular people who have access to jobs.

KNOWLEDGE: PREREQUISITES.

Prerequisites – everyday.

Prerequisites represent ordinary circumstances in the everyday lives of the graduates. To Siaka, it is the area in which he lives; for Rokia, it is her parents' means that allowed her to study; for Simone, it is specifically her travel opportunities; for Amadou, it is his academic conditions. Oumar and Madou point out friends and relatives. Prerequisites are external conditions considered to be positive and advantageous, such as education, traveling, or living conditions. Mostly, prerequisites are related to family situations.

Prerequisites – luck.

Luck comes by accident and is perceived as either good or bad (Rescher 1990). Prerequisites are also accidents, because they constitute primordial conditions which are randomly distributed amongst individuals. We cannot determine the circumstances of the life into which we are born nor can luck be enforced by an individual. There is no merit. The fact that Siaka or Simone, for instance, received that exact kind of socialization and education is good but completely random. Prerequisites are not reflected as taken for granted, but as something for which they are thankful. Graduates are aware of the fact that their circumstances could have been different, which is a way of acknowledging contingency (Bromber 2015). Prerequisites represent luck because they describe the appreciated conditions in which graduates happen to find themselves.

Prerequisites – capital.

Prerequisites are forms of capital in Bourdieu's sense. Just like prerequisites, capital makes the difference, and its distribution appears to us as a given. Bourdieu distinguishes between three forms of capital: economic capital (e.g. money, property, material objects), social capital (e.g. membership in a group), and cultural capital (e.g. education, diploma) (Bourdieu 1986, 6-8). When speaking about *la chance* in the sense of prerequisites, economic, social and cultural capital intertwines. The 'university graduate' is cultural capital. Rokia, for instance, considers herself "an intellectual", which "presupposes a process of embodiment" (Bourdieu 1986, 6). Most graduates' economic capital lies within their social capital, i.e. their parents' money, which ensured their education, their travels, and the environment in which they grew up. It is true that they acquired their diploma themselves; however, it was their parents who determined their educational circuit, which was again determined by their capital. Social capital signifies access to resources through the people we know, for example family, friends, fellow students, colleagues, neighbors, etc. Oumar's friendship with Adama is social capital, for instance.

All in all, prerequisites represent individual circumstances which are considered advantageous; they are distributed randomly and define an individuals' point of departure in the process of opening up *la chance*.

4 *La chance* | Emergence.

La chance is a sprout.

La chance c'est quoi ? L'être humain, l'être humain, ça veut dire quoi, mettre en jeu ses capacités sans *la chance* ? Quand moi je t'ai vu, je t'ai approché, je t'ai parlé, mais combien de personnes qui t'ont vu sont passés sans te parler ? C'est beaucoup, non ? Et moi quand je t'ai vu, je t'ai rapproché et je t'ai parlé et là, quelque chose est venu comme ça, paf, tu m'as donné l'opportunité, alors. Et si je ne t'avais pas approché, est-ce que tu allais me voir ? C'est un peu ça.

L1: predicate\sprout\moment\opportunity

La chance is also in human beings. What I'm saying is that humans come with all their capacities to the game of *la chance*. When I saw you, I came closer, I talked to you... but how many people have seen you too and simply passed by? I talked to you, we got to know each other and as soon as you had something... BAM! You gave me the opportunity. You think you would have given me the job if I hadn't talked to you in the first place? It's like that. (My translation, interview, 2015, with Siaka, graduated in English.)

Siaka knows that *la chance* is in people. He also knows that there are not a lot of people that approach and introduce themselves to a foreign person as he did when he talked to me. Consequently, *la chance* is in him. I assume the reason this matters to him is because ultimately, I offered him a job. Siaka interacts and connects easily with people. He initiated a conversation with me, while a lot of other people living in our neighborhood did not. Without him approaching me this job opportunity might not have been available to him. It was his qualification, in combination with his behavior, that distinguished him from others and "BAM", there was *la chance*, there was the sprout for which he was looking:

You needed someone to transcribe those interviews. That was *la chance* for me. You knew me already. That was an advantage. You did not know anyone else for that... and then, simple as that, you took me. (My translation, interview, 2015, with Siaka, graduated in English.)

My need to find someone to help with interview transcripts appeared as Siaka's *la chance*, he says. Because I did not know anybody else for the job, Siaka became an exclusive choice for me, and for him, it became his *la chance* (*ma chance*). It is interesting to note that he depicts this sprout as *la chance* to him, whereas it was "simple as that" to me. Even though he acknowledges that I was looking for someone to assist me, he does not speculate that knowing him might have been *la chance* to me as well. Obviously, *la chance* is a matter of perspective.

L2: *La chance* is in the encounter.

In "the game of *la chance*" (see chapter 5), human's bring their capacities to the table. People are different, they have different capacities. Some stop and talk, others pass by. He considers the job I gave him *la chance*. Player one: talking to player two; player two seeing player one and having an opportunity for player one at hand.

The moment of encounter can be *la chance* to both. It can be *la chance* to only one. Or nothing at all. In the moment of the encounter, it is *la chance* only if it corresponds to the players predefined goals about what it is they want and work for.

There is a difference between knowing people and finding friends, the difference is purpose. Obviously, he does not see me as a friend, but as a person that is potentially useful to know or to be in touch with. He approached me knowing I could be a valuable contact now or maybe at some point. We did not meet and become friends. It was enough for me to just know what he did for studies and that he was currently unemployed. This qualified him as an assistant.

How is this different from coincidence? How is this different from finding friends in accordance with a purpose "I know what I want, so I chose friends accordingly" and "I just walk around and talk to people with no particular goal in mind"?

Me taking him for the transcription of the interviews was *la chance* to him. My need *was la chance* to him. Player two's need is *la chance* to player one. The players know each other prior to the need occurring. Player one has an advantage, player one is the only person player two knows and who has that advantage. Player two picks player one. It is *la chance* for player one. Is this *la chance* for player two as well? Finding someone who can do the job?

The concrete matter of *la chance* here is the transcription of interviews. Qualifying for *la chance* is knowing player two (internal attribution as in what player one brings to the table and external attribution as in environment and coincidence), who is in need (external to player one) and being the only option for player two (external).

Player one is the receiver of *la chance*, player two distributes *la chance* to player one.

Knowing player two, who distributes *la chance*, is an advantage. Being the only one player two knows simplifies things.

Je me dis que j'ai une expérience déjà, je sais que je peux y arriver, il suffit de le vouloir et de travailler dur pour ça. Et c'est sûr que c'est Dieu qui donne de *la chance* et Dieu va me donner *la chance* d'accomplir cet acte-là parce que moi-même, je le veux et je vais travailler dur pour ça, donc ça se complète.

L1: predicate\sprout\moment\opportunity\success

I tell myself I already have some (professional) experience and I know that I can get there. If you know what you want and you are willing to work hard for it, God will help you to get there for sure. God is going to provide me with *la chance* to succeed, because I know what I want and I'll work hard for that. So, the two complement each other. (My translation, interview, 2015, with Simone, graduated in Law.)

La chance is to succeed. Simone knows that God provides *la chance* to those who know what they want and work hard for it. Consequently, if she works hard, she will be provided with *la chance* to succeed. In other words, to her, *la chance* is the result of both goal-oriented hard work and God's blessing. Simone knows her way already, and it is this knowledge that enables her to identify God's provision of *la chance*. Knowing what you want is presented here as the key criterion to *la chance* in the sense of an initial sprout.

L2: *La chance* is to succeed in what you want.

La chance is to succeed in what you want. Prior to success is the pursuit of success and knowing what defines success to the particular individual. In order to be able to identify *la chance*, one needs to know what *la chance* looks like, what success is relative to the person having it. *La chance* is not to just succeed in anything, but to succeed in what you want. And you can only succeed in what you want if you work hard for it. So, 1: dedication, 2: commitment, 3: *la chance* leads to success as defined by the initially formulated dedication.

She tells herself that is the case, talking it into existence. Her experience shows for two things: 1: dedication. She knows what she wants, i.e. becoming a journalist. And 2: commitment. She is working hard for it. That is all she can do. Now, *la chance* will come. God will help and provide her with *la chance*. God is the second player here: Help is contribution rather than 100 percent provision. Her dedication plus her commitment meet God's *la chance* and both elements together make up for success. She knows she cannot do it all on her own.

On a trouvé beaucoup de stagiaires là-bas, plus d'une vingtaine de stagiaires, mais nous, on a eu *la chance* de faire nos propres tournages, nos propres reportages alors qu'on est allé les trouver là-bas ; c'est une chance. (...) Les stagiaires, il y en avait aussi qui étaient vraiment intégrés, qui travaillaient dur aussi. Moi, je ne sais pas, je crois que c'est un coup de pouce. Un coup de pouce, c'est *la chance*. C'est vrai que nous avons contribué à cette chance-là, mais c'est une chance aussi.

L1: predicate\sprout\moment\special

There were a lot of other interns, more than 20, but we were the only ones allowed to produce our own reports. That was *la chance*. [...] The others were also honest and hard-working. I don't know, but I believe it's like an impulse for something to flourish. *La chance* is a *sprout*. It's true that we've contributed to it, but it was also *la chance* itself. (My translation, interview, 2015, with Simone, graduated in Law.)

Such sprouts create differences; they privilege some people while leaving others with what is considered to be normality. Generally speaking, "*la chance* is like an impulse for something to flourish". In her specific case, *la chance* is to be able to realize her own reports. Simone explains that she is not different from the other interns, but she and her friend were the ones to receive *la chance*; she became the exception. From this perspective, people are not perceived to be different, but it is *la chance* that creates difference. In this sense, *la chance* is like a sprout that enables something new. Now, the only difference between her and them is *la chance*. *La chance* distinguishes. She identified a norm, which is that interns do not usually produce their own reports. *La chance* is characterized by an exception to the rule. In other words, *la chance* exists in relation to the norm. To Simone, it is her own work, but even more so *la chance* that made her the exception.

L2: *La chance* is an impulse for something to flourish.

This is about the "why" of *la chance*. Why them? It is them, because they had *la chance* and they received *la chance* because of *la chance*. This explanation is indexical. It is *la chance* because it is *la chance*.

Creating journalistic reports is *la chance*, the reason why it happened is *la chance*. *La chance* is both part of the process (it was also *la chance* itself) and the outcome (realizing their own reports). As an outcome, *la chance* exists in a very concrete form, i.e. the opportunity to produce their own reports and as a part of the process *la chance* is like a sprout, like a catalyst that sets things in motion, an opportunity that allows people to get their things going. *La chance* is both the result and the driving force. There are more than twenty interns, all of them working hard. Only two of them get to realize their own reports. Realizing their own reports distinguishes them from all the other interns. It makes them special without them having to be special in the first place, because remember: all the others are hard-working, too.

La chance is like an impulse for something to flourish. *La chance* is a sprout. People can contribute to *la chance*, but there is also *la chance* itself. There are structural and agentive aspects about *la chance*.

Susann: Qu'est-ce que tu penses de *la chance*?

Mohamed: *La chance*? Mais ça existe.

Susann: Comment ça?

Mohamed: *La chance*, ça existe. Par exemple, je te donne un exemple. Madou vient de se marier... il a eu de *la chance*. Il y a beaucoup de mecs, qui proposaient à la fille de se marier avec eux. Mais c'est lui qui a eu *la chance* de se marier avec cette fille-là. Ça, c'est *la chance*. Voilà. Si moi, j'ai *la chance* aussi de marier celle-là... Parce que tout le monde aime une fille qui a reçu une bonne éducation dans sa famille. Tout le monde veut ça. Tout le monde veut proposer ça à son enfant ou bien à son petit frère. C'est comme ça. Si tu as *la chance*, tu peux l'avoir. Mais si tu n'as pas *la chance*... c'est quelqu'un d'autre qui va la prendre (se marier avec elle), hein.

L1: predicate\sprout\moment\opportunity\choice

Susann: What do you think of *la chance*?

Mohamed: *La chance*? It exists!

Susann: How so?

Mohamed: *La chance* exists. Let me give you an example: Madou just got married... he had *la chance*. There are a lot of guys who proposed to that girl. But it was him who had *la chance* to get married to her. That was *la chance*. Voilà. Everybody would like to have a wife like her, a woman coming from a good family. Everybody likes that. If you have *la chance*, you can have her. But if you don't have *la chance*... somebody else is going to take her, right?!

(My translation, interview, 2015, with Mohamed, graduated in Administration.)

Looking at his older brother's marriage situation, Mohamed has no doubt that *la chance* exists, referring to his older brother Madou as an example. Recently, Madou married the woman to whom he proposed – that is *la chance*. Mohamed is aware of the fact that she received a good education and that a lot of men proposed to her. She rejected all of these men and decided to marry his brother. That was *la chance* for Madou. Now, *la chance* distinguishes between the chosen one (his brother, who gets to marry her) and everybody else. Again, *la chance* is referred to as exceptional or especially valuable. Getting married is *la chance*, but even more so, it is to marry a woman like her. Though Madou was one of many interested in her, it was he who "got her". Speaking in more abstract terms, *la chance* means to get what is desired by many, but only given to a few. In this sense, a sprout of *la chance* distinguishes. It appoints a privilege to an individual. Mohamed speaks about *la chance* from an outside perspective, specifically his brother's *la chance*. It is interesting that this kind of *la chance* appears to him as a sprout Madou received. Mohamed doesn't mention any reason for Madou finding his future wife – other than *la chance*. During that time, Mohamed looked for his future wife as well. He visits her and her parents regularly, they always meet at her place in front of others, and they never go out. "I hope this will work out well. Because you cannot ever be sure, hein!" A year before, he was disappointed in his efforts to engage with a woman who in the end refused to marry him. He did not have *la chance*.

L2: The allocation of *la chance* is imperative.

La chance exists. Getting married to a woman lots of men propose to is *la chance*. If everybody likes to have something and you are the one to get it, it is *la chance*. Not the thing or the person itself, but the fact that you are the one to get it is *la chance*. Beating the odds is *la chance*. If you are not the one to have *la chance*, somebody else is going to have it. *La chance* is a singularity only for one person to own. *La chance* is either for you or for somebody else to get. *La chance* does not dissolve. *La chance* cannot be shared or distributed. *La chance* not being distributed is not an option. The allocation of *la chance* is imperative.

> *La chance*, c'est peut-être obtenir quelque chose que tu ne pensais pas avoir et que tu obtiens. Ça, c'est *la chance*. Tu désires quelque chose, tu sais en âme et en conscience, même en travaillant, que tu ne peux pas l'avoir et que tu n'as pas de chance de l'obtenir, mais le bon Dieu faisant bien les choses, il y a un petit truc qui va enclencher ça et tu l'auras. Ça c'est de *la chance*.

L1: predicate\sprout\moment\special

> *La chance* is maybe to achieve something that you never thought you could. Yeah, that's *la chance*. You want something, but you're aware you'll never get it if you don't have *la chance*. But there is God who provides you with just some little thing, but that gets things moving so you'll get it. That's *la chance*. (My translation, interview, 2015, with Simone, graduated in Law.)

Here, *la chance* exists beyond the realm of possibility and at the same time, as "just some little thing". *La chance* is provided by God. Simone knows there are things she will not ever achieve, and if she does achieve them anyway, it is because of *la chance*.

L2: *La chance* is unlikely.

La chance is achieving something which seemed unlikely to the person achieving it. To achieve something you thought you could achieve is not *la chance*. There is something you want and *la chance* is undeniably necessary to get it. In other words, it is impossible to get that something without *la chance*. It becomes possible though by God providing you with a little thing, which is not *la chance*, but it gets things going and ultimately leads to *la chance*. So, the process is this: 1: there is something that you think you do not get, 2: God provides a little thing, which gets things going, 3: *la chance*. *La chance* can only appear in unlikely circumstances. *La chance* is not taken for granted. God is able to provide the preconditions for *la chance*, but not *la chance* itself.

Si je viens en vacances, bon, je pars me promener... ça c'est clair. Mais, si je pars peut-être en Allemagne, je ne peux pas m'asseoir comme ça. Je vais aller jouer au foot, ça c'est sûr et certain. Si j'ai *la chance* d'intégrer un club là-bas, je vais jouer. (...) Tu peux jouer au foot, quand tu gagnes de l'argent, tu commences d'abord à faire un petit boulot. Donc, tu essayes un peu de travailler, étudier, travailler, étudier... et puis avec un club, si j'ai *la chance* seulement... fiiiiiiiu, ahahaha!

L1: predicate\sprout\moment\opportunity

If I go on vacation, well, I'll enjoy myself... of course. But if, for example, I go to Germany, I can't just sit around. I'll play soccer, that's for sure. If I have *la chance* to get contracted by a club, I'll play. [...] I could play soccer and once you start earning money... Well, I'd start off working a little job, then start studying, you know, work a little, study a little, work, study and then... with a club, if only I had *la chance*... pheewwww. Ahahahaha! (My translation, interview, 2015, with Mohamed, graduated in Administration.)

Mohamed imagines *la chance* somewhere in the future, when he will become a professional soccer player. The whole account is conditional: "if" he goes on vacation, "if" he goes to Germany, and so on. To Mohamed, *la chance* is becoming a contracted soccer player. He knows that becoming a contracted soccer player would make a big difference in his life, and for that difference to be made, *la chance* is needed. Let us get a little more into detail here: there is a difference between going on vacation, which is about walking around and going to Germany, where he cannot simply sit around. If he went to Germany, he would play soccer, which requires effort and is not the same as "walking around". So, becoming a member of a club where he can play is *la chance*, a kind of *la chance* that would enable him to do what he desires so much: play soccer on a professional level. His preference for playing professional soccer in Germany or the United States seems to be tied to his family: Mohamed was born in Bavaria, and his parents spent several years there and both speak fluent German; and, the States are interesting to him because his older sister lives in Maryland with her husband. He prefers Germany because of soccer's popularity there. Though his favorite team is Arsenal London, Mohamed does not mention England as an option, which I assume is because he does not know anyone there. Once he gets to either Germany or the States he plans to work, study, work, study.

Playing soccer in a professional team in Germany would be extraordinary, and it is beyond working in order to make a living and finance university studies. In order to get the extraordinary, in order to move beyond and towards the extraordinary, he would "only" need *la chance*.

L2: *La chance* is to be able to do or to have something.

La chance is to be able to do or to have something. To have *la chance* to do something. *La chance* allows individuals to do something they have not been able to do before. *La chance* is to get contracted by a soccer club. *La chance* is a precondition in order for something to happen. You need *la chance* in order to sign with a soccer club. Having signed with a club would allow him to do other things, i.e. work and study and pheeeewwww. "If only he had *la chance*". In other words, *la chance* is all that is missing for him to sign with a club. He needs *la chance* in order to get a contract with a club.

Susann:	Et pour le moment est-ce que il y a des gens qui te soutiennent financièrement?

Boubacar:	J'ai terminé les études depuis 2007, présentement nous sommes en 2011. Après, directement, j'ai eu *la chance* de faire le concours de la fonction publique que j'ai eu en 2008. J'ai terminé 2007, j'ai eu le concours de la fonction publique en 2008 en tant qu'inspecteur des services économiques.

L1: predicate\sprout\moment\opportunity\success

Susann:	Right now, is there anybody who supports you financially?

Boubacar:	I finished my studies in 2007. [...] Straight after that, I had *la chance* to participate in the concours for public administration. I got employed in 2008. I finished in 2007, passed the concours in 2008 and ever since I've been working as an inspector in economic services.

(My translation, interview, 2013, with Boubacar, graduated in Economics.)

I ask him if there are people that support him financially, and in response Boubacar recalls the time when he found employment, clarifying that he is not a student anymore. In 2007, he finished his studies, and in 2008, he had *la chance* to do the *concours* for public administration and passed. It is not clear whether it is *la chance* that he was able to participate in the *concours* or that he passed. Later, I would learn that the *concours* does not take place every year, and sometimes graduates must wait several years for the opportunity to participate. In many cases, about 5,000 people apply for 10 jobs in public service. He knows that concours take place irregularly and *concours* are difficult to pass. Therefore, I argue that *la chance* is about two things here: first, about the *concours* taking place exactly by the time Boubacar finished his studies – a sprout of *la chance* and, second, about him passing that *concours*. In other words, he transformed the sprout of *la chance* into an outcome when he passed it. Boubacar became administrator at the Ministry of Economy, but he was quickly transferred to the Ministry of Commerce, where he currently works. Being employed in public administration has quite an impact: as a civil servant, you get paid monthly, and if you get paid on a monthly basis, people depend on you, he explains. This was not the case before. First, he was dependent on his parents' money, but now that he works at the Ministry, they depend on his salary as well. Even though they don't need his money, he contributes to his parental household because this is how it is supposed to be, he explains. He is married now as well, which comes along with financial duties. He concludes, "One can say that my wife depends on me; my parents depend on me; my brothers and sisters depend on me because they are part of the family, and I pay for their food sometimes, so, somehow they depend on me as well." Boubacar's parents work for the government as well; all of his brothers and sisters (except his younger brother who is still studying at the University of Bamako) work for the government, as does his wife. As such, they all work in secure jobs that ensure their financial futures. And yet, Boubacar does not get tired of emphasizing his contribution and the fact that members of his family depend on him. Dependence does not seem to be an "everyone depends on me" scenario, but more of a "we are all dependent on each other" scenario. Every member contributes to the family's overall well-being. It is not important for him to be performant as a single person, but to be performant as one part of his family.

All in all, this short extract gives insight into the relationship between *la chance* and employment and security, which in this case is characterized by responsibility towards his family. Boubacar had *la chance*, and no matter what this *la chance* refers to specifically, it indexes towards fixed employment, which guarantees a fixed salary at the end of every month. In addition to Boubacar, it also provides security to his parents, his wife, and his brothers and sisters. His financial support is more about contribution, rather than dependence or help. His parents do not need his money, which means it is not about survival; rather, it is about the certainty that they will get a share of his money every month. With this money, they can make plans, spend, or save. In any case, it is money they will most certainly get. His job is connected with a certain amount of money, which switches the relationship between him and his parents. Whereas before he depended on his parents' financial support, now he no longer needs it as he works for the government himself. Thus, his contribution is a bonus to the household. Boubacar says that the concours was *la chance*, and that was the starting point of secured employment, which enabled him to take a second step to become not only independent from his parents, but also able to establish his own family.

L2: *La chance* is the ability to participate.

I ask a question about his financial status and he responds with a story of him getting a job that pays off. *La chance* is to be able to participate – in this case in the *concours*. This account is about timing: *concours* "straight after" university; employment the next year. It is also about the ability to participate, pass and ultimately, become an economic services agent. He attributes *la chance* to the participation rather than the passing or the timing of the *concours*.

J'ai fait du football, et en fait, j'ai eu la malchance de ne pas pouvoir être – parce que j'avais l'idée d'être un jour – un joueur professionnel. En fait, comme j'ai eu des blessures au niveau du genou, c'est ça qui m'a un peu ralenti. Mais je me suis dit avec cette petite connaissance sur le football : pourquoi ne pas aider les enfants qui veulent vraiment pouvoir devenir un jour professionnels ? Donc j'ai créé une petite équipe dans mon quartier.

L1: predicate\malchance

I used to play soccer. In fact, I've had *la malchance* to not have become a professional player because I injured my knee. That's what slowed me down. But I told myself that with my modest knowledge in soccer, I could help kids become professional players one day. So I set up a little soccer team in my neighborhood. (My translation, interview, 2015, with Amadou, graduated in International Law.)

To Amadou, *la malchance* was a knee injury, which kept him from becoming a professional soccer player. In this case of *la malchance*, which for Amadou means not being able to become a professional soccer player, we deal for once with the contrary of *la chance*. Because Amadou was injured, he could not become a professional player. This chain of events represents *la malchance*, but is *la malchance* the reason why his dreams did not work out? For instance, if we turn it around: even if Amadou had not been injured and had had *la chance* to become a professional player, we do not know if he would have actually become a professional player. Perhaps *la chance*, in the sense of a sprout, would have been needed for him to accomplish his goal. Since this very event definitively blocked his path, his injury is defined as *la malchance*. *La malchance* is just as definitive as *la chance*, but whereas *la chance's* connotation is genuinely positive, *la malchance* is intended to be understood negatively. Again, both concepts define crucial moments. *La chance* is not about a genuinely positive future, nor is *la malchance* about a genuinely negative future. Both have the capability to shape real futures, but while *la chance* enables, la malchance *disables*. With an injured knee, Amadou knew he could no longer become a professional player. *La malchance* is bad and undesirable, but it comes along with certainty – a certainty of the dead-end of one's chosen path. In addition, a moment of *la malchance* puts an end to the conviction that *la chance* is to be found on this path. In other words, *la malchance* puts end to the process of looking for *la chance*, and at the same time starts a new one.

Another aspect to consider is the temporality of *la malchance*. Amadou refers to it in retrospect, which makes it just as definite as *la chance*. Maybe at the time of his injury, he did not know that it was the end, but over time, he realized he became slower and wasn't good enough anymore to justify to himself that he was capable of achieving his dream.

L2: The opposite of *la chance* is la malchance.

La malchance seems to be the opposite of *la chance*; *la chance* in a bad sense rather than a positive sense. *La malchance* is different from the absence of *la chance*. *La malchance* is soccer players injuring their knee, so they will not be able to go professional. Healthy knees are preconditions of playing soccer.

He does not say that he would have become a professional soccer player if he had stayed healthy. However, his knee injury put an end to him potentially becoming a soccer player. Injuring his knee was *la malchance*. *La malchance* is final. *La malchance* closes the door on *la chance*. A healthy knee is a precondition to having *la chance* of becoming a professional soccer player.

KNOWLEDGE: SPROUTS.

Sprouts – special.

Some informants referred to the following constituent of *la chance* as 'a sprout' that suddenly appears. I like this metaphor because it conveys the sense that 'opening up *la chance*' is like planting seeds: university graduates are the ones who plant, and the seeds themselves need the conditions to grow as well. A sprout appears. It doesn't show up in a flashy and noisy fashion. It's small and fragile. Therefore, it can easily be overlooked by people who previously did not cast any seeds. But those who do see a sprout still have to take good care of it in order to make it flourish. University graduates refer to it in real life as opportunity, coincidence, or hazard. This sprout itself cannot be created by individuals though. Its very emergence is beyond individual influence, but it does require an individual to recognize it. Put differently, a sprout of *la chance* needs to be identified by the prepared individual.

Sprouts are positive ruptures, which enable impulses and trigger welcome change. Sprouts are a result of both external conditions and individual effort. For example, Simone receives the opportunity to do her own reports as a result of her previous journalistic work. Similarly, Siaka gets a job offer and Boubacar passes the concours. By these sprouts of *la chance*, change was introduced: Simone turned from a usual intern into one of the two to have her own project, Siaka turned from one of many into an assistant and Boubacar received a civil service job as one out of several thousand applicants. Simone worked hard, Siaka was qualified, and Boubacar was performant – as the chosen ones out of many, they were the ones to receive a sprout of *la chance*.

Sprouts represent a rupture of the everyday and describe an extraordinary event. The moment a sprout is identified, there is no more contingency; all possible futures are eliminated but one, and one specific future materializes. Therefore, moments like these are reflected as meaningful in retrospect, which is why they require an explanation. Rare events have "a greater emotional impact than common events do" and "we are especially likely to keep thinking about them" (Gilbert 2006, 207).

Sprouts – serendipity.

Sprouts are positive accidents – just like luck (Rescher 1990). Sprouts "can alter the course of our lives" (Becker 1994, 185) – just like coincidence. Sprouts of *la chance* are also similar to what Shanahan describes as "chance events", which are unlikely and unintended, causing change and warrant explanation (Shanahan 2006). In a much more narrow sense, Gladkova and Mazzucato, investigating migrants' trajectories, describe "chance encounters" as "a transitory social interaction with a previously unknown person that is perceived [...] as unintentional and can be viewed as a risk or an opportunity in the future" (Gladkova 2015, 4). All in all, luck, coincidence, chance events and chance encounters describe exceptional and defining moments, which is true for sprouts of *la chance* as well. In some cases, university graduates planted the seeds themselves and watered them, which means they kept their eyes open for the appearance of the sprout, while simultaneously playing a part in making the sprout appear. We saw that in Simone's case, when her journalistic efforts allowed her to realize her own reports, or when Boubacar chose to not go abroad for further studies but accept the job he received through the concours. Both familiarized themselves with an image of a sprout of *la chance*. In other words, sprouts of *la chance* require identification by the individual. The concept of serendipity (Merton 2004) does that. Serendipity is a "happy accident", "a mixture of wisdom and luck" (Merton 2004, xiv), a "eureka moment in the process of discovery" (ibid. xv). As much as serendipity is about the event, it is just as much about the individual involved. Serendipity has to be identified by an individual, which is essential to our discussion on sprouts of *la chance*. Merton and Barber connect the idea of serendipity with discoveries in sciences: "Obviously a chance discovery involves both the phenomenon to be observed and the appropriate, intelligent observer" (Merton 2004, 172). Put differently, serendipity needs recognition – just like sprouts of *la chance* start to matter through their identification by the prepared graduate:

> When having serendipity is considered meritorious, the component of luck in serendipity is minimized; when serendipity is regarded as discreditable, the factor of luck is thought to be of paramount importance. To put it another way, when serendipity is used to enhance the reputation of an individual, the component of luck is made dependent on qualities that are unambiguously admired. Luck or chance, according to these formulations, does not favor

people at random; rather, it is prepared minds who are able to benefit from luck, and to preparedness may be linked such qualities as alertness, flexibility, courage, and assiduity (Merton 2004, 171).

Serendipity is no hazard; it only appears to those who deserve it. Serendipity is about merit, as are sprouts of *la chance*, but they can be just as much about randomness (c.f. chapter *La chance*: Explained). In sum, sprouts are positive ruptures of the everyday routine that come into existence as a result of both an external force and individual effort.

La chance is an outcome.

On dit : quelqu'un qui a *la chance*, c'est quelqu'un qui a toujours quelque chose. Tu comprends ce que je veux dire ? S'il a quelque chose, on dit qu'il est chanceux, il est chanceux, parce qu'il a quelque chose. Si tu n'as rien, qui va dire ; il est chanceux ? Maintenant quand tu cherches... c'est comme ça.

L1: predicate\outcome\achievement\possession

We say that someone who's got *la chance* is someone who's got something. Do you understand what I want to say? If you got something, we say you have *la chance*. But if you don't have anything, no one is going to say that you have *la chance*. So, you have got to look for it. That's it. (My translation, interview, 2015, with Siaka, graduated in English.)

La chance is to have something. Siaka knows that possession is recognized by people and it is then identified as *la chance*. He also knows that people must look for *la chance* in order to have it – and in order for people to say that a person has *la chance*, this person must possess it. *La chance* is about possession.

L2: *La chance* is recognized by others.

This is what people say about people who have *la chance*: People say something about people who have *la chance*. People who have *la chance* have something. People recognize people who have *la chance*. They recognize them by seeing that they have something, which is *la chance*. People talking are player 3. They see and talk about another person's *la chance*. To have *la chance* is to have something. If you don't have anything, nobody is going to say you have *la chance*. When people say you have *la chance*, it means they see you have something.

Susann: D'accord et qu'est-ce que tu penses de ta vie?

Safiatou: Je pense que j'ai beaucoup de chance aujourd'hui. Il ne reste que la moitié de ce que tout le monde recherche. Aujourd'hui, j'ai un boulot plutôt stable, j'ai un bébé, j'ai un mari, je ne demande rien de plus que...

Susann: Tu ne demandes rien de plus que...

Safiatou: Que d'avoir encore plus de chance et arriver à mes fins, réaliser mes rêves, on va dire, mais sinon, tout le reste que je pense que je veux aujourd'hui c'est juste un surplus. Je trouve que ma vie, elle est belle, je suis chanceuse.

L1: predicate\outcome\achievement\possession

Susann: What do you think of your life?

Safiatou: Today, I think I've had a lot of *la chance*. I've got half of what everybody is looking for these days. I have a stable job, I have a baby, I have a husband, and I couldn't ask for more, but...

Susann: You couldn't ask for more but?

Safiatou: But for more *la chance*, so that I will be able to get to the end... 'To realize my dreams', we'd say. Other than that, I think that anything that adds to what I have already is a bonus. [...] I think [...] my life is beautiful. I'm very lucky.

(My translation, interview, 2015, with Safiatou, graduated in English.)

Safiatou has had a lot of *la chance*. Her life is beautiful, because of her job, her husband and her kid – to her, all of that was *la chance*. The realization of her professional dreams might be her *la chance* to come. She knows most people do not have all that, and this comparison of what she has and what others aspire to but do not have is essential to her perception of *la chance*. However, she is only halfway there. She could not ask for anything more, except *la chance*. She knows she is going to need *la chance* for her life to stay good or get even better. *La chance* pushed her to where she finds herself today, but she cannot resign from *la chance*. *La chance* is crucial to both maintenance and change. She needs *la chance* to stay with her in order to enable her to arrive at the end. The end means to fully realize her dream, which is to set up a communications agency – but that would be a bonus anyway. She acknowledges that she has had a lot of *la chance* already, and she just wants it to stay that way. The point is there is no ultimate outcome, but a continued process. One instance of *la chance* might enable another *la chance*. Opening up *la chance* is a process that has no finite end.

L2: La chance is a bonus.

Life (a setting?).

La chance is to have what everybody is looking for. *La chance* is to have a stable job, a husband and a baby. She has *la chance* to have a stable job, a baby and a husband. She looks at her life. Is life a setting, in analogy to "a professional setting?" In a way, she talks about herself as player one from a player three perspective and concludes that she had a lot of *la chance*.

La chance ensures people get to realize their dreams. At some point, when life is beautiful already, *la chance* is a bonus.

4 La chance | Emergence. 155

Bon, pendant mon temps libre, en fait, je suis obsédé par l'ordinateur. Comme tu vois, je n'ai jamais, je n'ai jamais eu assez de l'ordinateur. En fait, je suis toujours curieux, j'ai été toujours curieux de chercher à connaitre. (...) Je télécharge des livres, je lis ces livres sur le développement, comment on doit se développer, pour essayer d'avoir mes idées sur l'avancement de mon pays, tu vois, essayer de corriger l'expérience passée des autres. Si je fais l'analyse de ces trucs, j'ai forte chance d'avoir une solution, dans mon cas.

L1: predicate\outcome\achievement\potential\access

Well, during my time off... The truth is, I'm obsessed with computers. I just can't get enough of it. I'm always curious, curious to find out something new. [...] I download books. I read these books that problematize 'development' like how should we develop, try to develop my own ideas concerning my country's development, and try to correct peoples' past experiences. If I analyze stuff like that, I'll have strong *la chance* to find a solution for my case. (My translation, interview, 2015, with Amadou, International Law.)

In Amadou's case, *la chance* results from his efforts, which he hopes will enable him to move forward. *La chance* is to find a solution for his scenario. With knowledge of his skills with the computer and analyzing society, Amadou is confident he is in a good position to find "strong *la chance*". In other words, *la chance* is a consequence of his skill set. Amadou likes to discuss current issues with his friends and play soccer, though his main activity is researching on the Internet. Somehow, he hacked the wireless Internet code from a little company across the street, which ensures his connection to the Internet, provided the company pays the bill. When he offers to share the password with me, I am astonished and ask how he got hold of it. He just smiles like a little boy, saying "I did some research". Drawing from all of that, I suggest that the Internet enables him to find answers to anything he could possibly ask. He looks for solutions himself by researching, experiencing, and analyzing. Nevertheless, he positions *la chance* between his effort and finding a solution. He provokes *la chance* by his effort, and even increases his exposure to *la chance* as it becomes "strong chance". Internet access is the outcome of his search for *la chance*. Amadou provided himself with an Internet connection, which he sees as requisite for him to find a solution in the future. In other words, the achievement of an outcome of *la chance* might as well lie in its potential in terms of gained access or new possibilities.

L2: *La chance* is finding a solution.

To have *la chance* is to have a solution. For his case. What does he mean by "his case"? What is his case? Is the solution like player two? Finding a solution is *la chance*. Player one can go player two. Player one can be player two, too. Player one can look for *la chance*, see *la chance* and give *la chance* to him/herself. Here, *la chance* is in the computer and the books, in the analysis itself. Engagement. *La chance* is in the encounter with another player. It is also in the encounter with resources such as books. He asks himself for help and maybe he will see, he will help himself. He intentionally looks for something in books, he does not just read books because he enjoys it, like people meeting people just because they meet people without giving it any thought and it is only later that the relationship leads to *la chance*. The encounter with books in his case is intentional. He looks for *la chance* in these books.

Susann: Pourquoi as-tu décidé d'étudier la physique ?

Issa: Bon, en principe, en principe, mon ambition c'était d'être un cher-cheur. Bon, parce qu'en physique pure, quelqu'un qui choisit la phy-sique pure... il a *la chance* de pouvoir être un chercheur.

L1: predicate\outcome\achievement\potential\possibility

Susann: Why did you decide to study physics?

Issa: Well, my ambition was to become a researcher. Well, in basic phy-sics... somebody who choses to study basic physics... is able to have *la chance* to become a researcher.

(My translation, interview, 2013, with Issa, graduated in Physics.)

Issa reflects along similar lines about a past decision which offers him an opportunity today: *La chance* is the opportunity to become a researcher. Issa knows that people who study become researchers, so he decided to study phys-ics. He believed that if he studied physics, he would be capable of becoming a researcher or have *la chance* to do so. Here, *la chance* is connected with the idea of capability as well as qualification, which is represented by university studies, which is Issa's way to acquire knowledge himself. Again, *la chance* of being a researcher is situated further along in the future of the process – after the decision to study and after studying itself. By studying, he puts himself in a position to receive *la chance* to become a researcher later on. Issa transforms his studies into an outcome; a new prerequisite in looking for *la chance*.

L2: *La chance* is not guaranteed, despite all efforts.

Being able to fulfill one's ambitions is *la chance*. In order to be able to have *la chance* to become a researcher, people study. There are ways to qualify for *la chance*, which does not mean that *la chance* is guaranteed. Temporality is interesting here as well: he decides to study back then, thinking of unlocking an ambition situated in the future, i.e. *la chance* to become a researcher. "The ability to have *la chance*" – these are the preconditions, that is what player one either has or can work for.

Mohamed: J'ai eu *la chance* de remporter la coupe CAF ici. Ça, c'est une chance. (rire) j'ai eu *la chance* de marquer quatre buts.

Susann: Quatre!

Mohamed: Mais pas dans un match, mais hors compétition. Ça c'est *la chance*. (rire) j'ai eu *la chance* d'avoir mon baccalauréat. J'ai eu *la chance* de terminer l'école, d'avoir une licence. J'ai commencé avec le master. J'espère avoir *la chance* de terminer tout ça. J'espère avoir *la chance* de me marier avec la fille dont je t'ai parlé.

L1: predicate\outcome\achievement\possession

Mohamed: I've had *la chance* when I brought home the CAP cup. That was *la chance*. (laughs). I've had *la chance* to score four times!

Susann: Four!

Mohamed: Not in one game, but during the whole tournament. That was *la chance*. (laughs). And I've had *la chance* to get my bac (baccalauréat) and *la chance* to finish school, and graduate. I'm starting with my Master's. I'm hoping to have *la chance* to be able to finish all that. I hope I'll have *la chance* to marry the girl I told you about.

(My translation, interview, 2015, with Mohamed, graduated in Administration.)

La chance is winning a soccer tournament and scoring four times, finishing school with a Bachelor's degree, and starting a Master's program. All of these events and achievements are situated in the past. In the future, Mohamed hopes for *la chance* to finish his Master's degree and to get married to the woman he wants to marry. He does not mention why these are *la chance* to him. In both contexts, *la chance* is referred to as genuinely good and desired. The words he uses such as "finishing", "winning" as well as "having" share a commonality: the notion of accomplishment and success. Here, *la chance* is referred to in the sense of outcome. Both the victory in the tournament, as well as graduation from university, are outcomes of his personal effort in transforming sprouts of *la chance*. In other words, he was able to transform a certain play into a goal, and he was able transform his university studies into a certified qualification.

L2: *La chance* is not certainty.

This is similar to what Simone says on gratitude.

Winning a championship is *la chance*. Scoring four times in a tournament is *la chance*. *Le bac* is *la chance*. Finishing school is *la chance*. Being able to graduate with an MA is *la chance*. Being able to marry a particular woman is *la chance*. Accomplishing something successfully is *la chance*. Getting something desired is *la chance*. Accomplishing something is not just accomplishing something, it is *la chance*. Getting something desired is not just getting it; it is *la chance*. It is not something that is taken for granted. *La chance* is something out of the ordinary. In relation to those who did not win, those who did not score, those who did not finish school, those who won't graduate and those who won't get to marry that girl. You cannot be certain about *la chance*. *La chance* is not certainty.

Je suis économiste de formation. Maintenant après les études, comme je t'avais dit auparavant, j'ai eu *la chance* d'avoir la fonction publique, en tant qu'inspecteur. Bon, on a muté au niveau du Ministère du Commerce.

L1: predicate\outcome\achievement\civil service

I'm an economist. Right now, after my studies, like I said before, I've had *la chance* to get into civil service at the Ministry of Commerce. (My translation, interview, 2013, with Boubacar, graduated in Economics.)

La chance is getting into civil service. Boubacar knows that a lot of people apply, but only a few get in. He is one of the few, which makes that fact *la chance*. I think the difference between *la chance* in the sense of a sprout and *la chance* in the sense of an outcome becomes very clear in this example. Earlier on, Boubacar said: "I've directly had *la chance* to do the *concours* for *fonction publique*, which I got in 2008", whereas now he says: "I told you before that I've had *la chance* to have *la fonction publique*". Note that the emphasis switches from '*la chance* to do' to '*la chance* to have'. *La chance* to do the concours and *la chance* to have a job in public administration. In other words, the emphasis of *la chance* switches from opportunity (sprout) to result (outcome). First, *la chance* referred more to the opportunity to participate in the *concours*, with results that may lead to employment; then, *la chance* referred to the result of the *concours* itself, which is the employment in the public sector. There is a difference between doing and having. Both are *la chance*, but whereas "do" is connected with the idea of having something later, "have" refers to a requisite that is at one's disposal (for example a diploma and thus the precondition to participate in the *concours*).

L2: *La chance* is to get into the civil service.

La chance is to get into the civil service. To have *la chance* to get into the civil service. He said before that *la chance* is not in the professional world. *Le concours* is probably not part of the professional world, but a means to get into the professional world.

Juste après ma soutenance, en 2008, deux mois plus tard, j'ai eu *la chance* de trouver un emploi. Il y avait un concours pour la fonction publique et j'y ai participé. J'ai été accepté en 2008.

L1: predicate\outcome\achievement\civil service
Directly after my defense, in 2008, two months later, I had *la chance* to get employed. There was a *concours* for the civil service and I participated. I got accepted in 2008. (My translation, interview, 2015, with Boubacar, graduated in Economics.)

After he finished his studies in 2007, Boubacar says that a lot of things have happened in his private and professional life: "After my defense, right in 2008, two months later, I had *la chance* to have the job. There was a concours for public administration." "To have *la chance* to have something" is an important expression. One does not simply have *la chance*, but rather, one has *la chance* to have something. And accordingly, one does not have an employment, but rather, one has *la chance* to have an employment. Having a job and *la chance* is directly connected.

L2: *La chance* is the right timing.
The relationship between timing and *la chance* is important here. *La chance* is to get employment in time. In this case, directly, two months after graduation. *La chance* is to get employment fast, right when it is needed. Getting a job at the right time, i.e. directly when it is required, is *la chance*.

Nous avons fait connaissance, parce que... par sa cousine. Je travaillais chez sa cousine. J'ai travaillé avec elle pendant cinq mois. Elle m'aimait beaucoup, elle m'a beaucoup aidé, même à trouver un autre travail plus intéressant. Elle a tout fait... elle est une personne très, très gentille. C'est juste de *la chance* de la connaitre et de travailler pour elle. Et elle voulait faire des choses pour moi. Elle avait imposé des trucs bien. Voilà. Donc, elle nous a.... elle a échangé nos contacts. Et il y a eu des jours qu'on ne s'est pas appelés. Elle a insisté encore pour qu'on se parle vraiment. Donc, c'est comme ça que c'est venu. Mon mari, il n'était pas encore là. Il ne vivait pas encore au Mali. Mais on a fait connaissance en avril. En juin il est venu... Il est venu et tout se passait aussi bien que quand on se parlait à distance. Donc, on a attendu un mois et un mois et quelques jours après, on s'est mariés religieusement.

L1: predicate\outcome\achievement\possession\by-product

We got to know each other because of his cousin. I worked with his cousin for five months. She liked me a lot and also helped me find another job which I'd find more interesting. She did everything. She's a very nice person. It's *la chance* that I know her and that I worked for her. She wanted to do good things for me. Voilà. So she gave us each other's number. She made us talk on the phone. She insisted sometimes so that we would really talk. So that's how it happened. My husband wasn't here in Mali yet. We got in touch in April, he arrived in June, and it went just as well when he was here as from a distance. So, we waited a few months, and then we married religiously. (My translation, interview, 2015, with Safiatou, graduated in English.)

Safiatou refers to an outcome of *la chance* in a way she did not at all antici-pate – an outcome as a by-product shaped by her unintended action. She was looking for a job, but along the way, she met her husband.

I ask her how she decided to marry her husband Abdoul. "Moi, je crois beaucoup au destin" – "I believe very much in destiny", she answers. You are going to receive those signs and you cannot resist them, you just understand them. Those signs point your way to the person that is made for you. Their story is full of such signs, starting from the way they were introduced to each other. Abdoul was doing his Bachelor in economics in France; he was also looking for a woman in Mali to marry and told his cousin about it. At the time, Abdoul's cousin is the head of a communications agency for which Safiatou worked as an intern. Safiatou did not identify with her job there at all, but it served a different purpose she did not expect: she met her future husband.

She hadn't initially planned on marrying him, but she read the signs: she and her husband-to-be got in touch through his cousin and because of her insistence; they stayed in touch at the beginning. Maybe the whole thing would have ended early if it had not been for Abdoul's cousin. This woman provided Safiatou with *la chance*. Safiatou did not look for that contact, but this woman insisted on the two of them getting in touch and made sure they would talk to each other regularly. "In Mali, there are men running after you; they will promise you anything: 'I want you to be my wife! I will do this for you and I will do that for you!' But that doesn't ever happen", she says. But he was special somehow. "I've trusted him from the very start. I believed in what he told me. And it's because of the way everything happened that I speak of destiny." It was not necessarily Abdoul who was different, but her perception of him. She wasn't one of these women; she did not believe in what men told her they would do for her, but with Abdoul it was different. Even though they only met on the phone and it was all about talk and promises, she felt trust rather than rejection.

Safiatou was looking for *la chance* as she began that internship. Though the internship did not turn out as she wanted, something she did not antic-ipate happened: she met her future husband. While she did not transform the sprout of *la chance* into an outcome at her work, she found a different outcome along the way.

L2: *La chance* is knowing particular people.

Knowing her is *la chance*. Player one knows player two. Player one works for player two. Their relationship is characterized by work. Player two wants to do good things for player one; these things have nothing to do with their work relationship. Player two gives player one a contact for a potential love relationship. Player two insists sometimes that player one and the external person be in touch and talk. Player one and the external person, player three, get married. Their relationship was initiated and established by player two.

KNOWLEDGE: OUTCOMES.

Outcomes – merit.

Outcomes are sprouts made one's own; they are about possession. Outcomes are positive; they are a reward for personal efforts. Outcomes can be different in nature: they signify change (e.g. improvement, new conditions, defining decision), maintenance (status quo, a closed deal), or something completely unexpected (by-product).

Outcomes are transformed sprouts of *la chance*. To transform a sprout of *la chance* means to transform an event into a property. Speaking in Bourdieu's terms, outcomes can be considered as products of capital conversion (Bourdieu 1986). The principal conversion of one type of capital "is nothing other than labor-time (in the widest sense); and the conservation of social energy through all its conversions is verified if, in each case, one takes into account both the labor-time accumulated in the form of capital and the labor-time needed to transform it from one type into another" (Bourdieu 1986). Capital conversion is based on effort. Outcomes are products of individual effort as well. However, outcomes are not simply prerequisites converted into something new or more; they are also the product of prerequisites plus a sprout converted. In Bourdieu's world, capital is based on its own and it is its own result or, as he puts it: "Everything is not equally possible or impossible" (Bourdieu 1986, 1). This means that difference is not only determined, but also persistent; it is apparent and there to stay. He describes a world without sprouts. In Bamako, there are sprouts. For instance, Boubacar got a secure employment in the civil service (outcome) as a result of his performance in the *concours* (sprout). Safiatou married a wonderful man and is pregnant (outcome) as a result of an internship she did not like; her boss, however, liked her and introduced her to her nephew (sprout). Mohamed won a trophy he will be forever proud of (outcome) and Moussa took the right decision that will now allow him to be flexible (outcome). Only those who identify and transform sprouts of *la chance* benefit from it. There are many people living in the same area, but not all of them are considered to have *la chance* –only some. *La chance* is not for everyone; it is distinctive. Once it is possessed, it is recognized in retrospect, if it has been grasped or transformed from sprout to possession, from 'la chance' to 'sa chance' ('her or his chance'). Others would only recognize *la chance* when in the state of possession.

In sum, outcomes are an accomplishment as they substantiate an individual's prerequisites – their new prerequisites. Outcomes are the product of an individual's work with *la chance*. Outcomes are, therefore, not randomly distributed, but individual merits.

[Tracings]

Tracing L1: KNOWLEDGE: prerequisites, sprouts, outcomes.

I presented a systematization of *la chance*: prerequisites, sprouts, and outcomes. Prerequisites are categorized by graduates' social context, their families, the environment they grew up in and their education. Graduates possess their prerequisites; they have been assigned to them. Prerequisites have the potential to enable further *la chance*, namely, sprouts of *la chance*. Sprouts of *la chance* are opportunities appearing; they need to be identified by graduates. Sprouts potentially advance new paths which can be established by graduates as they turn sprouts of *la chance* into outcomes. Outcomes of *la chance* are sprouts that have been turned into possession by the graduates themselves, e.g. an employment contract based on an internship or civil service employment based on the successful participation in a *concours*.

Prerequisites, sprouts and outcomes of *la chance* differ from each other when it comes to how they are perceived by individuals and their origin.

	la chance		
	prerequisites	sprouts	outcomes
state	possession	event	possession
perception			
positive	yes	yes	yes
everyday	yes	no	yes
special	no	yes	no
origin			
randomness	yes	yes/no	no
merit	yes	yes/no	yes

Figure 4.1 Overview of the constituent parts of la chance

La chance is generally perceived as positive. Prerequisites, sprouts, and outcomes are positive. Prerequisites are ordinary; outcomes are made ordinary. Sprouts, on the other hand, are special. In terms of origin, each part is different. Whereas prerequisites are mostly random, outcomes are mostly merit. Boundaries blur when it comes to sprouts, which are both random and merit. The three parts of *la chance* are not simply parts of *la chance*, but they also presuppose one another. In fact, their connection describes a process of how a state changes through an event into a different state. Prerequisites and outcomes define a status; a sprout is an event. Individuals possess prerequisites; they might also own outcomes, which then again changes their prerequisites, but only if there was a sprout in between. Simply put: no sprout, no outcome.

Sprouts are special; they are a rupture of the everyday, which is why they require an explanation: "infrequent or unusual experiences are often among the most memorable" (Gilbert 2006,3 219). Certainly, the day *la chance* showed up in Amadou's life was crucial, as he remembers and explains. In other words, memories of sprouts come to our mind quickly, exactly because they are uncommon (Gilbert 2006, 219). Sprouts are also special because of their origin, which is contested in terms of its explanation. Whereas prerequisites are attributed to randomness and outcomes to merit (see figure below), sprouts of *la chance* are contested in that regard. Sometimes sprouts are attributed to individual effort, sometimes to randomness[3] (Lewis 1998, 108). Either view has different impacts on the way we see ourselves as agents in the present and our influence on the future.

---

3 "We need to recognize that randomness really does exist. Although chaos theory suggests complexity, it does not argue that truly random events or chance exists and affects our lives. Given the existence of chance, no predictive course of development is likely to be possible" (Lewis, 1998).

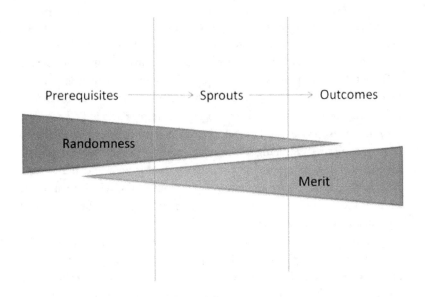

Figure 4.2 Randomness and merit in la chance.

To conclude, in this chapter I established a differentiation of *la chance* and thus defined this thesis' exact research object. Based on the analysis of graduates' knowledge about *la chance*, I identified and described prerequisites, sprouts, and outcomes. These constituent parts of *la chance* are connected, but not necessarily so. For instance, a sprout does not necessarily emerge from prerequisites, but it can. *La chance* represents knowledge (prerequisites), knowledge about the unknown (sprouts), and knowledge of how to get to know (outcomes).

How does this differentiation of *la chance* contribute to research on the future and uncertainty? To put it in perspective, there are aspects about *la chance* that are very certain, i.e. the prerequisites. Graduates know what their prerequisites are, how theirs relate to others', and what they can do with them.

Sprouts are a little more complex; they are uncertain. Sprouts are rare; they are ruptures and they are desired prospectively, yet, they are explained in retrospect. In a way, sprouts relate to the idea of "black swans" (Taleb 2007). A black swan is defined by its rarity, extreme impact, and retrospective predictability (Taleb 2007, xviii). The swan story goes as follows: every swan is white and we are certain about our knowledge that every swan is white, until we see a black one. Seeing a black swan is a surprise, because we are proven wrong in thinking they did not exist. Black swans represent the unexpected. We realize that our knowledge was incomplete. Nevertheless, we do not transfer this finding into other contexts, i.e. we do not project that experience into the future, for instance. As a result, we are always surprised by events we did not expect to happen – not only because of their impact, but more importantly because of them happening in the first place. Taleb puts it this way:

> Black Swans being unpredictable, we need to adjust to their existence (rather than naively try to predict them). There are so many things we can do if we focus on antiknowledge, or what we do not know. Among many other benefits, you can set yourself up to collect serendipitous Black Swans (of the positive kind) by maximizing your exposure to them. [...] We will see that, contrary to social-science wisdom, almost no discovery, no technologies of note, came from design and planning – they were just Black Swans. [...] The strategy is, then, to tinker as much as possible and try to collect as many Black Swan opportunities as you can (Taleb 2007, xxv).

In other words, we continuously refuse to expect the unexpected. Taleb claims the assumption that we are able to predict the future based on what we already know is the major source of uncertainty, because it leaves us vulnerable to surprise. Back to *la chance*: the appearance of a sprout marks a rupture from the everyday; yet, it is a desired rupture. Sprouts are desired and anticipated, yet not expected to appear. In other words, to know that there are sprouts of *la chance* is to acknowledge the possibility of seeing a non-white swan at some point in the future. And this impacts graduates' knowledge of their everyday practices, such as the preparation for sprouts of *la chance*. The next chapter will focus precisely on these practices.

Tracing L2: Clues on *la chance*.

What is *la chance*?

1 *La chance* is the preferred option, not just an option.
For instance,
La chance is getting the job you want, not just getting a job.
La chance is to have many jobs, not just one job.
La chance is getting a paid job, not just a job.
La chance is not money, but having money.
La chance is to be able to share money.
La chance is a privilege.
La chance is to know people, who have access to jobs, not just to know people.

2 *La chance* is special.
La chance is the exception, not the norm.
For instance,
For a girl, going to school is *la chance*.
For a boy, going to a good school is *la chance*.
La chance is unlikely. *La chance* beats the odds.
La chance is beneficial.
La chance is popular.
La chance is rare.
La chance is an important factor in peoples' lives.
La chance is a driving force and a result. *La chance* is process and outcome.

3 *La chance* makes a difference.
La chance plays by its own rules.
La chance cannot be enforced.
La chance cannot be predicted.
La chance emerges in relation to others and to one's own particular situation. In both relations, *la chance* is special. From an individual perspective, *la chance* is highly unlikely. From a collective perspective, *la chance* is very likely to emerge for certain people. And individuals draw from these observations and sometimes gear their actions accordingly.

La chance's agency is characterized by its presence and its absence. In other words, the agency of *la chance* shows in its emergence. Graduates' agency is constituted by practices of preparation for *la chance* and the identification as well as transformation of it. *La chance* is neither the graduates, nor the circumstances only. *La chance* emerges in an assemblage of the graduate and the circumstances. *La chance* is the product of an assemblage which is decomposable into its parts, i.e. graduate and circumstances, but not reducible to them.

What is NOT *la chance*?

Religion is not *la chance*.

Work is not *la chance*. Paid work is *la chance*.

Money is not *la chance*. Having money is *la chance*.

What is la *malchance*?

La malchance is negative *la chance*.

La malchance is the absence of *la chance*.

La malchance precludes the possibility of *la chance*.

5   *La chance* | Encounter.

Layer 1: Members' activities: *La chance* is practiced.

This layer explores the question: How is *la chance* accessed? Drawing from Membership Categorization Analysis, I analyze category-tied activities articulated in the accounts of university graduates in order to grasp their knowledge on *la chance* in terms of a practice they call "opening up *la chance*".

Just like in the previous chapter, I concentrate on the members' category "la chance", but this time I investigate how university graduates approach *la chance* in terms of practice. For that purpose, I coded my informants' accounts for a different device in relation to *la chance*, namely category-bound activities. As a result of first-cycle coding, categories such as "attitude", "applying", "building relations", "knowing", "deciding", "continuing" and "anticipating" emerged. This means that graduates approach *la chance* by their attitude, for instance, by being flexible or persistent, by applying for jobs, by knowing what they want to do, by making decisions or by anticipating future events. Later on, I compared between these categories and spliced them in accordance with their differences and commonalities (Dey 2003, 148). I realized the categories differ with regard to their temporal orientation in relation to *la chance*. In other words, some activities are conducted prior to *la chance* and others in response to and, therefore, after *la chance*. I recognized that activities like "applying", "qualifying/improving" and "attitude" are characterized by their pursuit of *la chance*, i.e. by graduates "looking for *la chance*". The activities "knowing" and "deciding" are about graduates "finding *la chance*", provided that *la chance* appears. Furthermore, I grouped "proving oneself worthy", "taking advantage", "continuing" and "anticipating" as devices which categorize the practice of "working with *la chance*" once it has appeared. Based on these compiled categories of activities, I conceptualized three ways in which graduates approach *la chance*, i.e. "preparation", "identification" and "transformation".

Layer 2: Clues: *La chance* emerges in the encounter.
***La chance* and the encounter: How does *la chance* emerge?**

Drawing from the clues extracted in layer two through an explorative content analysis, I carve out the idea of a game. Please note that as opposed to game theory, playing games is not about the strategic decision-making in anticipation of a desirable outcome prior to action, but rather about the continuation of action itself. In other words, the game of *la chance* is not about winning, but about playing. As graduates open up *la chance*, they play what I call "the game of *la chance*".

How do people engage with *la chance*?

La chance is found in the encounter, i.e. in relationships and in collaboration between the players. I describe the players and their relation to *la chance*. I focus in particular on the relationship player one and *la chance*, which is characterized by knowledge and practices of deciding, preparing, seeing and influencing.

Furthermore, I introduce various plays (workplace, friendship, business, success, by-product and parenthood) in which *la chance* emerges in the encounter between the players. This is also where we find out about the difference between having *la chance* and having the ability to have *la chance*, the co-constitutive relationship between the players characterized by the difference between players seeing and being seen as well as the interchangeability of players one and two.

Example.

Original Interview Extract in French.

Layer 1: Coding Scheme.

Narrative Interview Account.

Interpretation 1:
Membership Categorization Analysis focusing on predicates (chapter 4) and activities (chapter 5) of "la chance" as an empirical phenomenon.

Layer 2: Clue.

Interpretation 2:
Explorative Content Analysis focusing on predicates (chapter 4) and activities (chapter 5) of la chance as a concept.

La chance, ça existe, mais moi, chez moi ça n'existe pas trop.
On dit qu'on cherche trouve, en cherchant tu vas trouver, mais lorsque tu ne cherches pas, tu ne peux pas parler de chance.

L1: activity\preparation\looking_for

La chance exists, but in my life, there is not a lot. We say that if you look for la chance, you'll find la chance. But if you don't look for it, you cannot speak of la chance. (my translation, Interview 2015 with Siaka, graduated in English).

Siaka distinguishes between *la chance* in general and *la chance* in his life. He did not experience a lot of *la chance*; yet, he is convinced of its existence. He knows that it is only by looking for *la chance* that one will find it. It is the practice of "looking for" that defines *la chance*. To put it differently, la chance as a sprout is the result of practices of preparation. It is only *la chance* if it has been looked for in the first place. So, there is a difference between "looking for" and "finding" *la chance*. *La chance* exists, but only those who look for it will be able to find it.

L2: *La chance* is distributed unequally.

So, *la chance* exists, but not in his life. There are differences between *la chance* existing and being, between *la chance* in general and in his life, and between what people say and do when it comes to *la chance*. People say things about la chance and they identify la chance, and they also look for and find *la chance*.

La chance comes in different amounts. *La chance* is distributed unequally. "We" speak about *la chance*. Sometimes people seem to speak about *la chance* when it actually is not. There are two things "we" say about it: There is a relationship between looking and finding. If you look for *la chance*, you find *la chance*. One follows the other consecutively. So, one has to look for la chance prior to finding it.

So, for us, it is important to keep in mind that if you find *la chance* and you have been looking for it, it is *la chance*. If you find la chance without looking for it, it is *not la chance*. He does not explicitly connect *la chance* in his life and what is said about *la chance*. Maybe there is no connection. Maybe he does not look for *la chance* a lot and maybe he does look for *la chance*, which means he is going to find it.

Assemblage: Opening up *la chance.*

Looking for *la chance.*

University graduates know they do not simply receive *la chance*, but they are "looking for" or "provoking" *la chance* as a means of preparing for *la chance* to appear. They are preparing, not because it is guaranteed that *la chance* will emerge like a sprout, but because graduates know that otherwise it is unlikely for them to find it. However, *la chance* is not only about getting or finding it, but also about preparing for it.

La chance, ça existe, mais moi, chez moi ça n'existe pas trop. On dit 'qui cherche trouve, en cherchant tu vas trouver', mais lorsque tu ne cherches pas, tu ne peux pas parler de chance.

L1: activity\preparation\looking for

La chance exists, but in my life, there is not a lot. We say that if you look for *la chance*, you'll find *la chance*. But if you don't look for it, you cannot speak of *la chance*. (My translation, interview, 2015, with Siaka, graduated in English.)

Siaka distinguishes between *la chance* in general and *la chance* in his life. He did not experience a lot of *la chance*; yet, he is convinced of its existence. He knows that it is only by looking for *la chance* that one will find it. It is the practice of "looking for" that defines *la chance*. To put it differently, *la chance* as a sprout is the result of practices of preparation. It is only *la chance* if it has been looked for in the first place. So, there is a difference between "looking for" and "finding" *la chance*. *La chance* exists, but only those who look for it will be able to find it.

L2: *La chance* is distributed unequally.

So, *la chance* exists, but not in his life. There are differences between *la chance* existing and being, between *la chance* in general and in his life, and between what people say and do when it comes to *la chance*. People say things about *la chance* and they identify *la chance*, and they also look for and find *la chance*.

1. *La chance* comes in different amounts. *La chance* is distributed unequally.
2. "We" speak about *la chance*. Sometimes people seem to speak about *la chance* when it actually is not. There are two things "we" say about it: There is a relationship between looking and finding. If you look for *la chance*, you find *la chance*. One follows the other consecutively. So, one has to look for *la chance* prior to finding it.

So, for us, it is important to keep in mind that if you find *la chance* and you have been looking for it, it is *la chance*. If you find *la chance* without looking for it, it is not *la chance*.

He does not explicitly connect *la chance* in his life and what is said about *la chance*. Maybe there is no connection. Maybe he does not look for *la chance* a lot and maybe he does look for *la chance*, which means he is going to find it.

But what about *la chance* one has not looked for?
And who constitutes the "we" he refers to?

> Je prends l'exemple du football : pour avoir *la chance* de marquer, il faut savoir jouer. Voilà, donc dans ce sens, on peut provoquer *la chance*. Mais dans la vie courante, comme pour aussi avoir beaucoup de chance, il faut avoir *la chance* d'avoir du travail, un bon travail. Pour ça, il faut avoir fait les bonnes études, après ça, il faut chercher du travail. Voilà, comme ça, tu pourras avoir *la chance* d'avoir un peu de boulot, donc dans ce sens, on peut provoquer *la chance*. Mais elle peut venir aussi comme ça, d'elle-même, voilà. Par exemple quand j'ai rencontré Adama, je ne savais pas quel type de personne il était.

L1: activity\preparation

> Let's take soccer as an example: if you want to have *la chance* to score, you need to know how to play first. So, it is in this sense that you can provoke *la chance*. In real life, you need *la chance* to have a good job, and for that, you need a good diploma in the first place. [...] So, in this sense you can provoke *la chance*, but *la chance* could also show up just like that. For example, when I met Adama. (My translation, interview, 2015, with Oumar, graduated in Economics.)

Oumar gives an example based in soccer: scoring is *la chance*, and if you want to score, you need to know how to play. In reverse, if you are not fit and are unable to lead the ball or read the game, you cannot score. Figuratively speaking, there are skills required in order to open up *la chance*, skills that are informed by preparation and practice. "In real life," *la chance* is to have a job, Oumar says. If you want that *la chance* of being employed, you have to be qualified and well-educated. Mastering the game of soccer or holding a university degree render individuals capable of provoking *la chance* (sprout), and therefore more likely to receive *la chance*.

To provoke *la chance* is to look for *la chance* in the sense that individuals provide themselves with the skill set required to make sure they are able to identify *la chance* (sprout) when it appears. But there are also sprouts which come "just like that". Oumar connects this kind of *la chance* with his friendship with Adama. We remember that to him, friendship is *la chance*. He did not provoke it. It just is. There is no rule for meeting great people. "We met just like that and we became friends just like that." Friendship, it seems, cannot be provoked, only fostered. Oumar appreciates their friendship for everything it is, and his employment opportunity was not expected. While it is true that the opportunity for employment originated in that friendship, it was not the reason that he cultivated the friendship. Oumar did not establish his relationship with Adama with the intention of finding employment. Nevertheless, Oumar found *la chance* without having genuinely looked for it. The intention to provoke *la chance* is outside of the scope of intention in friendship. When it shows up through friendship, it comes as a surprise and it is experienced as having 'just happened'.

L2: *La chance* appears just like that.

In soccer, scoring is *la chance*. In real life, *la chance* is to have a good job. Scoring is preconditioned by knowing how to play. Knowing how to play does not necessarily lead to scoring. You provoke *la chance* by knowing how to play. Having a good job is preconditioned by a diploma. However, a diploma does not necessarily lead to a good job. You provoke *la chance* by qualification. There is a difference between the provocation of *la chance* and the actual event of *la chance*. La chance does not show up just like that.

La chance shows up just like that. Meeting Adama was *la chance*. Who is Adama? And why was meeting him *la chance*?

La chance does not appear just like that, except when it shows up just like that.

Graduates can provoke it by knowing how to play the game of soccer or by virtue of their studies.

La chance can show up.

La chance shows up just like that, for instance, when meeting someone.

La chance shows up under certain conditions, but not necessarily.

He knows that *la chance* has the last word here, he can provoke, but not enforce. *La chance* plays by its own rules.

Mohamed: Tu ne peux pas influencer *la chance* d'avoir beaucoup d'années, hein, d'avoir une longue vie. Tu ne peux pas influencer ça. Tu ne peux pas influencer non plus *la chance* d'avoir, par exemple, d'avoir de l'argent.

Susann: Tu ne peux pas influencer ça?

Mohamed: Non, non.

Susann: Pourquoi pas?

Mohamed: Il y a des pauvres qui travaillent plus que les riches. Il y a des riches qui sont comme ça. Comme moi... l'argent, ça rend comme ça : fou, fou fou, fou fou... ils n'ont rien fait. Par exemple, prenons l'exemple d'un cultivateur ici au Mali. On suppose qu'il n'a même pas 100 francs. Il ne fait que subvenir à ses besoins. Il est pauvre. Il n'a pas assez de revenus. Ça, c'est un travail dur. Et celui qui s'assoit au bureau... il a beaucoup d'argent. Ça, c'est peut-être la chance... d'être pauvre et *la chance* d'être riche. Personne ne sait si... Toi, tu ne sais même pas, si toi tu vas être riche ou pauvre. C'est seulement *la chance* qui peut déterminer ça. Quand tu fais l'école seulement, *la chance* peut venir, parce qu'il y a des concours, il y a des examens : quand tu passes, tu as *la chance*.

L1: activity\preparation\looking for\attitude

Mohamed: You can influence *la chance*, but not in every case. You cannot influence *la chance* to grow old. You cannot influence that. And neither can you influence *la chance* to have a lot of money.

Susann: You can't influence that?

Mohamed: No.

Susann: Why not?

Mohamed: Because there are poor people, who work more than some rich people. There are people, they are just like me and the money is just coming in...just like that, they don't do anything. Just look at a farmer here, he doesn't even have 100 francs, everything he owns, he needs for living. He is poor. He's working hard though. Then there are people sitting in an office and they earn a lot of money. That's his *la chance* maybe... being poor or having *la chance* of being rich. Nobody knows, nobody knows if he's going to be rich or poor. It's only for *la chance* to determine... but if you go to school, there is a little *la chance*. If you go to school, *la chance* might come, because there are concours, exams and if you pass, you have *la chance*.

(My translation, interview, 2015, with Mohamed, graduated in Administration.)

Mohamed talks about cases of *la chance* that people cannot influence. *La chance* is to grow old and *la chance* is to have a lot of money. Both kinds of *la chance* are beyond individuals' influence, which is the conclusion Mohamed draws from his observation of the difference between poor people and rich people. The difference between them is not effort, but *la chance*. The farmer works a lot and is poor; an office worker sits around and is rich. Therefore, the amount of money a person makes is independent from their workload and is dependent on the person's *la chance*. To Mohamed, influence equals work. Consequently, people cannot influence the amount of money they earn through work. Effort is detached from money; and money is attached to *la chance*. "Nobody knows if he is going to be rich or poor" means that one's *la chance* is also unknown. He does know though that *la chance* does not come with effort only. However, *la chance* might come with education, which then again offers potential access to the *concours*. Consequently, going to school might encourage *la chance*.

L2: *La chance* can and cannot be influenced.

There are two different cases of *la chance*: some of which you can influence and others which you cannot. You cannot influence *la chance* when it comes to aging and having a lot of money.

People are rich because they have *la chance*. People are poor because they do not have *la chance*. The difference between rich and poor people is *la chance*; not hard work. *La chance* is not hard work paid off, *la chance* is *la chance*. If being rich were the result of hard work, farmers would be rich and people who work equally hard would earn equal money, people who do not work hard would be poor. *La chance* is the determining factor for the money people have. When it comes to the distribution of money, *la chance* does not evaluate people's efforts. In other words, you can work as hard as you want, but if you do not have *la chance* your work will not pay off. If you work hard and you are poor, it is because you do not have *la chance*. If you work hard and you are rich, it is because you do have *la chance*. The essential reason for being rich is *la chance* and again, not work. Farmers are considered to work hard, office jobs are considered to not require hard work. It is not about being rich or poor, but about being poor and having *la chance* of being rich.

"Nobody knows, nobody knows if he is going to be rich or poor. It's only for *la chance* to determine." There is no connection between knowledge and money people make. People do not know if they are going to make money or not. If they do, it is *la chance*. *La chance* determines. *La chance* is unknown. *La chance* determines, randomly though. People do not know if they will have *la chance* of being rich. *La chance* ultimately determines your financial status. Going to school might be followed by *la chance*. Going to school, qualifying for the *concours*, passing the concours is *la chance*. Passing the concours is *la chance*. However, this is preconditioned by going to school and participating in the *concours*. People who pass the *concours* have *la chance*, not because they have the job, but because they are going to have money.

La chance is essentially about money. There is a lot of work and people do work a lot, but there is no money that pays for their work.

Bon, j'ai envie d'être polyvalent. Quelqu'un qui a appris... voilà. Quelqu'un qui a *la chance* d'avoir mille et mille travails. Quelqu'un qui est monovalent, si ce n'est pas dans un domaine bien précis, il a des difficultés pour avoir un travail. Mais un polyvalent, tu sais, dans n'importe quelle situation, il a une connaissance adéquate.

L1: activity\preparation\attitude

I'd like to be polyvalent, somebody that is educated... voilà, somebody that has *la chance* to have thousands of different jobs. Somebody who is monovalent, if he's not specialized, he'll face huge difficulties finding a job. But being polyvalent means to know a little something on everything. (My translation, interview, 2013, with Moussa, graduated in Physics.)

Moussa believes it is best to invest in multiple qualifications. He likes to be "polyvalent." In this case, *la chance* is referred to as enabling; it leads to "thousands and thousands of jobs." Being educated in many domains leads to *la chance* to have a lot of jobs. *La chance* here is a factor for possibilities – a sprout. However, *la chance* is preconditioned by polyvalence. Again, a sprout is an exception; *la chance* is the possibility to choose here. Moussa distinguishes polyvalent and univalent people: whereas polyvalence comes up with *la chance* to have a lot of jobs, univalence comes with difficulties of finding a job at all. His itch to be polyvalent is part of the attitude demanded by the process of opening up *la chance*. We continue the conversation, as I am curious why he is talking about polyvalence, even though he knows pretty well that he wants to become a researcher, which is in my understanding quite univalent. He explains to me that he found out that there are no studies in electrical engineering in Mali and going abroad did not work out for him. Electrical engineering is his biggest wish ("mon vœux le plus cher") and he still wants to accomplish that, but he found out that he would not get far by sticking only to that wish. Out of necessity ("forcément"), he changed directions and decided to consider every emerging opportunity. Polyvalence is an attitude which describes the ability to take advantage of whatever employment opportunity shows up. Based on the general direction he chose in the past, he prepares for everything he can possibly do. Since he studied physics, he is now looking for employment in that particular domain: ENI, ENSUP, the private university was an attempt to look into another field of study that he assumed to have a future, and several other internships at Energie du Mali.

L2: *La chance* is to have options.

He likes to be that polyvalent person who has thousands of different jobs. Which is also a way of saying that he is not yet that kind of person. He seems to be working on it though, at the time we discussed this he was employed as a physics teacher and studying electrical engineering. He contrasts two ideas in relation to finding a job: polyvalence and univalence.

Polyvalence is a trait of a person who is educated, who knows a little about everything and therefore has plenty of different jobs. Having lots of different jobs is *la chance*.

Univalence is not specialization. To fill out the blanks in analogy to his point on polyvalence: To be specialized is to know a lot about something and to be univalent is to know a little bit about something. Univalence leads to difficulties finding a job.

La chance is having thousands of different jobs; polyvalence gets you there. Univalence does not.

Polyvalence leaves a person with thousands of options, univalence with one option. Having thousands of options is *la chance*.

> Dans la vie, il y a toujours de *la chance*, mais *la chance* aussi, on peut aussi la provoquer. Comment on peut provoquer *la chance* ? Par exemple, toi et moi on se connait. Tout de suite, toi, en Suisse on te demande : "Est-ce que tu connais déjà quelqu'un au Mali qui a fait ça, qui a fait ça, qui a fait ça" et toi, tu vois que le profil que la personne te demande correspond à mon profil. Toi, tu m'appelles directement. Je sais comment j'ai eu beaucoup de temps avec toi. Moi, je peux dire qu'il y a des gens qui peuvent dire que ça c'est *la chance*, parce que j'ai eu *la chance* de te connaitre, c'est grâce à ça que j'ai eu le boulot. Il y a tout ça, mais *la chance* en tant que telle, par exemple tu postules quelque part, tu postules pour un boulot, tu ne connais personne là-bas, on t'appelle... On t'appelle pour quelle raison ? Selon moi, ce n'est pas *la chance*, parce que ça c'est grâce à ton CV. Peut-être qu'en envoyant le CV et puis la lettre de motivation, on voit que ton CV c'est un très bon CV, les gens te prennent en fonction de ça, moi je vois *la chance* en tant que telle. Moi je ne vois pas, selon moi il n'y a pas *la chance*.
>
> ---
>
> Mais *la chance*, peut-être ce sont les connaissances, et puis tout ce qui fait *la chance*. Les gens disent aussi souvent : même les examens, ça c'est *la chance*.

5 *La chance* | Encounter.   185

Les gens ont des examens grâce à *la chance*. Mais si tu travailles bien, tu n'as pas besoin de *la chance* ; quand tu bosses très bien à l'école, tu n'as pas besoin de *la chance* pour passer à l'examen, parce que tu sais déjà tous les sujets qu'on va donner ; toi, tu peux traiter les sujets. Mais ça ce n'est plus *la chance* !

Boubacar: Dans le milieu professionnel, *la chance*, je pense que moi je ne vois pas *la chance* parce qu'il faut chercher aussi. Quand tu es bien, les gens vont courir derrière toi. Par exemple, toi, tu es un jeune, tu viens dans un département ministériel ; toi, tu ne connaissais personne, mais les gens t'ont reconnu, parce que toi tu aimes travailler. Si tu aimes travailler, les gens vont t'aider même s'il y a des gens qui sont un peu méchants, ils savent que tu es une fille qui est bien, qui veut travailler. Même s'il faut venir chaque fois chez eux, même s'ils te ferment la porte, tu viens, tu tapes : "Bonjour, ça va, j'ai besoin de ça, j'ai ça, j'ai ça". Les gens seront obligés de t'ouvrir leur cœur. Bon, il y a les milieux, il y a des endroits aussi, où il n'y a pas grand-chose. Il n'y a rien en tant que bon dossier, il n'y a rien en tant que formation, il n'y a rien en tant que tel. Selon moi ce n'est pas *la chance*.

Susann: Et toi, est-ce que tu avais *la chance* dans la vie?

Boubacar: Je n'accorde aucun crédit à *la chance*.

L1: activity\preparation\looking for\applying

In life, there is always *la chance*. But one might as well provoke one's *la chance*. How? For example, you and I, we know each other. Now, if somebody in Switzerland asks you: 'Do you know anybody in Mali who does X?' And you see that my profile corresponds with what he is looking for, you're going to call me. I know that the two of us have known each other for quite a while now. But there are people who are going to say: "That's *la chance*!" and that it was *la chance* for me to know you and that it's because of this I got a job. There's all that. But *la chance* per se... for example, you apply for a job and you don't know anybody over there and they call you. Why do they call you? I think that is not because of *la chance*, but because of your CV. Maybe they saw that your CV is

> a pretty good one and they take you because of that. But *la chance* per se... I don't see it. To me, there is no *la chance*. (My translation, interview, 2014, with Boubacar, graduated in Economics.)

For Boubacar, it all comes down to one's own qualification represented in a strong CV. He starts out saying "there is always *la chance*" and ends saying "there is no *la chance*". What happens in between? Boubacar makes a distinction between *la chance* and provoking *la chance*. He uses an example to make his point, and it turns out that there are two things behind *la chance*: knowing people and a good CV. In this account, *la chance* is a job, which he does not say explicitly. Now, if the graduate gets a job, because of his or her CV, it is not *la chance*. If the graduate gets a job, because of somebody he or she knows, it is *la chance*. Whether the reason for getting the job is the CV or a contact depends on the knowledge people have about the situation. Sometimes people say that something is *la chance* when it is not. Consequently, *la chance* is a matter of perspective. Back to Boubacar's opinion on *la chance*: it is not *la chance* if people get a job because of their application. It is *la chance*, though, if people get a job because of their contacts. To him, *la chance* is connected with networks; it is about knowing people and knowing people who know people or people you think might know people. There is a crucial distinction between what is *la chance* and what is not: merit. In his network example, somebody else created the sprout for him; he did not create it himself but received it just like that. In other words, Boubacar has no merit in this. There is no connection between effort and job, so it is *la chance*. If there is a connection between effort and job, it is not *la chance*, but merit. Merit is to get something for a direct reason, e.g. a strong application, while *la chance* is to get something for an indirect reason, e.g. a friend contact – both exist. On the other hand, getting something for no reason is *la chance* per se ("en tant que telle"), which does not exist. Put simply, since there is no *la chance* per se, people always merit their jobs for some reason. He goes on talking about that issue:

> But *la chance*, maybe knowing people... Sometimes people say even that exams are passed by *la chance*. But if you work hard, you don't need *la chance*. If you study, you don't need *la chance* in order to pass an exam. You know already which subjects they're going to ask for, so you can prepare, but that's not *la chance* anymore! (My translation, Interview 2014 with Boubacar, graduated in Economics.)

5 *La chance* | Encounter.   187

Boubacar considers again what people say, which is that passing an exam is *la chance*. He further elaborates on the idea of need when it comes to *la chance*. You either need *la chance*, or you do not. You do not need *la chance* when you study and prepare for an exam. On the other hand, if you do not study, you do need *la chance*. In that regard, *la chance* seems to be a substitution for studies and preparation. According to Boubacar, it all comes down to two ways of passing an exam: by la chance or by preparation. Put differently, preparation or knowledge make *la chance* unnecessary. The prepared individual does not need *la chance*, because he or she achieves something by merit. To Boubacar, *la chance* is at the other end of merit. Again, people get employed because of their qualification, as he did:

> Boubacar: In professional settings, I don't see *la chance* because you need to look for it as well. If you're good, people will approach you. For example, you're young and you go to a ministry, for example, you don't know anybody, but people there get to know you and they see that you like working and they're going to help you. Even if there are some bad people, they'll see that you're a good person who is willing to work. So, you've got to keep going, even if they'll sometimes close their doors in front of you, you go there again and say: 'Hey, how are you? I need your help.' People are forced to open their hearts for you. Now, there are settings that don't have much to offer for you. So even if they open their doors and hearts for you, there won't be anything. However, the most important thing is a good application and a decent education. To me, there is no *la chance*.

> Susann: Would you say there was *la chance* in your life?

> Boubacar: I don't give any credit to *la chance*.

> (My translation, interview, 2014 with Boubacar, graduated in Economics.)

There is no *la chance*, unless people look for it. *La chance* does not come alone; it exists only in connection with a person looking for it. But how do graduates look for *la chance*? Boubacar takes the example of employment research: you need to be good, work hard, keep going, and convince people, and you will get a job. If you do all these things and still you do not get a job, it is because there is no job. But what about *la chance*? Boubacar does not give credit to *la chance* ("Moi, je n'accorde pas la place à la chance."), but rather to good applications and education. He has been working in the civil service ever since he graduated from university and passed the official entrance exam. We remember that sprouts of *la chance* need to be looked for, otherwise it is not *la chance*. To Boubacar, random distribution of jobs would be *la chance*, which means that jobs are an accomplishment to those who receive it – they deserve it. Qualification entitles to a job; *la chance* is for those who are not entitled to it. The difference is merit. In the beginning of this part, Siaka introduced us to the same idea: *la chance* is for those who prepared for it; it is a reward for their efforts.

L2: *La chance* you see and la chance you look for are not necessarily the same.

In professional settings, he does not see *la chance*, which is different from "there is no *la chance*." In professional settings, you need to look for *la chance*, so there is no *la chance*. There is a difference between *la chance* you see, *la chance* you do not see and *la chance* you need to look for.

Player one has particular traits: young, goes to a ministry, is unfamiliar with the people there, likes working and players two see that player one likes working, they help. Player one comes with traits which player two sees and reacts to by helping. When it comes to seeing player one, it does not matter if player two is good or bad. They cannot not see. However, they can still say no. So, there are two scenarios: 1: player one is seen, and player two says yes and helps or, 2: player one is seen, but player two says no and does not help. In that case, player one keeps going and forces player two to act on what s/he sees already and help. The third option is independent from what the players are doing, because they have nothing to offer. These are professional settings which have nothing to do with *la chance*. Instead these settings are about player one not showing up, player two's closed heart or the fact that there are no jobs. Player one showing up with a good application and a decent education is the most important precondition. There is no *la chance* in a professional setting.

La chance does not emerge in professional settings.

The *la chance* he describes before I put my question to him is specific to professional settings. He does not give any credit to *la chance*. If you say you got a job because of *la chance*, it's like saying you are not qualified and you did not submit a good application or that you did not show you are willing to work.

Giving credit to *la chance*. Attributing the cause of events to *la chance*.

Shortly afterwards though, he talks about *la chance* to participate in and pass the concours. There are different kinds of *la chance* and different settings for *la chance*.

Maintenant, je ne devrais plus penser qu'à moi. Ce voyage, je veux le faire pour mon enfant et aussi pour mon mari. Pour faire ma propre agence de communication... Ça peut attendre dans trois ans. Mais le fait est que je veux que mon bébé, il connaisse d'autres choses, il naisse dans un autre pays pour lui donner une chance de pouvoir étudier après. Ça ne peut pas attendre. Pour ça, il faut que je le fasse au début pour que mon mari, il fasse sa formation lui aussi, et quand on rentre ensemble, lui aussi il avance dans ses affaires... Ça aussi, ça ne peut pas attendre. Donc, la priorité maintenant, c'est le voyage, mais si ça ne marche pas, je dirai que on n'était pas faits pour ça et qu'il y a certainement une autre solution pour mon enfant.

L1: activity\preparation\looking for\attitude

Safiatou already shared her thoughts on *la chance* in her life with us. She is confident about the level of *la chance* she has always had. Now, she is trying to look for *la chance*, but not for herself: she and her husband are planning to go to the United States so that he can finish his studies and for their yet unborn baby to get American citizenship.

> Right now, I can't think of myself only anymore. This trip... I want to do that for my kid and my husband. My own communications agency has to wait... three years maybe. But I want my baby to be able to see other things and if it's going to be born in a foreign country, it will have *la chance* to be able to study there later. This can't wait. And my husband also needs to finish his studies and once he's done doing that, we will return together. This can't wait. The trip is our priority right now. If it's not going to work out, well, then I'd say it wasn't meant to be and I'll have to find another solution for my kid. (My translation, interview, 2014, with Safiatou, graduated in English.)

She wants to provide her kid with *la chance* be able to study in the United States. She knows that if she gives birth in the States, her baby will be an American citizen, and it is much easier to travel with an American passport. Additionally, it is easier and cheaper for American nationals to study at US universities, she tells me later in the conversation. Now, in order for that to work, she stops thinking of herself and her agency; instead, the trip becomes her priority. She wants to do this for her new family. Safiatou is planning way in advance: her baby is not born yet and she already anticipates its urge to study at a foreign university. Safiatou is trying to open up *la chance* for her baby; she is looking for a sprout of *la chance*. This account is also about setting priorities straight. Their trip to the States cannot wait, because she will give birth soon and once the baby has arrived the opportunity will be gone. Her husband Abdoul needs to finish his studies, in order to "move forward", so it is necessary for her to make that adjustment for her loved ones now. They both applied separately for their visas. Abdoul received his student's visa already. Safiatou was still waiting for her tourist visa by the time we had this interview. She anticipates the possibility that her application might be denied; she knows most visa applications are denied.

L2: *La chance* can be provided for somebody else.
La chance is for the kid to be able to study in a foreign country. Player two is providing player one with *la chance*. This is a mother-child relationship. Here, the parent does not have to see the kid do anything specific in the first place, but it is about the parent, player two, initiating *la chance* for the kid, player one, to take or not to take. *La chance* here is something player two thinks is *la chance* or might be *la chance* for player one. In order to be able to provide *la chance*, parents have to do something, i.e. organize a trip to the US in this case. The temporality is interesting here: In order for their kid's *la chance* to exist in about 18 years from now, it is on them as parents to make their kid's *la chance* their priority today.

KNOWLEDGE: PREPARATION.

Looking for *la chance* is about preparing for *la chance*.

Looking for *la chance* means to prepare and to be attentive. Graduates prepare for sprouts of *la chance* as they sharpen their attention and provide themselves with the skills required to take advantage of them by working on their education, their networks, or their attitude. Oumar prepares for a sprout of *la chance* as he improves his skillset, Moussa is extending his qualification as he keeps on studying, and Madou is staying persistent in his efforts. Both Moussa and Boubacar emphasize the importance of education and a strong application in order to convince future employers. Safiatou is looking for her future child's *la chance* as she is trying to modify his prerequisites.

There are several concepts in literature similar to the idea of "looking for *la chance*." For instance, "straining" in Freetown, Sierra Leone "is an everyday practice of young men at work" (Finn 2015, 41) which describes the process of 'getting by' and "refers to a type of work that is innovative and opportunistic" (ibid. 39). Straining is directed towards better employment, more education, or more support for their families. We find something similar in the emic concepts "trying" and "hustling" in Monrovia, Liberia (Kaufmann 2017) as well as "dubriagem" in Guinea Bissau (Vigh 2010), "débrouillage" in Ngaoundèrè, Cameroon (Waage 2006) and "managing" in Accra, Ghana (Langevang 2008). These concepts describe daily income practices and struggles that are both embedded in the present in terms of "getting by" and directed towards the future. "Managing", for example, includes "making a plan, but not necessarily implementing it, and the ability to adapt to the moment. It involves a delicate balancing act between keeping in line with long lasting ideals while at the same time being able to envision, accept and adopt new paths" (Langevang 2008, 2046). Put differently, "managing" is essentially about dealing with and reacting to present circumstances. The temporal focus of these practices of "getting by" is the present, and they are undoubtedly part of graduates' lives in Bamako. To look for *la chance* highlights practices that are embedded in the present but much more geared towards *la chance* situated in the future. Put simply, to look for *la chance* means to prepare in the present for *la chance* in the future. Along the same lines, Jeffrey emphasizes the purposefulness and the intentionality of "timepass" to which his informants in India refer as "the opposite of 'seri-

5 *La chance* | Encounter. 193

ous' practice" (Jeffrey 2010, 77). According to him, the "timepass" period is crucial for his informants as they use it to acquire skills (Jeffrey 2010, 4) and develop "social contacts and acquire information pertinent to their search for employment"[1] (Jeffrey 2010, 97).

Preparation ensures that graduates are ready when *la chance* appears, but it neither guarantees the timing nor the appearance of *la chance*. Archambault makes an interesting point concerning timing with regard to the future: her informants in Mozambique anticipate with pleasure their monthly payday by making plans and projects with the money in the near future (Archambault 2015). It is crucial for them to know the date and the amount of money they are going to get paid; that constitutes predictability.[2] The appearance of *la chance* is anticipated, yet not predictable – and unlike with a monthly salary, graduates cannot plan and project with *la chance*. In contrast to a positive connotation of anticipation, Vigh discovered the notion of "apprehension" in a context of war and danger in Guinea Bissau. Apprehension "generally defines an experience of disquiet and anticipation of misfortune. [...] an attempt to sense, to understand, and to control the way that our surroundings engage us" (Vigh 2015, 112). While graduates do not anticipate misfortune, they do understand the ways in which their surroundings engage them.

Again, graduates anticipate *la chance* as they are preparing, though sometimes it is not clear what exactly they are looking for – like which job position or which study program, or like Archambault's informants, longing for payday. Along these same lines, Di Nunzio's informants in Addis Ababa "embrace uncertainty" (Nunzio 2015) as they expose themselves to chance. Or, as he puts it: "Before you get a chance, they argued, you do not know what the future will look like. When you get one, you start to know where your life could be heading" (ibid. 155). My informants do not know the future either, but they relate to the future with reference to *la chance*.

---

1 This was reported by informants who, by the time of the interview, were working in government positions (Jeffrey 2010, 97).

2 Her main claim is that uncertainty is a temporal experience instead of an omnipresent circumstance: "I propose to think about uncertainty as an experience broken up and shaped by moments of respite, by recurrent interludes set to the tempo of payday, as well as by more ad hoc ones, such as when one gets a lucky break (bolada). Key to my discussion is the idea that particular rhythms shape and modulate experiences of material uncertainty in ways that translate into experientially distinct temporalities" (Archambault 2015, 129).

Consequently, they do not expose themselves to any chance, but to a very particular one. Graduates know they need to prepare in order to be able to recognize their *la chance*, which is what I will now turn to.

Finding la chance.

Finding *la chance* means identifying a sprout of *la chance*; it describes the moment in which *la chance* is recognized. Finding *la chance* is strongly connected to the practices of looking for *la chance* – as we have seen already in some of the accounts presented. Finding *la chance* is connected with the practices of working with *la chance* – as we will see in the following accounts. In fact, the identification of *la chance* is right at the intersection between preparation and transformation; it marks a transition. Despite that strong connection, I somehow insist on this distinction because it enables us to see that these practices have different purposes, as well as a different temporal orientation.

Susann:	D'accord, comment est-ce que tu as reçu l'opportunité de faire ce travail?
Boubacar:	J'ai fini directement les études. (...) Je me suis dit que je vais même partir en Europe pour continuer les études. (...) Je me suis dit que si je le dis à mon papa, de me financer les études, qu'il faut le faire, ça va jouer peut-être sur le financement de la famille. Après, je me suis dit que soit je vais en Europe, soit je reste ici pour faire le concours. (...) Maintenant j'ai postulé pour ça, on a fait le concours et heureusement pour moi, j'ai été reçu. Je me suis dit que ça, c'était ma chance, ma chance c'était ici, ce n'était plus la peine d'aller en Europe faire encore des études. Maintenant que j'ai eu le concours, je vais rester finalement pour faire le travail ici.

L1: activity\identification\finding

Susann:	How did you get the opportunity to do this job?
Boubacar:	Directly after finishing my studies [...] I told myself that I might as well go to Europe in order to continue my studies. [...] I thought I could ask my father to pay for my studies, which he would have done, but that would have influenced my family's finances. So, I thought I'd either go to Europe or stay here in order to do the concours. [...] So, I did the concours and luckily, I passed. I told myself that this was ma chance. Ma chance, it was here! It wasn't necessary anymore for me to go to Europe for studies, because I passed the concours. Ultimately, I'm going to stay here for work.

(My translation, interview, 2014, with Boubacar, graduated in Economics.)

Boubacar reflects on a moment in his life in which he identified a sprout of *la chance*. It determined his future. After finishing his studies, Boubacar was not sure how to proceed: continue studying in Europe or get a government job in Mali by *concours*. Shortly after his defense, the government announced a *concours*, and he succeeded: "Heureusement pour moi, j'ai passé" – "Luckily for me, I passed". All of a sudden, his decision was clear, because he told himself it was *la chance*. In other words, it was not passing the *concours*, but rather, him telling himself that it was *la chance*. He was the one who identified *la chance*. This is important because he could have ignored the *concours* never mind the consequences, and he could have gone to Europe instead, but he didn't. Yet, he decided this was *la chance*, so he stayed in Mali and became a civil servant. "*Ma chance* was here (in Mali)," Boubacar said. That was the moment to determine his future. Until then, Boubacar imagined two possible futures: the 'Europe future', a continuation of his studies, and the 'Mali future' a fresh start into wage labor. Financially, the 'Europe future' implied that his father would pay for everything, while the 'Mali future' instead implied he would become financially independent. The 'Europe future' was dependent on his father's willingness to pay, while the 'Mali future' was dependent on the availability of government jobs and his performance in the *concours*.

L2: *La chance* decides.

I ask about opportunity; he answers with *la chance* of him passing the concours. So, there is a relationship between opportunity and *la chance*.

Let us look at the details of this account: There is a before and an after, the timeline is interrupted by passing the *concours*. Boubacar has two options: continuing his studies in Europe with his family carrying the financial load, or doing the *concours* not knowing whether or not he is going to pass. Going to Europe for studies takes a couple of years, participating in the *concours* takes a day. Going to Europe is preconditioned by his family's means and ultimately his decision to take advantage of them. The variables of the *concours* are less calculable, however, simple participation is an investment of a solid day's work. Luckily, he says, his attempt to pass the *concours* was successful. Passing the *concours* is *la chance*. Why? This is specific to his situation, because it allowed him to stay in Mali with a job earning his own money. Two issues dissolve: him leaving for Europe and his family paying for it. *La chance* is passing the *concours*, because it comes with employment in Mali. Passing the *concours* is *la chance* because of the odds of passing, but also because of the government employment that comes with it. *La chance* is marked by the *concours*, yet it signifies secure employment in Mali.

Susann: Tu penses que *la chance* joue un grand rôle dans ta vie?

Abdrahamane: Oui, *la chance* joue un grand rôle dans ma vie. C'est *la chance* qui a fait que je suis arrivé. Parce que quand j'ai postulé pour ce programme, on m'a dit que les agents seraient déployés au mois de juin, j'ai postulé en mai. Je suis resté en juin, ils n'ont pas appelé ; en juillet, ils n'ont pas appelé. C'est en août qu'on m'a appelé. Avant ça, j'avais... Dans le même mois, j'ai postulé pour un poste d'animateur, pour ne pas rester comme ça. Sinon, ce n'est pas un poste que j'ai voulu. On ne peut pas rester toujours au chômage. On m'a appelé pour faire le test écrit, et... Là où je suis présentement, ces gens-là m'ont appelé pour passer l'interview directement et j'ai été retenu. Donc, de l'autre côté, le même jour on m'a appelé pour me dire de faire l'interview, donc, vous voyez, donc les postes aussi, n'était pas pareils. Là où je suis, je suis conseillé technique, de l'autre côté c'était animateur, et je crois aussi que les salaires aussi n'étaient pas du tout pareils, il y a une grande différence, donc c'est *la chance*.

L1: activity\identification\finding

Susann: Do you think *la chance* plays a role in your life?

Abdrahamane: Yes, *la chance* plays a huge role in my life. *La chance* made me get where I am right now. You know, when I applied for this program, they told me they were going to recruit people in June. I applied in May. In June, they didn't get back to me. In August though, they called me. And well before that, I had applied for another job as an animator so I would not be sitting around unemployed. Other than that, it really was not the job I wanted. Meanwhile, the people at the place where I am right now called me, wanted me to write an exam, but then decided to just interview me and I passed and I did get that job as well. That's the job I wanted, I wanted to work as a technical advisor. And the salary is so much better as well. That was *la chance*.

(My translation, interview, 2015, with Abdrahamane, 27, graduated in English.)

Abdrahamane mentions *la chance*, which he happened to find in a moment he did not look for it anymore. *La chance* made him get his current job, one that he wanted and is better paid than his previous job. In addition, he did not assume he was going to get it, according to the information he initially received. Abdrahamane applied for the position as a technical advisor, and once he thought he would not get it, he applied for another position, and successfully so. Though it is unclear what exactly *la chance* did that made him get the job, he does know that it was *la chance*. The ability to choose between two jobs is rare and so is the opportunity for getting the job you wanted. He applied a long time ago and the fact that they got back to him after such a long time with the job offer caught him by surprise.

L2: *La chance* matters.

La chance is an important actor in his life; *la chance* made him get to where he is today. So, where is he today? He is working in the job he wanted as a technical advisor. The job also pays a lot better than the one he had at the time. He tells the story of how it all happened: This is not a causal sequence of events, it is rather an accumulation of unlikely circumstances: the hiring period was up, he found closure in his new job and then received an unanticipated call, which sent him straight to the interview process and ultimately, his desired, well-paid employment.

   La chance in his case does not seem to be about the circumstances within which he received the job, but more about the fact that he got the job and the job being his preferred option both in terms of content and salary.

Oui, j'ai toujours dit, j'ai de *la chance* avec mes amis, parce que j'ai choisi les amis, donc je sais ce que je devrais choisir. Souvent, on parvient à faire des choses ensemble que j'aime bien. Donc, c'est *la chance*, mais *la chance* d'abord ça vient de la personne : il faut choisir ce que tu veux. Mais je pense que le choix est difficile, mais il faut savoir ce que tu veux faire. En ce moment, tu parviens à trouver ton chemin, et en le parcourant, tu vas avoir une chance.

L1: activity\identification\finding\knowing

I've always said that I've had *la chance* when it comes to my friends, because I chose them. And I am what I chose to do. Oftentimes, we organize things together, which I like. That is *la chance*. First of all, you need to know what you want and then there will be *la chance*. I think the choice is difficult, but it's easy if you have priorities, then you'll find your way and as you go along, you're going to have *la chance*. (My translation, interview, 2015, with Siaka, graduated in English.)

Siaka is an active member of several associations. His passion is the English language and he wants to become a translator. He is a founding member of a network of English speakers in Mali, which enables him to participate in professional language courses, organize official activities, collaborate with well-known NGO's, as well as to access information on current job offers. His closest friends are fellow members of that association. Siaka's friends are *la chance*. He had his priorities which influenced him until his friends came along. In other words, he knows that his friendships are a result of the choices he made.

L2: *La chance* is relative to what you want.

Friends are *la chance*. Friends are a choice. You can choose friends and you can choose *la chance*.

People are defined by their choices.

Organizing things together is *la chance*. Knowing what you want is a precondition to *la chance*.

You can provoke *la chance* by knowing what you want. Choosing what you want is difficult.

There are things you can do for *la chance* to show up: 1: knowing what you want and 2: making decisions accordingly. He chose his friends based on what he wants in life. They are *la chance*. The fact that he found them and is able to appreciate them for the things they do together is based on him knowing what *la chance* is to him in the first place. Doing things. He is able to identify things as *la chance* because he knows what he wants. Getting what he wants is *la chance*. He only knows what *la chance* is because he has predefined *la chance* by knowing what he wants.

La chance is preconditioned by knowing what you want.

In other words, if you want to become an actress and receive a role in a movie, you know that this is *la chance*. If you receive an offer to manage a large hotel chain, you do not consider that *la chance*.

La chance is relative to what you want. Therefore, in order to know what *la chance* is, you need to know what you want. If you do know what you want, you can choose *la chance*.

Susann: Utile...Comment est-ce que toi, tu te rends utile pour ta famille?

Youssouf: Je me rendis utile parce que ma famille, aujourd'hui je suis pas une charge pour ma famille, Dieu merci. Depuis que j'ai commencé ce stage, je ne suis jamais allé chez mes frères, mes parents, ma maman ou bien mon père pour demander : "donne-moi ça". Au contraire, si j'allais, je partageais. Dieu m'a donné cette chance, cette opportunité. Je n'ai jamais demandé de services après le départ de l'école.

L1: activity\identification\finding\knowing

Susann: How do you make yourself «useful» for your family?

Youssouf: I am useful for my family because today I don't need their financial support anymore, thank God. Ever since I've started this internship, I didn't need to ask my brothers or my parents for any money. On the contrary, I go there and share. God gave me that *la chance*, this opportunity. Ever since I finished school I didn't need to ask for anything.

(My translation, interview, 2014, with Youssouf, graduated in Law.)

Youssouf knows that his financial independence is due to God providing him with *la chance*. *La chance* is an opportunity that established Youssouf's comfortable economic situation. Ever since he started his internship as a law student writing his thesis he worked at the ministry. For years, he has been a non-contracted intern without an official salary. In order to get a contract, he would have to pass the *concours*, which has not taken place yet. He knows that his ability to provide for himself and his family as an intern with no contract is special. Therefore, this opportunity, i.e. the internship, is *la chance* to him. We saw already that *la chance* represents the ability to work the job you wanted.

L2: *La chance* is to be able to share money.

Being useful for the family is to be able to support them financially. Usefulness is connected to money. He is able to do that because he has an internship. He started the internship when he finished school. And it changed his financial situation: Prior to the internship, he asked some family members for money, now that he has the internship, he is able to even share some of the money he earns. God gave him that *la chance*, this opportunity. *La chance* is an opportunity. Is *la chance* an opportunity to share money or an opportunity to have an internship? I would say both is adequate here. It is not simply about the internship, but about the opportunity that comes with the internship, which is the ability to share money. The ability to share money is *la chance*. Internships do not necessarily come with salaries, so not all internships are *la chance*. He also accounts for the fact that earning money provides the opportunity and not an obligation to share.

He does account for the timing of the internship as the moment which changed his financial situation. Yet, this is not about the emergence of an event, i.e. the internship, but the significant changes caused by an event, i.e. financial status.

> Susann: La dernière fois, tu as dit «je vais le faire, même si c'est pas ce que je veux.» Ça m'a étonnée. C'est toujours comme ça ?

> Madou: Oui, c'est toujours comme ça, mais ça a un tout petit peu changé, parce qu'il y a des trucs que je ne connaissais pas, que je commence à connaitre maintenant. Il y a des domaines dont je n'avais même pas connaissance, donc j'ai commencé à faire ces études-là et ce n'était pas ce que j'avais souhaité faire dans la vie, mais c'était ma chance, donc. Mais ça commence à changer. Maintenant, j'aime ce que je fais.

L1: activity\identification\finding\deciding

> Susann: Last time you told me that what you're doing right now is not what you want to do. Do you still feel that way?

> Madou: Yeah, I still do. But it has changed a little, now that I start to understand certain things. I was totally new in the field, I didn't know what I was doing. Now that I've started studying... It was not what I wanted to do in life, but that was *ma chance*. So now things are starting to change and now I like what I'm doing.

(My translation, interview, 2015, with Madou, graduated in Physics.)

To Madou, *la chance* is a job he actually did not want to do, but he decided that this was going to be his *la chance*. Madou would have preferred to do his PhD in Germany, and he knew that this would have been his *la chance*. We know already that he did not get to do this, and in response, he started looking for other opportunities. Receiving an internship at the telecommunication agency allowed him to restart studies in another field, which he did because it was his *la chance*. Committing to that job was a decision based on the idea that this was his *la chance* now.

L2: La chance is (in)visible.

It was not what he wanted to do in life, but that was *la chance*. Events can turn out to be *la chance* in retrospect. Something happened, he did not think of it as *la chance*, but it later turned out to be *la chance*. It is because he thought he knew what he wanted that he did not consider the events to be *la chance*. The reason why he initially was not able to see *la chance* was because he was new to the field. He did not know what he was doing and he did not want to do it in the first place. Now that he studied a bit, he comes to understand and enjoy what he is doing. Looking back, it was *la chance*. Doing something he did not want and did not foresee for himself was *la chance*. *La chance* was invisible to him when it happened. It is only afterwards that *la chance* becomes visible to him.

KNOWLEDGE: IDENTIFICATION.

Finding la *chance* is about identifying *la chance*.

Similar to sprouts of *la chance*, there is another concept which captures the aspects of preparedness and chance in connection, i.e. the "serendipity pattern" (Merton 2004). Robert Merton, who researched the process and event of discovery in science, defines it as follows:

> The serendipity pattern refers to the fairly common experience of observing an unanticipated, anomalous, and strategic datum which becomes the occasion for developing a new theory or for extending an existing theory. All three elements in the pattern are essential to an accidental discovery, that is, to the unanticipated development or extension of theory – the observation in and of itself is no discovery (Merton 2004).

I will now establish the parallel between the serendipity pattern and the process of opening up *la chance* (sprouts). Let us therefore look more closely at the three elements "unanticipated", "anomalous" and "strategic".

"Unanticipated" refers to an observation which was initially unexpected. In other words, the observation is a by-product of the actual experiment (Merton 2004); it is what people find along the way. Safiatou's account (4.2.3) highlights this perfectly: while she was looking for a job she found the man she wanted to marry. That was *la chance* – an unanticipated by-product. But what about Boubacar's account? His stable job in government administration was not a by-product of his participation in the *concours* because he participated in the *concours* in order to get that job. More importantly though, he did not expect to pass the *concours* at all. Passing the *concours* was *la chance*; it was unanticipated. Sprouts of *la chance* are specifically looked for and desired; they might be imagined, yet not expected.

"Anomalous" describes a surprising observation which is in contrast to common knowledge and, therefore, stimulates the observer to make sense of the observation (Merton 2004). Boubacar, for instance, knows that it is highly improbable to pass the *concours*. He reflects on the fact that he passed as *la chance*, an anomaly. Sprouts make the difference – Boubacar becomes one of a few as he gets the job. Furthermore, sprouts of *la chance* are extraordinary; they constitute a rupture of the everyday routine. We recall Madou's account which offers the established routine of passing by his uncle's house every day for more than a year. This was interrupted one day by Madou getting the internship he was looking for. It was normal for him to hear his uncle say "come back here tomorrow" until he said something different, namely, "we got you an internship" – *la chance*. Second, the anomaly stimulates the individual that identified it to make sense of that very anomaly. Graduates make sense of their identified sprouts of *la chance* as they work with them, i.e. both Boubacar and Madou accept the jobs offered.

"Strategic" genuinely relates to the individual observing rather than to the observed event itself. "For it obviously requires a theoretically sensitized observer to detect the universal in the particular" (Merton, 2004). In other words, the ability to identify an anomaly is preconditioned by an understanding of what is normal. It is precisely because of that strategic element that the identification of *la chance* is not an accident. It is not an accident because graduates prepare in order to be able to identify *la chance*. Madou prepared as he continued to ask his uncle for a job, which demonstrated persistence. Boubacar prepared to pass the *concours* as he participated. When it comes to finding *la chance*, the graduate is as important as *la chance* itself. Chance accidents in scientific discoveries are discussed in that exact manner as interaction of chance with the prepared mind: "the value of the accident depends on the kind of man, on the kind of mind, by whom or by which it is first observed. If the soil is not sufficiently prepared, the seed will not grow" (Merton, 2004).

To sum up, looking for *la chance* means to prepare for and to anticipate sprouts of *la chance*. The nature of that anticipation might be very concrete, i.e. an unlimited contract in a communications agency, or rather abstract, i.e. being able to get thousands of jobs. Now, the practices of preparation depend on what is anticipated. As we have seen, Safiatou, looking for a contract in communications, is applying for related internships, and Siaka, who is looking for a job, is working on his polyvalent qualification.

Working with *la chance.*

Finding a sprout of *la chance* does not end the process. After having identified a sprout, it can be transformed into an outcome. It is important to note that working with *la chance* is different from looking for *la chance*. Looking for *la chance* refers to practices that are not directed towards a specific goal (e.g. becoming a researcher), but more towards a general idea (e.g. finding an employment). Practices of looking for *la chance* result in finding *la chance*. Working with *la chance*, by contrast, is directed towards a specific and anticipated outcome that has been inspired by the sprout of *la chance*. The product of working with *la chance* is the very possession of *la chance*.

Dans la vie quotidienne, bon, en tout cas quand je suis au boulot, je le fais correctement et dans ce sens-là, je suis en train de provoquer ma chance parce que le jour où ils vont faire les évaluations, ils diront : "celui-là il travaille très bien, on pourrait le mettre ici, on pourrait ceci, on pourrait faire cela". Dans ce cas, c'est ce qui la provoque.

L1: activity\transformation\working with\proving oneself

In my daily life, well, I'm at work and I work correctly. It's in this sense that I'm provoking *ma chance* right now. You know, one day, when they'll do their evaluation, they'll say: "this guy is working well, we should put him in another position"... So, it is in this sense that I'm provoking *ma chance*. (My translation, interview, 2015, with Oumar, graduated in Economics.)

La chance here signifies 'another position'. Oumar does not mention a concrete position, but he anticipates the possibility within the company. How does he get there? By provoking *la chance*, which means to 'be at work and work correctly'. Thus, it also requires 'them' to recognize that he is working well. In short, for *la chance* to come into existence, it requires a twofold process of him working and his work being recognized. Oumar's quality of work thereby tries to provoke *la chance* of being considered for another job. He is working for an anticipated outcome, i.e. *la chance*, yet he cannot enforce the outcome itself or create a vacant job position by himself.

L2: *La chance* is seeing and being seen.

Oumar provokes *la chance* in a particular sense: He does something, which then allows "them" to say something about his work and do something about his position. Oumar works, "they" recognize his work and as a consequence put him in another position. Oumar provokes his *la chance* by working, but it is for somebody else to recognize it and act on it.

Time: Oumar works every day and one day, every single day of him working well will matter. Daily life is working well in his position, one day is evaluation day, the day they evaluate his work. He provokes his *la chance* by making sure they will be able to see that he is working well and therefore put him in another job. It's not about the better position, but about them recognizing his good work and acting on it, which is prerequisite to his promotion.

Oumar's ability to provoke *la chance* is focused on working correctly every day and evaluation day will come at some point in the future.

Constant work as opposed to one particular day, i.e. evaluation day. Evaluation day is the day they recognize that he is working correctly every day and draw desirable conclusions from it.

Timing. Doing and seeing.

First, he does and second, others, who have the capacity to do something, see him doing something. So, it is not about Oumar identifying *la chance*, but it is about others providing *la chance* in response to him looking for it in a – to them – convincing manner (convincingly to them) in the first place.

It takes two parties for *la chance* to work out for one party.

En faisant des relations sérieuses, c'est-à-dire, quoi, quand toi et moi nous sommes en train de collaborer, je vais faire du sérieux avec toi. Si je dis sérieux, de ne pas faire le malhonnête avec toi, je vais être honnête avec toi. Mais si tu as quelque chose dans ce sens qui correspond à mon profile, tu ne vas pas hésiter à me contacter, n'est-ce pas ?

L1: activity\transformation\working with\anticipating

By creating serious relationships, I mean, we are collaborating right now and I'm going to be serious about it, and I'm not going to lie to you, I'm going to be honest. If you find something that corresponds to my profile, you surely won't hesitate to contact me, right? And that's it. (My translation, interview, 2015, with Siaka, graduated in English.)

La chance here is an employment that corresponds to his qualification. He anticipates that as he keeps working on his current sprout of *la chance*, which is his current job as research assistant. In this framework, he creates a professional relationship which requires him to work in a serious and honest manner. This is his means of establishing himself as a present collaborator and proving himself worthy for possible future collaboration. This is how he makes sure I would think of him if an opportunity arises for him in the future. But in order for this or *la chance* to work out, it requires some activity from my side as well: recognizing the quality of his work, as well as not hesitating to inform him. Again, this is a twofold process, which includes him working and his work being recognized, and, first of all, a vacant position.

L2: *La chance* is found in collaboration.

La chance is to be found in relationships and in collaboration. Within this relationship player one is serious and honest. In case player two (me) finds something (probably a job) that corresponds to player one, player two contacts player one. So there are three things involved: two players and "something". The two players have an established relationship (serious, honest) already. "Something" shows up, which has player two think of player one. The players are collaborating; the relationship is present. There is nothing new about the relationship, but "something" relates back to that relationship. Players know each other, their traits, i.e. seriousness and honesty as well as their professional profiles. The profile connects to "something", but the relationship allows for that associative connection to happen in the first place. In other words, three things are required for player two to be contacted by player one: collaboration, "something", and the combination of the two, i.e. no hesitation.

> Ces genres d'opportunités, c'est Dieu qui m'a donné *la chance* d'être parmi les cinq premiers de ma classe, d'être resté là-bas en tant que stagiaire et tout. Eeeeeh, *la chance* a été que on a bien étudié, on a compris nos leçons et on avait la soif de connaitre le savoir, on s'inquiétait et on a pu s'en sortir. C'est grâce à nous aussi que cette chance a pu fonctionner.

L1: activity\transformation\working with\continuing

> This kind of opportunity... it's God that gave me *la chance* to be amongst the best in my class, and to be able to do an internship there and to be allowed to stay there voluntarily. *La chance* was that we studied hard, we understood our lessons, and we were thirsty for knowledge. We were worried and we managed to get out and it's because of us as well that this chance did work out. (My translation, interview, 2015, with Simone, graduated in Law.)

As Simone reflects again on her and her friends *la chance* to become interns at the TV station she speaks of three different *la chances*: there is *la chance* provided by God, i.e. her being amongst the best students in her class and her becoming an intern at the station; *la chance* of her (and her best friend) studying well and staying at the station as an intern without getting paid that made *la chance* work; and *la chance* that "a pu fonctionner" – that worked out. It is because of God, as well as her own efforts, that *la chance* worked out, she says. *La chance* is not something that is supposed to work just like that, but it is something for people to work with. *La chance* is presented as an opportunity that has been recognized and exploited as such by Simone. In consequence, she had her part in transforming *la chance* from being a private school student to becoming an intern at the station and to "being allowed to stay there voluntarily".

L2: *La chance* is a combination of structural and agentive factors.

La chance is an opportunity given by God: being the best in the class, doing an internship, being allowed to stay. These things are consequential and accumulative. These are external factors.

La chance was them studying hard, understanding lessons and being hungry for knowledge. These are factors within her control.

La chance was given by God.

La chance is a combination of structural and agentive factors.

On fabriquait des petites voitures pour les enfants. (...) Tu sais ce qu'on faisait pour le marketing ? Il y avait un petit marché, on savait qu'il y a des enfants là-bas et leurs mères. Donc, on partait avec nos nouvelles voitures qui étaient sorties, on roulait avec ça, on faisait, on faisait la publicité avec ces enfants-là. Donc, dès qu'ils voyaient ces voitures : "Maman, il faut m'acheter ça, il faut m'acheter ça". C'était une publicité. On sait profiter de la situation, tu vois, on était tellement malin. (On vit cette capacité) ? si on partait voir ces enfants avec leurs mères, on avait plus *la chance* être assis et puis seulement ceux qui les voient les collectionnent et puis les achètent.

L1: activity\transformation\working with\taking advantage

[...] we built a little matchbox. It was a company. [...] Want to know what we did for marketing? There was a little market; we knew there were kids with their moth-ers. So, we went there as well. As soon as we had new cars ready, we took them there and played with them... we advertised them. Kids that saw these cars... 'Mom, please buy that for me! I want it!' [...] That was advertisement! We took advantage of the situation. You know? We were smart. With that capacity, we went out there, saw the kids with their moms and, of course, we had even more *la chance* simply by sitting around playing. People saw the cars and bought them. (My translation, interview, 2014, with Amadou, graduated in International Law.)

Amadou talks about *la chance* as a result of smart advertisement. What started out as a playful way of selling their self-manufactured toys, *la chance* is now reflected as the origin of his entrepreneurial skills. To Amadou, *la chance* is selling toy cars. This *la chance* constitutes two groups of people conducting activities. The first group is Amadou and his friends who built the matchbox cars, did the marketing, went to the market, and played with the cars as advertisement. The second group is mothers with their children who saw the product, recognized it as desirable and ultimately bought it. It is customers reacting to the company's actions. This interplay creates *la chance*. As the youngsters saw their strategy working, they simply sat at their spot and played with their toys in order to sell more cars. Ever since his early childhood, Amadou ran businesses. First, he sold oil to the Bozo, so they had light during the night. The Bozo lived on the riverbed during the fishing sea-son and, therefore had no electricity in their housing. Later, he had a little business with some of his friends. They produced little toy cars for younger kids. He describes it as "une societée bien organisée" – "a well-organized enterprise". Some of his buddies were responsible for the fabrication of the product, and some gave it a new design, while Amadou was responsible for the marketing and selling part of their business. There was a little market where Segou women went on a daily basis in order to buy fresh vegetables and meat, and most of them were accompanied by their children. The only thing Amadou and his friends had to do was to play with their cars. This attracted the kids' interest, and as soon as their mothers became aware, Amadou would tell them that the toys are for sale. They were not expensive, 75 to 100 francs, he says, so that really everyone could afford it. They took advantage of a situation that was already there – and it was almost effortless. "Tu vois, on était tellement malin" – "You see, we were really clever." This form of advertising made them have more *la chance* than they would have had if they were sitting around with people passing by looking at their product. By playing with their self-made toy cars they attracted future clients, which is different from simply exposing the product, Amadou argues. The decision to approach the marketing differently is what ensured the outcome of *la chance* in terms of regular sales. Amadou speaks of "more *la chance*" – "increased *la chance*", which refers to a kind of reward for cleverness and their courage to approach the market a little differently.

L2: *La chance* is selling something.

Having "even more *la chance* simply by sitting around and playing". Sitting around and playing is advertisement for the toy cars they are selling. Them selling cars is based on people seeing them playing with the cars. Being seen playing and selling cars are two actions linked to each other, it is making people buy cars. Selling cars is *la chance*. Player one sits and plays, player two sees player one and is attracted to it. Player two buys the cars, thereby increasing *la chance* of player one.

> Bon, *la chance* me sourit chaque fois. Je te dis, je suis avec Dieu. Je suis un croyant quoi. Chaque fois, il y a des opportunités qui se créent et j'ai de l'argent dedans. Souvent, j'ai des amis qui préparent des choses, donc je participe et il y a de l'argent. Je suis dans les associations, tu vois, je ne m'assois pas. Souvent même, il y a mon tonton qui est à l'Université. S'ils font des examens, il m'appelle pour aller surveiller ses étudiants, et donc, il me paie. Tu vois ? Souvent aussi, on part faire du business pour pouvoir gagner un peu, par exemple aller acheter un ordinateur pour quelqu'un. On va te donner de l'argent : parce que tu es dans le

domaine, tu connais mieux que n'importe qui, donc on va te donner l'argent et puis tu vas partir pour aller acheter. Donc, tu te fais des bénéfices, tu vois ? Tout ça, les marchés, les business comme ça, les petits business, on le fait !

L1: activity\transformation\working with\continuing

Well, *la chance* nurtures me every time. I'm telling you that I am with God; I'm a believer. Every time, there are opportunities that show up and I find some money in them. Sometimes, there are friends doing something. I participate and get some money. I'm in some associations, you know? I don't sit around. Sometimes, my uncle calls me to supervise his students at the university. He pays me. Sometimes, we go do some business in order to earn a little. For example, I buy a laptop for somebody. People give me jobs like these because they know that I'm into computers. So, I buy one and take some advantage. You see? These are all little businesses... we do them all. (My translation, interview, 2014, with Amadou, graduated in International Law.)

For Amadou, doing business is a learning process encouraged by appropriated skill. I ask how he makes his living. *La chance* nourishes him and ensures his living. He connects *la chance* with himself and various agents: God, his uncle, and other people. Either combination leads to money, which is *la chance* nurturing him. God provides him with opportunities that generate income, his uncle invites him to supervise exams, and people ask for his advice when buying technology. Amadou accepts all of them; he does not sit around. "There are little markets like that, little businesses," Amadou concludes later on. An uncle supported Moudou with the job at the phone stand, an auntie employed him in her restaurant, and yet another uncle funded his new company in Segou.

L2: *La chance* is a little business regularly.

La chance nurtures every time. There are opportunities to make money, not by one player two, but by several players two, for instance, friends who are in associations, his uncle who works at the university, people who need assistance with their computers. Player one does not sit around, but finds money in doing things, little businesses. Player two needs assistance, which is an opportunity for player one to do some business. Player two knows player one is good at computers, so player one qualifies for the gig. Little business every time is *la chance*. *La chance* is timing.

KNOWLEDGE: TRANSFORMATION.

Working with *la chance* is about the transformation of *la chance*.

A sprout of *la chance* is much more like an opportunity than a done deal. Once a sprout of *la chance* has been identified, it requires work. Working with *la chance* is a concrete response to the sprout identified and therefore describes practices with a concrete intentionality.

In anticipation of a promotion or future job opportunities, Oumar and Siaka both try to work hard in their current position. That worked out pretty well in Simone's case: as a result of studying hard, she received the opportunity to do a journalism internship, which ultimately enabled her to present her own reports on air. Amadou started to believe in his entrepreneurial skills, as it was usually rewarded with *la chance*. He kept working on that up until now. Safiatou, who said she just wants to keep *la chance* in her life, is working with the sprout of being married to the man she loves and pregnant as she is stepping back from her professional goals for now.

To identify and work with *la chance* is similar to what Johnson-Hanks describes as 'judicious opportunism' (Johnson-Hanks 2005), which talks about actors seizing promising chances in contexts of uncertainty (Johnson-Hanks 2005, 363). It is about evaluating and anticipating a "chance" to be "promising", and also about acting accordingly by "seizing" such a "promising chance". "Judicious opportunism" requires adaptation, flexibility, and evaluation based on "contingent, sudden, and surprising offers that life can make. On the basis of these offers, the aspirations, once vague, will be concreticized" (ibid. 376). In other words, "judicious opportunism" is a reaction in response to an opportunity arising, which represents the idea of a sprout being identified and worked with. However, there are opportunities which are not considered as sprouts and, therefore, left untouched. A conscious decision not to take a certain opportunity is pre-conditioned by the fact that it has been identified as an opportunity in the first place. This is part of what Jeffrey describes as "timepass", which is sometimes a conscious decision made by his informants; it is a "form of an "investment" – prioritizing long-term goals instead of short-term success (Jeffrey 2010, 4).

All in all, the practices of working with *la chance* are about transforming sprouts into an outcome. It is about possessing and holding onto *la chance*. Let us take employment as an example: graduates work with sprouts of *la chance*, such as an internship or a limited contract and, thereby try to maintain or transform their position into an unlimited contract, another job, or whatever it is they want it to grow their sprout into. A sprout of *la chance* is something to work with, something to cultivate. Figuratively speaking, it is something they can extract cuttings from and plant anew. Both looking for and working with *la chance* requires effort, but whereas "looking for" is about preparing the soil and inspecting it for sprouts, "working with" *la chance* is all about collecting the harvest.

[Tracings]

Tracing L1: KNOWLEDGE: preparation, identification, transformation

Looking for *la chance* is about preparing for *la chance*.
Finding *la chance* is about the identification of *la chance*.
Working with *la chance* is about the transformation of *la chance*.

> Sprouts of *la chance* – just like serendipitous events – cannot be planned, so "[a]ll we can do is [...] put ourselves into a favorable position to profit by unexpected occurrences" (Merton 2004, 191).

In this chapter, I explored university graduates' knowledge and understanding about how to put themselves into such positions – they open up *la chance* (*ouvrir la chance*). By applying membership categorization analysis to the accounts, I was able to systematically examine graduates' knowledge about practices (category-bound activities) connected with *la chance*. As a result, I presented the practices "looking for *la chance* (sprouts)" or preparation, "finding *la chance* (sprouts)" or identification and "working with *la chance* (sprouts)" or transformation. Looking for *la chance*" means to anticipate *la chance* in a concrete or abstract manner and prepare for it accordingly. These practices of preparation are conducted in the present based on their prerequisites, but they are geared towards the future – towards a sprout of *la chance*. They need to be identified and evaluated by graduates, and again, their ability to do so depends on their preparation. Once identified, graduates work on the sprout's transformation into a concrete and anticipated outcome. In contrast to preparation, transformation is not an activity directed toward a sprout of *la chance*, but a response to a sprout. The intersection of these two kinds of activities is marked by the identification of a sprout.

Throughout this chapter, I have discussed some of the concepts in the literature on youth practices in uncertain contexts in Africa, and I have contrasted the identification of *la chance* to "the process of discovery" (Merton 2004, 196). Concepts such as "dubriagem" (Vigh 2010), "embracing uncertainty" (Nunzio 2015), "timepass" (Jeffrey 2010, 77) and "straining" (Finn 2015, 41) emerge out of rich ethnographic descriptions of practices in contexts of uncertainty. Indeed, there are many parallels to my findings based on graduates' accounts on how they open up *la chance*, though the main difference is a result of the question addressed in this chapter. I did not ask what graduates do; instead, I asked what graduates know they need to do. Graduates open up *la chance*: they prepare, they identify, and they transform *la chance*. Though the bottom line is that they know they need *la chance* in order to succeed in their projects, they also know that *la chance* will not necessarily come. They know preparation might not be enough for *la chance* to appear. They know they cannot force or enforce *la chance*. In other words, graduates are not uncertain about whether or not they will find *la chance*; they know that only some of them will have *la chance* to find *la chance*. They know that their efforts might not pay off, but they also know that it will not get worse if they try.

Tracing L2: The game of opening up *la chance*.

La chance is found in the encounter, in relationships and in collaboration between at least two players. *La chance* is the (1) motivation, (2) the game itself and (3) the potential outcome of the game:

1. *La chance* makes players play. *La chance* is the reason players play.
2. *La chance* can and cannot be provoked by the players.

For *la chance* to emerge it takes at least two players: one player doing something and another player with the ability to do something.

3. *La chance* is what a player is looking for. It can be anything: a stable job, a husband, a baby, a vacation.

To some players, *la chance* is a bonus, to others, *la chance* is everything.

The Players.

Player one.
Characteristics: Serious, honest, dedicated to the game.
Aware of the fact that she cannot play alone.
Activity: Opening up *la chance*.
Capacities: the ability to provoke, but not enforce of *la chance*.

Player two.
Characteristics: helpful, recognizing, rewarding.
Activities: Contributing to someone else's *la chance*.
Capacities: provision of *la chance*.
Acknowledgement of *la chance*

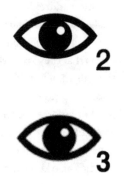

Player three.
Characteristics: knowledgeable.
Activities: observation and evaluation of player one.
Capacities: recognition of *la chance*.

The Plays.

We recall:
La chance is highly unlikely.
Achieving something unlikely is *la chance*. Achieving something likely is not *la chance*. Likeliness depends on the person and the circumstances.
La chance emerges in the encounter.
La chance emerges in the encounter between two players. So let me recapitulate some of the situations from layer two of the assemblage in which two players meet and the highly unlikely, i.e. *la chance*, potentially emerges. There are patterns emerging, but in order to stay true to the idea of the game, I call them plays (I-VI).

I In the workplace.

Compare:
L1: predicate\prerequisite\networks (see page 127)
L1: predicate\sprout\moment\opportunity\success (see page 143)
L1: predicate\outcome\achievement\civil service (see page 161)
L1: activity\preparation\looking for\applying (see page 185)
L1: activity\transformation\working with\anticipating (see page 211)

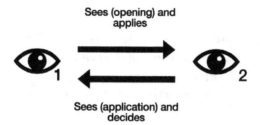

Player two posts an opening. Player two sees player one (her education and her application.) And decides whether or not to work with player one. Getting a job is highly unlikely, therefore, it is *la chance*.

II Friends.

Compare:
L1: *predicate\prerequisite\friendship (see page 125)*
L1: *activity\identification\finding\knowing (see page 200)*
L1: *activity\preparation (see page 178)*
L1: *activity\transformation\working with\continuing (see page 216)*

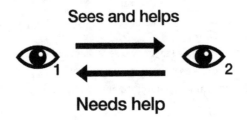

Player two needs help. Player two sees player one (her education and her application) and decides whether or not to work with player one.
The unlikeliness and, therewith, *la chance*, depends on the amount of people for player one to choose from.

III Doing business.

Compare:
L1: *activity\transformation\working with\taking advantage (see page 214)*

Player one is selling a product. Player two sees player one and decides whether or not to buy the product player one offers.
   Since the majority of the people does not buy, actually selling one's product is *la chance*. The more players player one engages with the higher the chances of making money.

**The difference between having the ability to have *la chance*
and having *la chance*.**

There is a difference between having the ability to have *la chance* and having *la chance*. To have the ability to have *la chance* is to be visible to other players. Remember, it is only in the encounter with another player that *la chance* emerges. Seeing player one is the precondition for player two to make a decision. Therefore, it is essential for player one to make herself visible and she does so by providing herself with the ability to have *la chance*. Though *la chance* requires the participation of a second player. In other words, being seen indicates the possession of the ability to have *la chance*.

IV Success

Compare:
L1: predicate\prerequisite\companion (see page 115)
L1: predicate\prerequisite\networks (see page 127)
L1: predicate\sprout\moment\opportunity\success (see page 143)

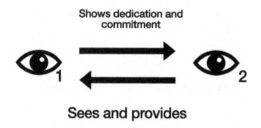

Player one is dedicated and committed to succeeding in her endeavors. Player two either does or does not see player one and if so, decides to whether or not provide success.

Player two can be anyone or anything player one can engage with and relate to, i.e. a friend, a family member, a random person, God or a material object like a book, a computer or a passcode. For player two to play along with player one requires player two to see player one in the first place. It is unknown to player one if there is going to be a player two.

So, no matter what player one does, two unknowns remain: being seen by player two and the emergence of *la chance*.

V By-product

Compare:
L1: *predicate\outcome\achievement\possession\by-product (see page 162)*

Player one is qualified and works. Player two sees yet another and different quality in player one and decides to put player one in touch with player three. *La chance* here is something player one wanted, but did not look for in that context.

So, from the perspective of player two the situation looks different.

A co-constitutive relationship and the interchangeability of the players.

Depending on one's perspective, one player appears to be passive, but actually both players are active. Players are interchangeable in a sense that any player can be either player one or player two depending on our focus. That focus is a random choice and we need to keep that in mind. Otherwise, we end up reducing the emergence of *la chance* to a plain cause-and-effect relationship, which it is not due to the fact that a cause does not necessarily lead to an effect and if there is a cause and an effect, it seems impossible to determine which one is which.

VI Business

Compare:
L1: predicate\prerequisite\social context (see page 118)
L1: activity\transformation\working with\continuing (see page 216)

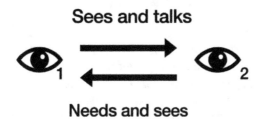

Player one sees a particular feature of player two (new to the area) and talks to player two. Player two responds.

Years later, player two needs a job done and remembers a particular feature (qualification and looking for a job) of player two.

Player one puts herself in a position to have *la chance* in the encounter with player two. Player one did not know if player two would see him; neither did he know if she would have a suitable job to offer. Player one just played. Player two only joined years later. *La chance* emerges for both players, yet in different shapes: to player one, player two and his skills are *la chance*; to player two, player one and the job he has to offer is *la chance*.
La chance is characterized by a co-constitutive relationship between the players who provide *la chance* for each other. It is only in the encounter of the two players that *la chance* potentially emerges.

VII Parent-child relationship

Compare:
L1: activity\preparation\looking for\attitude (see page 190)
L1: predicate\prerequisite\means (see page 120, 123)

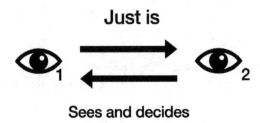

Player one (the kid) is seen by player two (the parent) and being put in a position to potentially have *la chance* at some point in the future. Player one is a kid and is seen by its parents who play for the kid's *la chance*. It is in that sense, for example, that Safiatou thinks about giving birth in the US, which would provide the kid with the future *la chance* of being able to study in the US and travel on a US passport, for instance. However, it is on player one in the future to evaluate whether or not that passport is *la chance* and potentially act on it.

Playing.

The knowns.
Depending on how the game is set up, there are different ways to open up *la chance*, i.e. to play the game of *la chance*, all of which are connected to what players know and what they know they do not know.

Knowing and Deciding.
Player one knows *la chance* she wants and makes decisions accordingly.

Knowing and Preparing.
Player one knows *la chance* she wants and qualifies accordingly. In other words, player one looks for education, qualification and networks in order to be able to have *la chance* in the future.

Knowing and Seeing.
Player one knows what *la chance* she wants, therefore she sees only a certain kind of *la chance*. Here, knowing comes at a cost, because sometimes *la chance* remains invisible to the player who already knows what *la chance* is supposed to look like. Graduates are aware of that, therefore they play not knowing what *la chance* is.

So, there are two ways of playing the game: 1 knowing *la chance* prior to playing, i.e. playing towards a particular goal (*la chance*), or 2 getting to know *la chance* while playing, i.e. playing towards an elusive goal (*la chance*).

1. When playing, players know what *la chance* is. They play towards it. That is how they see *la chance* once it emerges. This way, certain manifestations of *la chance* remain invisible to them. They might miss out on a *la chance* they do not want and are not looking for. Remember that if a player does not want it, it is not *la chance*. Yet there is change to what players want and *la chance* (past or still present) becomes visible.
2. When playing, players do not know what *la chance* is. They play anyway and they know what *la chance* is, when they see it.

The known unknowns.
There are two unknowns for each player. The first unknown relates to the visibility of the players to each other, i.e. to a player having the ability to have *la chance*. And the second one relates to the emergence of la chance, i.e. to a player having *la chance*:

1: Player one makes herself visible, but she does not know if she will be seen by player two.

At the same time, player two, looking for another player, does not know if she is going to find one.

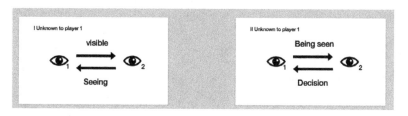

2: Once player one is seen by player two, player one does not know if player two is going to act on what she sees.

At the same time, the consequences of an engagement with player one are unknown to player two.

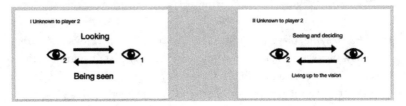

Particularly, plays V (business) and VI (parent-child relationship) point to another factor, namely temporality, which is an unknown to the extent that it cannot be strategically approached. Every encounter might or might not count. Both the reception and the outcome of the plays are unknown, and so is their temporality. Yet, players know what they are doing now and in doing so potentially put themselves in a position to have *la chance*. Players play now.

GAMEPLAY: The game of opening up la chance.

[Argument]

After having shown some plays which account for how the idea of the game of *la chance* emerged from my data, I will now move on to describe the characteristics of playing a game, as opposed to any other kind of practice.

My main point is that it is against the backdrop of difficult and uncertain circumstances, particularly the labor market situation in Mali, that university graduates are playing the game of *la chance*.

I now turn to (I) describing what I mean exactly by gameplay and, thus, the game of opening up *la chance*. I then (II) discuss the implications of looking through that lens and, ultimately, I (III) highlight what that lens allows us to understand about university graduates' knowledge and practices.

(I) Gameplay:

(1) Through the lens of the game, we see that despite their knowledge of their circumstances graduates keep trying.
(2) Through the lens of the game, we see graduates are striving towards dif ferent goals and succeed in doing so.
(3) Through the lens of the game, we see that graduates play the game of *la chance*, not because they have no other choice, but because they want to.
(4) Through the lens of the game, we see that university graduates do un derstand their situation and do not resign themselves to it.

(II) Implications:

1 The goal of the game is prelusory (Suits). This implies that the goal of the game is *la chance* rather than employment, for instance.
2 The constituent rules of the game allow for the activity of playing (Suits). This implies that it is only within the rules of the game of *la chance* that *la chance* is an accomplishable goal.
3 The players engage in the game voluntarily (Suits). That implies that graduates are not playing because they have no other option, but they play because they want to.

(III) We see:

(1) action, (2) disobedience (3) the actual puzzle and (4) a different kind of success,

I Graduates are playing the game of *la chance*

Overall argument:

The practice of opening up *la chance* is a game. In other words, graduates are playing the game of *la chance*. When graduates open up *la chance*/play the game of *la chance*, they "voluntarily attempt to overcome unnecessary obstacles" (Suits 2014 (1925), 41).

Definition and application to *la chance.*

Inspired and guided by Suits, I define the traits of a game and, in a second step, apply that definition as a lens to the practice of opening up *la chance*. As a result, I come up with a description of the game of *la chance*.

> "(P)laying a game is the voluntary attempt to overcome unnecessary obstacles" (ibid.)

According to Suits' conceptual analysis, games consist of three consecutive traits: (1) games have a prelusory goal, meaning that the goal of the game can be achieved apart from the game, (2) games have constitutive rules within which the goal can be achieved and these rules forbid the most efficient means to achieving the goal and (3) games require its players to have a lusory attitude, meaning the players have to be willing to accept the rules of the game.

This might sound a bit abstract, so here is an example which illustrates the three traits of playing games:

Prelusory goals and constitutive rules.
The Marathon.

Running a marathon is a game (see Nguyen 2020). Its goal is to cross the finish line. It is prelusory in a sense that crossing a finish line does not matter outside of the game within which it is achieved. Anyone can cross a finish line, but the marathon is about crossing the finish line after running 42,19 kilometers. Running that distance before crossing the line is a marathon, a game, the voluntary attempt to overcome an unnecessary obstacle. The marathon would not exist if it was not for the unnecessary obstacle of 42,19 kilometers prior to the finish line. However, it is that distance, that obstacle, that rule that allows for the marathon to exist.

Running a marathon is the voluntary attempt to overcome unnecessary obstacles.

For the purpose of playing the game, i.e. running a marathon, not for the purpose of crossing the finish line.

In fact, if you do not run the 42,19 kilometers, you do not run a marathon. All you do is cross a finish line. And that can be a game, too, but one that is different from that of a marathon.

The game of opening up *la chance*.

Now, how does this relate to what we know about the relationship between graduates and *la chance*?

If we look at the practice of opening up *la chance* through the lens of game playing, this is what we see:

Opening up *la chance* is a game. Its goal is to have *la chance*. However, to have *la chance* does not matter outside of the game of *la chance*, because what matters outside of the game is employment, for instance. Outside of the game, it does not matter if the job is *la chance* or not. It is a job. The point here is that every graduate can have a job, but the game of *la chance* is about having the job they want. Playing the game of *la chance*, graduates need to open up *la chance* prior to having *la chance*. To simply get the employment is not the same as getting the employment having opened up *la chance* before. It is that practice of opening up, the circumstances and obstacles graduates have to overcome that allows for the game of *la chance* to exist. Opening up *la chance*, i.e. playing the game of *la chance*, is the voluntary attempt to overcome unnecessary obstacles.

The purpose of playing the game of *la chance* is not to have *a* job, but to have *the* job, which is *la chance*. A graduate who does not open up *la chance* does not have *la chance*, even if they get a job. They get a job as a result of a job hunt, which can be a game, too. However, that is a different game, not the game of *la chance*.

Lusory attitude.

"There is always something in the life of a player of a game more important than playing the game" (Suits 2014 (1925), 30). This also implies that if a game becomes more important than anything else in a player's life, it ceases to be a game. Playing the game of *la chance* is not the most important activity in graduates' lives and, therefore, getting the employment they want is not the most important activity. Graduates can always stop opening up *la chance*, i.e. stop playing the game of *la chance* (compare Suits, 29) and still have a job. The fact that they usually do not stop, but keep trying does not account for the fact that they have no choice, rather, it points towards the voluntary attitude with which they are approaching the game.

Playing the labor market.

Playing the game of *la chance* is part of graduates' everyday life. However, it is different from going to work every day (compare Suits, 41). Whereas going to work requires graduates to obey the rules of the labor market, the game of *la chance* allows them to escape these rules. At this point it is important to remember that the game of *la chance* is not primarily about getting employment, but about getting *la chance*. The game of opening up *la chance* is different from looking for employment because it is not restricted by the rules set by the labor market, but by the rules of the game of *la chance*.

And these rules are accepted by the players "for the sake of the activity they make possible" (Suits, 32). In other words, the rules of the game of *la chance* allow them to play a game that is not the labor market game. Here we see that graduates do not obey the rules of the labor market, but the rules of the game of *la chance*. In doing so, they play with the rules of the labor market. I will get to that implication later, but first things first:

The labor market is a necessary obstacle, at least when it comes to getting a job. However, when it comes to getting *la chance*, the labor market is an unnecessary obstacle which has to be overcome in order to get *la chance*, which again, can be a job. What might sound complicated here is actually quite simple: those who get the job they want right away did not play the game of *la chance*. They crossed the finish line, but they did not run the 42,19 kilometers.

"But they do have a job", you might say now and that is true. Think about saying "but they did cross the finish line", which is also true. Yet again, playing games is not about the goal, but about the activity prior to reaching the goal.

To sum up,

I argue that graduates are playing the game of *la chance*. I am not saying that life is a game or that work is a game, instead, university graduates approach the labor market like an infinite game (see Carse 1986). And the elusiveness of *la chance*, being the goal of the game, is key in doing that. Since graduates aware of the elusiveness of the goal, it allows them to focus on playing the game itself rather than on the goal. Neither does this imply that all they do is play games. It merely means that in situations in which they find themselves within limits not set by themselves (like the labor market or the marriage business) they provide themselves with the freedom to play.

Of course, the labor market is not intended for play. However, it is by means of attitude that graduates' appropriate it (compare Sicart, 27). "Appropriation implies a shift in the way a particular technology or situation is interpreted. The most usual transformation is from functional or goal oriented to pleasurable or emotionally engaging" (ibid). In other words, graduates transform the rules of Mali's labor market as they play the game of *la chance*. Playing the game of *la chance*, graduates transform their contexts; they do not simply act within it.

II Implications of Gameplay

Three Implications of Gameplay.

To say that graduates are playing the game of *la chance* has three other significant implications on our understanding of what graduates are doing:

1 The goal of the game is prelusory (Suits). This implies that the goal of the game is *la chance* rather than employment, for instance.

In the game of *la chance*, *la chance* is the goal of the game. In chapter four, we will see that *la chance* is elusive, which is the key to playing the game and enjoying it. Because the goal is elusive, the success of playing is not defined by winning, but by playing itself. Due to the nature of the goal employed by the game they play, graduates do not fail and neither do they feel like they are. Their goal is not to get an employment, but their goal is to explore, to be busy, to be doing things. It is about figuring stuff out as they go along. They do not have to do that because most of them do have jobs or a family who is taking care of them and they, too, are aware of the precarious labor market situation. So graduates are not judged by the job they do not have, but they are recognized by the game they play.

It is also the nature of the goal that distinguishes the game of *la chance* from playing the lottery, for instance. The lottery is about winning and the only way to be in a position to win something is to buy a ticket. The goal of the lottery is not playing, but winning. In playing in the lottery, the goal is not prelusory, but all about the money and therefore success is measured only by the amount of money won or lost. In contrast, the game of *la chance* is about playing towards a goal, which is prelusory and therefore success is measured by playing.

Playing the game of *la chance* is not primarily about fun and enjoying it, but much more about graduates doing something they do not have to do.

GAMEPLAY: The game of opening up la chance. 237

2 The constituent rules of the game allow for the activity of playing (Suits). This implies that it is only within the rules of the game of *la chance* that *la chance* is an accomplishable goal.

In other words, the combination of the goal of the game being *la chance*, and *la chance* being prelusory enables graduates to succeed. Let me use the Myth of Sisyphus (see Camus 1955) to explain what I mean by this: Sisyphus is punished by having to push a rock up a mountain. He is doomed to continue with this activity forever, never actually reaching the top of the mountain. His life is a punishment, a struggle. He is aware of the meaninglessness of his actions. At least, they are meaningless in relation to the goal of getting the rock on top of the mountain. He is aware of the fact that he will not reach the top. He knows. And in response to that knowledge he just lets go of the goal in favor of his action. In other words, he turns the pushing of the rock into his thing. Consequently, his purpose is no longer to reach the goal, rather his purpose is to push the rock. In relation to that purpose, or that goal, his actions are no longer meaningless, his actions are impactful, his life is no longer a struggle imposed by somebody else, but his own created by himself. We just have to imagine Sisyphus happy (Camus). Sisyphus redefined the mountain top. Success is no longer reaching the top, but pushing the rock and enjoying it.

Now, what about graduates? Are they Sisyphus? For the sake of analogy: graduates are punished by the political, economic and educational system, which forces them to push a rock and they know that it is highly unlikely for them to reach the top with the rock. Graduates, too, have let go of the concrete goal of getting a particular employment a long time ago. If your goal is not to become a professor, but to be happy, there are plenty of ways to attain it. If the goal is to become a professor, there is only one way. However, there are many ways to being happy, earning money or making an impact, for instance. Graduates understand that, so they keep pushing their rock, but they also look for other rocks. That is part of what I call the game of *la chance*.

Remember the physics graduate Madou, who in 2013 wanted to become a professor in physics, a big shot in telecommunications in 2014 and a farmer in 2015? I was amazed and puzzled by the fact that his goals changed both so quickly and significantly. I remember asking him if he was serious and, of course, he was. In 2021, he did work as a manager in telecommunications and selling home grown veggies and chicken. He knew of three different ways to get to where he wanted to be, and to him, it was never about the concrete goal of a profession, but about the idea he thought would come with these professions, i.e. business and fame. So, it is not about the professional activity, but about the goal to which these activities are directed.

3 **The players engage in the game voluntarily (Suits). That implies that graduates are not playing because they have no other option, but they play because they want to.**

And that seems like an actual surprise, but only if the primary assumption – perhaps related to the precariousness of the labor market situation in Mali – is that they cannot engage in an employment activity of their own choice. For instance, why do people run a marathon? More than 45'000 people run the Berlin Marathon every year, only one person wins it. Except for a couple of participants, nobody runs to win it. The majority of the runners run for a purpose that is not winning in terms of crossing the finish line first. Winning is measured in relation to every runner. People won because they finished. Some won because they got a new personal best. Some won because they had to realize this was not their day, but they kept going anyway. Some won because they got to the starting line. Some won because they tried. There are so many ways to win.

So again, why do graduates play the game of *la chance*? Because why not? The only answer to "why?" is "why not!" And the more revealing question is: why is "why not?!" not a satisfying response? Why do we go to work every day? Because we have to and we need the money to make a living. Obligation is a satisfying response. Survival is one, too. However, there is a lot less agency in obligation and survival. For some people the answer to why they show up for work every day is: because they can. And because it makes them feel good about themselves. Graduates ask "why not go to work?" and go for it, not because they have to due to financial reasons (remember: some of them are not even getting paid for extended periods of time, if at all), but because they want to.

Other than questioning assumptions on an abstract level, graduates' behavior might lead to concrete changes, too. By playing the game of *la chance*, graduates do not obey the rules of the labor market ultimately targeted to getting an employment, but rather the rules of the game of *la chance* targeted to the continuation of playing. In doing so, they play with the rules of the labor market. Playing the game of *la chance*, graduates know they can-

GAMEPLAY: The game of opening up la chance.   239

not win against the background of the labor market. However, within the game of *la chance*, they do succeed and thereby appropriate the labor market.

III What we see now

(1) We see action.
Through the lens of the game, we see that graduates play the game of *la chance*, not because they have no other choice, but because they want to.

Practices such as making do, getting along, muddling through, actively waiting (see for instance Honwana 2012) usually accounts for people doing things despite the circumstances. These perspectives on practice challenged and changed common assumptions about work (formal and informal work) and what it means to do things (waiting is doing, practices that usually escape our eyes). With reference to practice and what people are actually doing on an everyday basis, research now knows that people do things, how they do them, and argues for the significance of the process. Nevertheless, ongoing practices tend to be evaluated as liminal vis-a-vis measurable outcomes of success and failure in conducting these very practices and a lot less research is devoted to how people keep doing the things they do.

Waiting for a bus, waiting for someone, waiting for a job is thinking in relation to a future-oriented outcome (getting on the bus, meeting someone or getting a job), which is a kind of framing and, consequently, a kind of thinking that requires an evaluation of every situation. The goal has been achieved, the goal has not, or not yet been achieved. That kind of thinking values the process much less than the ultimate outcome. Waiting appears to describe the lack of researchers' ability to imagine process without progress much more than the actual practices they investigate. Now, in order to take the practice itself just as serious as the outcome, we need to take graduates' practices of *la chance* in Bamako just as seriously. I argue that the idea of game-playing allows us to do that.

Playing the game of *la chance* is not about making do despite the circumstances, but about acting because of and in response to what they have come to understand about their situation. Game-playing is intentional and therefore requires players not only to be able to do things and to actually do them, but also to be aware of the practices they are exercising. Ultimately, game-playing is a practice which accounts for graduates' agency *par excellence* in the sense that it presumes agency rather than concludes it.

(2) And we see disobedience.
Through the lens of the game of *la chance*, we see that university graduates do understand their situation and do not resign themselves to it.

Graduates are not raising their voice out in the streets; they are not protesting. In fact, they do not seem to be doing anything, despite the fact that they understand. So why is that?

Precisely because they understand their situation, they are not out in the streets protesting, but out there playing the game of *la chance*.

In "Weapons of the Weak", rather than big movements, James Scott (1985) focuses on everyday forms of resistance and non-cooperation of peasants in rural contexts against oppression. He shows seemingly invisible forms of resistance, arguing that the agency of the weak is subtle, mute and involves individual acts (Scott 1985,137) for two main reasons: one, because the weak cannot afford it to be otherwise, because in a situation of powerlessness survival is on the line; and two, just as "fish do not talk about water", people do not talk about their everyday, routine actions because they take them for granted.

So, just because resistance failed at winning by overthrowing the system (Scott, 289), this does not mean that it lost in general. There are other ways to resist without directly confronting elite norms: "in ridicule, in truculence, in irony, in petty acts of noncompliance, in root dragging, in dissimulation, in resistant mutuality, in the disbelief in elite homilies, in the steady, grinding efforts to hold one's own against overwhelming odds – a spirit and practice that prevents the worst and promises something better" (Scott, 350).

Playing games is another way of resisting: "Play becomes political action when the interplay between the context and the appropriation leads to an activity that critically engages with the situation without ceasing to be play. ... Because it is play, it can thrive in situations of oppression; because it is play,

GAMEPLAY: The game of opening up la chance.

it can allow personal and collective expression, giving voices and actions when no one can be heard" (Sicart, 80f.).

(3) We see the actual puzzle.
Through the lens of the game of *la chance*, we see that despite their knowledge of their circumstances graduates keep trying.

The description of professional practices as play is by no means new. Richard Rottenburg (2001), for instance, examines development work with Africa as a game in which the participating parties agree on the reduction of complexity for the benefit of measurability and ultimately, for the purpose (or the goal) of improving the conditions in developing countries. There is an agreement about the necessity of improvement in one of the two partner countries. Rottenburg argues that the primary assumption is that translation is possible, i.e. the translation of an idea from one context to another and, therefore, countries can change from undeveloped to developed. He describes a game, which is about winning or losing because it is evaluated in accordance with the measured efficiency and success of the project at stake.

The puzzle Rottenburg is confronted with is this: How come the practice of development work is kept alive even though it keeps failing? Approaching the puzzle, he examines the game, its framework (or rules) and practices (means by which the parties follow the rules) and based on an analysis thereof distinguishes between a code of practice and a code of reflection. He argues that these codes are kept separate, and have to be kept separate in order for the game of development work with Africa to be played. Put differently, playing the game, players do not question the game.

The actual puzzle is not how graduates deal with uncertainty and how they find their ways into the future. The puzzling question is: why even try?

In other words, if the labor market situation is so precarious and graduates understand that even prior to starting their studies, why do they even try? Why do they keep going? Most of them do not seem to be frustrated, they do not take their criticism to the streets, they just keep going. They keep signing up for the *concours*, they keep trying to extend their arms. How come they keep going when the reality of the situation stays the same and gets even worse?

Hirikazu Miyazaki (2006) asks a similar question in "The Method of Hope", which focuses on Fiji's Suvavou people, who have, for generations, been seeking the promised government compensation for the loss of their ancestral land almost 150 years ago: how do they keep up hope when reality continues to prove them wrong? (Miyazaki 2006, 3) The Suvavou people keep up hope by practicing "the method of hope", which is a practice Miyazaki discovered when examining ritual practices and their process rather than their effects. This method allows people to keep prospective momentum; an idea of the present in a state of the "not-yet" future (Bloch in Miyazaki 2006), rather than a not at all. It is this prospective momentum that allows them to keep going. The situation in Mali is similar, yet, radically different: Graduates do not work towards an anticipated future; they know about the state of the present and they engage in game-playing. The game is not about gaining prospective momentum, game playing is about momentum for the prospect of *la chance*, which is elusive.

Graduates keep going through the practice of opening up *la chance*, which I refer to as "the game of *la chance*". In doing so, they do succeed individually. And their individual success is a product of a practice they exercise as a collective: they are "opening up la *chance*", as they would call it; they are "playing the game of *la chance*". The game of *la chance* is not about winning, so they are not trying to win, but they are playing the game. Graduates are not looking for any employment, but they look for *la chance*, which is the employment they want. They are not looking for work, but they look for *la chance* of getting paid for their labor.

(4) And we see a different kind of success.
Through the lens of the game, we see graduates are striving towards different goals and succeed in doing so.

University graduates are not playing the game of employment, but the game of *la chance*, in which the goal is a different one. In the game of *la chance*, the goal is opening up *la chance*. What matters within the game of opening up *la chance* is playing it.

Think about Amadou's phone cabin for a second. Think about this business not being about the money, but about doing the business itself. It is about getting up in the morning, opening the doors of the business, putting the bench in front of the door and sitting on it, ready to sell units to passers-by. It makes so much more sense to think about it like that, simply because there is not enough money to be gained by running a phone cabin.

GAMEPLAY: The game of opening up la chance.   243

Graduates practice game-playing in real life, which does not distract from the seriousness of life, rather from the seriousness of assumed goals. Graduates are aware that the imposed goals are not achievable for most of them; they are playing for a different goal. Graduates know they most likely will not get a stable employment that corresponds to their qualification and they act according to that knowledge.

If we approach university graduates as engaging in game-playing, we see them not as victims doomed to failure, but as people achieving goals that matter to them and they have defined for themselves.

The game of *la chance* is about *la chance*, which is elusive. And because graduates know about the elusiveness of the goal of the game they are playing, the game of *la chance* is not so much about winning, but much more about playing. The future is elusive, too, and so is everything we place in the future, i.e. our imaginations, our dreams, our goals.

Playing the game of *la chance* allows for a perspective on the present which is less influenced by normative ways of imagining the future and outcome-oriented evaluations of present practices. Success or failure are no longer a criterion for the evaluation of present actions once we stop putting so much emphasis on the outcomes, but rather on the process of actions.

Bibliography

Aneesh, Aneesh. 2017. "'Relocating Global Assemblages': An Interview with Saskia Sassen." *Science, Technology and Society* 22 (1): 128–34. https://doi.org/10.1177/0971721817694927.

APEJ. 2015. "Présentation de l'agence Pour La Promotion de l'emploi Des Jeunes." Bamako: APEJ Agence pour la Promotion de l'Emploi des Jeunes (private copy).

Archambault, Julie Soleil. 2015. "Rhythms of Uncertainty and the Pleasures of Anticipation." In *Ethnographies of Uncertainty in Africa*, edited by Elizabeth Cooper and David Pratten, 129–48. London: Palgrave Macmillan UK.

Bandura, Albert. 1998. "Exploration of Fortuitous Determinants of Life Paths." *Psychological Inquiry* 9: 95–99.

Bargatzky, Thomas. 2010. "Contemplativus in Actione." In *Glück Hat Viele Gesichter–Annäherungen an Eine Gekonnte Lebensführung*, edited by Alfred Bellebaum and Robert Hettlage, 113–24. Wiesbaden: VS Verlag.

Beck, Ulrich. 1986. *Risikogesellschaft*. Frankfurt am Main: suhrkamp.

Becker, Howard S. 1994. "'Foi Por Acaso': Conceptualizing Coincidence." *The Sociological Quarterly* 35: 183–94.

Behrends, Andrea, and Carola Lentz. 2012. "Education, Careers, and Home Ties: The Ethnography of an Emerging Middle Class from Northern Ghana." *Zeitschrift Für Ethnologie*, 139–64.

Berger, Peter L., and Thomas Luckmann. 1991. *The Social Construction of Reality: A Treatise in the Sociology of Knowledge*. London: Penguin UK.

Bernard Suits. 2014. *The Grasshopper. Games, Life, and Utopia*. Toronto: Broadview Press.

Bille, Mikkel, Frida Hastrup, and Tim Flohr Soerensen, eds. 2010. *An Anthropology of Absence*. New York, NY: Springer New York. https://doi.org/10.1007/978-1-4419-5529-6.

Birzle, Maike, Michelle Engeler, Noemi Steuer, and Elísio Macamo. 2017. "Ça va Aller: The Role of Hope in Burkinabe University Graduates' Navigation towards the Future." In *Dealing with Elusive Futures – University Graduates in Urban Africa*, 53–68. Bielefeld: Transcript.

Bourdieu, Pierre. 1983. "Ökonomisches Kapital, Kulturelles Kapital, Soziales Kapital." In *Soziale Ungleichheiten*, edited by R. Kreckel, 183–98. Göttingen: Otto Schwartz und Co.

Buchanan, Ian. 2021. *Assemblage Theory and Method*. London: Bloomsbury Academic.

Calkins, Sandra. 2016. *Who Knows Tomorrow?: Uncertainty in North-Eastern Sudan*. Oxford: Berghahn Books.

Camus, Albert. 2014. *Der Mythos Des Sisyphos*. Reinbeck: Rowohlt-Taschenbuch-Verlag.

Carse, James P. 1986. *Finite and Infinite Games*. New York: Free Press.

Chimanikire, Donald P. 2009. *Youth and Higher Education in Africa. The Cases of Cameroon, South Africa, Eritrea and Zimbabwe: The Cases of Cameroon, South Africa, Eritrea, and Zimbabwe*. Dakar: CODESRIA.

"Communique N° 2016-000024 / MTFP-CNCFP Du Ministre Du Travail et de La Fonction Publique, Charge Des Relations Avec Les Institutions." 2016. (private copy).

Cooper, Elisabeth, and David Pratten. 2015. *Ethnographies of Uncertainty in Africa*. London: Palgrave Macmillan UK.

Cooper, Elizabeth, and David Pratten. 2015. "Ethnographies of Uncertainty in Africa: An Introduction." In *Ethnographies of Uncertainty in Africa*, edited by Elizabeth Cooper and David Pratten, 1–16. London: Palgrave Macmillan UK.

Daou, Alou. 2010. "Problématique de l'effectif de l'enseignement Supérieur: Plus de 70 000 Étudiants, l'université de Bamako Est Au Bord de l'implosion." Maliweb.Net. 2010. http://archive.wikiwix.com/cache/?url=http%3A%2F%2Fwww.maliweb.net%2Fcategory.php%3F-NID%3D55362.

DeLanda, Manuel. 2006. "Deleuzian Social Ontology and Assemblage Theory." *Deleuze and the Social*, 250–66.

Deleuze, Gilles, and Félix Guattari. 1987. *A Thousand Plateaus: Capitalism and Schizophrenia*. Minneapolis: Bloomsbury Publishing.

Dey, Ian. 2003. *Qualitative Data Analysis: A User Friendly Guide for Social Scientists*. London: Routledge.

Diakite, Fatoumata N'Diaye. 2011. "Conseil Des Ministres Du 28 Septembre 2011." Journal Du Mali. 2011. http://archive.wikiwix.com/cache/?url=http %3A%2F%2Fwww.journaldumali.com%2Farticle.php%3Faid%3D3674.

Ehn, Billy, and Orvar Löfgen. 2012. *Nichtstun: Eine Kulturanalyse Des Ereignislosen Und Flüchtigen*. Hamburg: Hamburger Edition HIS Verlagsgesellschaft.

Engeler, Michelle. 2016. "Between Afropolitans and New Sankaras. The Reproduction of Academics and the Making of Middle Class Status in Ouagadougou, Burkina Faso (Draft)."

Engeler, Michelle, and Noemi Steuer. 2017. "Elusive Futures: An Introduction." In *Dealing with Elusive Futures – University Graduates in Urban Africa*, edited by Michelle Engeler, Noemi Steuer, and Elisio Macamo, 9–28. Bielefeld: Transcript.

Finn, Brandon Marc, and Sophie Oldfield. 2015. "Straining: Young Men Working through Waithood in Freetown, Sierra Leone." *Africa Spectrum* 50: 29–48.

Fisher, Josh. 2016. "The Unemployed Cooperative." In , edited by Jong Bum Kwon and Carrie M. Lane, 191–211. Ithaca: Cornell University Press. https://doi.org/10.7591/9781501706134-012.

France, Alan. 2007. "Youth Transitions in the Age of Uncertainty." In *Understanding Youth In Late Modernity*, edited by Alan France, 59–77. Berkshire: Open University Press.

Francis, David, and Stephen Hester. 2004. *An Invitation to Ethnomethodology: Language, Society and Interaction*. London: SAGE Publications.

Furlong, Andy. 2009. *Handbook of Youth and Young Adulthood: New Perspectives and Agendas*. London: Taylor & Francis.

Furlong, Andy, and Fred Cartmel. 2009. *Higher Education And Social Justice*. Berkshire: Open University Press.

Geertz, Clifford. 1975. "Common Sense as a Cultural System." *The Antioch Review* 33: 5–26.

Gilbertson, Adam. 2015. "Food Security, Conjugal Conflict, and Uncertainty in 'Bangladesh', Mombasa, Kenya." In *Ethnographies of Uncertainty in Africa*, edited by Elizabeth Cooper and David Pratten, 84–108. London: Palgrave Macmillan UK.

Gladkova, Nataliia, and Valentina Mazzucato. 2015. "Theorising Chance: Capturing the Role of Ad Hoc Social Interactions in Migrants' Trajectories." *Population Space Place*, 1–13.

Graeber, David. 2012. "The Sword, the Sponge, and the Paradox of Performativity. Some Observations on Fate, Luck, Financial Chicanery, and the Limits of Human Knowledge." *Social Analysis* 56: 25–42.

Hänsch, Valerie, Lena Kroeker, and Silke Oldenburg. 2017. "Uncertain Future(s): Perceptions on Time between the Immediate and the Imagined." *TSANTSA* 22: 4–17.

Hansen Tranberg, Karen. 2005. "Getting Stuck in the Compound: Some Odds against Social Adulthood in Lusaka, Zambia." *Africa Today* 51: 3–16.

Haram, Liv, and C. Bawa Yamba. 2009. *Dealing with Uncertainty in Contemporary African Lives*. Uppsala: Nordiska Afrikainstitutet.

Have, Paul ten. 2004. *Understanding Qualitative Research and Ethnomethodology*. London: SAGE Publications.

Henrik Vigh. 2010. "Youth Mobilisation as Social Navigation. Reflections on the Concept of Dubriagem." *Youth and Modernity in Africa* 18: 1–18.

Hester, Stephen, and Peter Eglin. 1997. *Culture in Action: Studies in Membership Categorization Analysis*. Lanham: University Press of America.

Hettlage, Robert. 2010. "Das Prinzip 'Glück.'" In *Glück Hat Viele Gesichter – Annäherungen an Eine Gekonnte Lebensführung*, edited by Alfred Bellebaum, 11–28. Wiesbaden: Verlag für Sozialwissenschaften.

Hine, Christine, ed. 2005. *Virtual Methods: Issues in Social Research on the Internet*. Oxford: Berg.

Honwana, Alcinda Manuel. 2012. *The Time of Youth: Work, Social Change, and Politics in Africa*. Sterling: Kumarian Press Pub.

Imperato, Pascal James, and Gavin H. Imperato. 2008. *Historical Dictionary of Mali*. Lanham: Scarecrow Press.

Jeffrey, Craig. 2010. *Timepass: Youth, Class, and the Politics of Waiting in India*. Stanford: University Press.

Johnson-Hanks, Jennifer. 2002. "On the Limits of Life Stages in Ethnography: Toward a Theory of Vital Conjunctures." *American Anthropologist* 104: 865–80.

Jones, Rachel A. 2007. "'You Eat Beans!': Kin-Based Joking Relationships, Obligations, and Identity in Urban Mali." *Anthropology Honors Projects* 2: 1–134.

Kaufmann, Andrea. 2017. "Crafting a Better Future in Liberia: Hustling and Associational Life in Post-War Monrovia." *TSANTSA* 22: 37–46.

Krüger, Fred, and Elísio Macamo. 2003. "Existenzsicherung Unter Risikobedingungen. Sozialwissenschaftliche Analyseansätze Zum Umgang Mit Krisen, Konflikten Und Katastrophen." *Geographica Helvetica* 58: 47–55.

Kuhn, Thomas. 1962. "1970. The Structure of Scientific Revolutions."

Kwon, Jong Bum, and Carrie M. Lane. 2016. "Introduction." In , edited by Jong Bum Kwon and Carrie M. Lane, 1–17. Ithaca: Cornell University Press. https://doi.org/10.7591/9781501706134-002.

Lane, Carrie M. 2016. "The Limits of Liminality." In , edited by Jong Bum Kwon and Carrie M. Lane, 18–33. Ithaca: Cornell University Press. https://doi.org/10.7591/9781501706134-003.

Langevang, Thilde, and Katherine V. Gough. 2009. "Surviving through Movement: The Mobility of Urban Youth in Ghana." *Social & Cultural Geography* 10: 741–56.

Leccardi, Carmen. 2005. "Facing Uncertainty: Temporality and Biographies in the New Century." *Young* 13: 123–46.

Lewis, Michael. 1998. "Altering Fate: Why the Past Does Not Predict the Future." *Psychological Inquiry* 9: 105–8.

Ludwig, Susann. 2011. "Feldforschungsbericht Bamako/Mali August-September 2011." Unpublished Work.

— 2013. "'Je Me Débrouille' – Ein Beitrag Zum Zusammenhang von Neoliberaler Wirtschaftspolitik Und Arbeit Unter Jungdiplomierten in Bamako/Mali." MA Thesis, Martin-Luther-Universität Halle/Wittenberg.

Luhmann, Niklas. 1991. *Soziale Systeme: Grundriß Einer Allgemeinen Theorie.* Frankfurt am Main: suhrkamp.

Macamo, Elísio. 2017. "On Uncertainty." In *Dealing with Elusive Futures – University Graduates in Urban Africa*, edited by Michelle Engeler, Noemi Steuer, and Elísio Macamo, 179–91. Bielefeld: Transcript.

Mains, Daniel. 2016. "Youth Unemployment, Progress, and Shame in Urban Ethiopia." In , edited by Jong Bum Kwon and Carrie M. Lane, 135–54. Ithaca: Cornell University Press. https://doi.org/10.7591/9781501706134-009.

Malmström, Maria Frederika. 2019. *The Streets Are Talking to Me: Affective Fragments in Sisi's Egypt.* Oakland: University of California Press.

Mannheim, Karl. 2016. "Das Problem Der Generationen." *Faksimile:Kölner Zeitschrift Für Soziologie Und Sozialpsychologie*, August, 1–41.

Masquelier, Adeline. 2013. "Teatime: Boredom and the Temporalities of Young Men in Niger." *Africa* 83: 470–91.

— 2019. *Fada: Boredom and Belonging in Niger.* University of Chicago Press.

Merton, Robert K., and Elinor G. Barber. 2004. *The Travels and Aventures of Serendipity.* Princeton: University Press.

Ministère du Travail et de la Fonction Publique. 2016. "LISTE DES CANDI-DATS AU CONCOURS DIRECT D'ENTREE DANS LA FONCTION PUB-LIQUE: Adjoint d'Administration." (private copy).

Miyazaki, Hirokazu. 2006. *The Method of Hope: Anthropology, Philosophy, and Fijian Knowledge*. Stanford: University Press.

Moseley, William G. 2017. "The Minimalist State and Donor Landscapes: Livelihood Security in Mali during and after the 2012–2013 Coup and Rebellion." *African Studies Review* 60: 37–51.

Munive, Jairo. 2010. "The Army of 'Unemployed' Young People." *Young* 18: 321–38.

Nguyen, C. Thi. 2020. *Games: Agency As Art*. Oxford: Oxford University Press. https://doi.org/10.1093/oso/9780190052089.001.0001.

Nunzio, Marco. 2015. "Embracing Uncertainty: Young People on the Move in Addis Ababa's Inner City." In *Ethnographies of Uncertainty in Africa*, edited by Elizabeth Cooper and David Pratten, 149–72. London: Palgrave Macmillan UK.

Oldenburg, Silke. 2016. "'I Am an Intellectual'. War, Youth and Higher Education in Goma (Eastern Congo)." *AnthropoChildren* 2016: 1–19.

Pankoke, Eckart. 1997. "Modernität Des Glücks Zwischen Spätaufklarung Und Frühsozialismus." In *Glücksvorstellungen – Ein Rückgriff in Die Geschichte Der Soziologie*, edited by Klaus Barheier Alfred Bellebaum, 75–105. Opladen: Westdeutscher Verlag GmbH.

Pollner, Melvin. 1974. "Sociological and Commonsense Models of the Labelling Process." In *Ethnomethodology: Selected Readings*, edited by Roy Turner, 27–40. Harmondsworth: Penguin.

Powell, Walter W. 1990. "Neither Market nor Hierarchy: Network Forms of Organization." *Research in Organizational Behaviour* 12: 295–336.

Ralph, Michael. 2008. "Killing Time." *Social Text* 26: 1–29.

Readings, Bill. 1996. *The University in Ruins*. Cambridge: Harvard University Press.

Rescher, Nicholas. 1990. "Luck." *Proceedings and Adresses of the American Philosophical Association* 64: 5–19.

Rottenburg, Richard. 2001. "Kultur Der Entwicklungszusammenarbeit Mit Afrika." In *Entwicklungspolitische Perspektiven Im Kontext Wachsender Komplexität. Festschrift Für Prof. Dr. Dieter Weiss*, edited by Steffen Wippel and Inse Cornelssen, 349–77. München: Weltforum Verlag.

Sambaiga, Richard. 2017. "Negotiating the Future: Young Graduates Respond to Career Uncertainty in Tanzania." In *Dealing with Elusive Futures – University Graduates in Urban Africa*, edited by Michelle Engeler, Noemi Steuer, and Elísio Macamo, 29–52. Bielefeld: Transcript.

Scott, James C. 1985. *Weapons of the Weak: Everyday Forms of Peasant Resistance*. New Haven: Yale University Press.

Shanahan, Michael J., and Erik J. Porfeli. 2006. "Chance Events in the Life Course." *Advances in Life Course Research* 11: 97–119.

Sicart, Miguel. 2014. *Play Matters*. Playful Thinking. Cambridge: The MIT Press.

Silverman, David. 1998. *Harvey Sacks: Social Science and Conversation Analysis*. Oxford: University Press.

Sommers, Marc. 2012. *Stuck: Rwandan Youth and the Struggle for Adulthood*. Athens: University of Georgia Press.

Spittler, Gerd. 2001. "Teilnehmende Beobachtung Als Dichte Teilnahme." *Zeitschrift Für Ethnologie*, 1–25.

Steuer, Noemi. 2017. "Of Murdered Mozarts – Processes of Identity Repair in the Narratives of the Second Malian Student Generation." Presented at the European Conference on African Studies, Basel.

Stokoe, Elisabeth. 2012. "Moving Forward with Membership Categorization Analysis: Methods for Systematic Analysis." *Discourse Studies* 14: 277–303.

Susan Reynolds Whyte. 2009. "Epilogue." In *Dealing with Uncertainty in Contemporary African Lives*, edited by Liv Haram and C. Bawa Yamba, 213–16. Uppsala: Nordiska Afrikainstitutet.

Taleb, Nassim Nicholas. 2007. *The Black Swan: The Impact of the Highly Improbable*. New York: Random House.

Tali, Margaret. 2017. *Absence and Difficult Knowledge in Contemporary Art Museums*. New York: Routledge. https://doi.org/10.4324/9781315114118.

Thaver, Beverly. 2004. "Private Higher Education in Africa: Six Country Case Studies." In *African Universities in the Twenty-First Century: Liberalisation and Internationalisation*, edited by Paul Tiyambe Zeleza and Adebayo Olukoshi, 69–83. 1. Dakar: CODESRIA.

Till Förster. 2013. "On Urbanity: Creativity and Emancipation in African Urban Life." In *Living the City*, edited by Brigit Obrist, Veit Arlt, and Elisio Macamo, 235–51. Zürich: LIT.

Vigh, Henrik. 2006. *Navigating Terrains of War: Youth and Soldiering in Guinea-Bissau*. Vol. 13. New York: Berghahn books.

— 2009. "Motion Squared: A Second Look at the Concept of Social Navigation." *Anthropological Theory* 9: 419–38.

— 2015. "Mobile Misfortune." *Culture Unbound: Journal of Current Cultural Research* 7: 233–53.

Waage, Trond. 2006. "Coping with Unpredictability. Preparing for Life in Ngaoundèrè, Cameroon." *Navigating Youth, Generating Adulthood: Social Becoming in an African Context*, 61–86.

Walanta. 2016. "Fonction Publique: Communiqués d'ouverture Des Concours Directs de Recrutement et Des Concours Professionnels 2016." Malijet. Com. 2016. http://malijet.com/actualite-politique-au-mali/flash-info/168836-fonction-publique-communiqu%C3%A9s-d%E2%80%99ouverture-des-concours-directs-d.html.

Whitehouse, Bruce. 2017. "Political Participation and Mobilization after Mali's 2012 Coup." *African Studies Review* 60: 15–35.

Whyte, Susan Reynolds, and Godfrey Etyang Siu. 2015. "Contingency: Interpersonal and Historical Dependencies in HIV Care." In *Ethnographies of Uncertainty in Africa*, edited by Elizabeth Cooper and David Pratten, 19–35. London: Palgrave Macmillan UK.

Zeleza, Paul Tiyambe, and Adebayo Olukoshi. 2004a. *African Universities in the Twenty-First Century: Knowledge and Society*. Bd. 2. Dakar: CODESRIA.

— 2004b. *African Universities in the Twenty-First Century: Liberalisation and Internationalisation*. 1. Dakar: CODESRIA.

Zeric Kay Smith. 1997. "'From Demons to Democrats': Mali's Student Movement 1991-1996." *Review of African Political Economy* 24 (72): 249–63.

Acknowledgements

Wow! What a ride! This is it: this is the thesis. (And now the book.) Aw ni ce, Bamakomogow! Thanks for your time, thoughts and company. Thanks to my supervisors Elisio Macamo and Richard Rottenburg for being an inspiration – both to this thesis and to me as a scholar in the making. I am grateful for your thoughts, comments and your support. Thanks to the Centre for African Studies in Basel and all the people who make it such an awesome place to do a PhD. Thanks to Veit Arlt, in particular, for making things happen. Thanks to the project team "Construire son Avenir" and its members Michele Engeler, Manfred Perlik and Noemi Steuer. Thanks to my dear colleague Maike Birzle. To all my colleagues and friends at the Centre for African Studies in Basel: High five! Thanks for your thoughts and critical comments that have helped shape this thesis: Carole Ammann, Stephanie Bishop, Lydia Linke, James Merron, Joschka Philipps, Haddy Sarr and Susanne Schultz. Special thanks to Julia Büchele and Bognan Valentin Koné for your continuous support. Go team! (Thanks to all the members of the African Studies Institute at the University of Leipzig for your support, your ideas and thanks for the inspiration, the discussions and the companionship.) I am thankful for the financial contributions made by the Schweizerische Nationalfonds (SNF) as well as to Freiwillige Akademische Gesellschaft (FAG), the Travel Fund of the University of Basel and the Graduate School of Social Sciences (G3S). Thanks to Grace Tran for language suggestions, to Alassane Keita for interview transcriptions. (Thank you, Matthias Müller, for editing this book with so much care and patience.) (Thanks to the publishing team at transcript and thanks again to the SNF for funding the publication of this book.)

Thanks to la famille à Faladie. Thank you, Mama. And to Flo (and Tilda): Love! Thank you!

Basel, November 2017 (and Leipzig, 2023.)